GREEK FOR BEGINNERS

by
L. A. WILDING, M.A.

Late Senior Classical Master, Dragon School, Oxford
Formerly Scholar of Oriel College, Oxford

SECOND EDITION

faber and faber
LONDON · BOSTON

First published in 1957
by Faber and Faber Limited
3 Queen Square London WCIN 3AU
Second edition revised 1959
First published in this edition 1973
Reprinted 1977, 1982, 1986 and 1991

Printed in England by Clays Ltd, St Ives plc
All rights reserved

ISBN 0-571-10402-9

Preface to the Second Edition

I am grateful to reviewers who have been good enough to mention any inaccuracies or defects in the first edition, and I hope that I have now taken account of them.

Oxford, 1958

Preface to the First Edition

The aim of this book is to enable the pupil to enjoy Greek, both the reading of it and the writing of it, as soon as possible. An attempt is made to introduce Grammar and Syntax in a comprehensible sequence, chapter by chapter; Greek precedes English both in the examples and in the exercises. Continuous translation is begun as soon as sufficient grammatical forms have been mastered; the pieces are all made-up in the sense that the exact words of the original authors have often had to be altered, but they are original in the sense that, with one exception, they have been drawn and adapted from the actual texts of Herodotus, Thucydides, and Xenophon. The limitations imposed by the pupil's knowledge of Grammar and Syntax made it impossible to set down the episodes in chronological order, but for the beginner to reach some of the best stories after a few months' work may be felt as a compensation for this.

Most teachers of Greek like their pupils to become familiar as soon as possible with the pages of a definite 'Grammar'. For this reason it is only at the start that grammatical forms are set out in this book, i.e. in the first eight chapters; they include the Indicative Active of λύω, the scheme of the 3rd Declension, and Adjectives of the 1st and 2nd Declensions. After this point reference is made to pages of Abbott and Mansfield's *Primer of Greek Grammar* (by permission of Messrs. Duckworth, to whom is due my grateful acknowledgement); those who are used to

5

other grammars will readily find the relevant pages. Much might have been included concerning philology and the laws of sound, but it has been thought better to plunge *in medias res*; most grammars contain a good deal of information on these matters and may be consulted by those who are interested. The beginner is generally more concerned with etymology and this interest should be constantly stimulated by tests in derivation.

It is for the individual teacher to decide how far the pupil should have advanced in Latin before beginning Greek. It is assumed that he will at least be familiar with the Subject-Verb-Object relationship in an inflected language and the rules of the Four Concords; it is also assumed that his study of Latin will always be kept rather in advance of his study of Greek; in this book usages in Greek are not elaborated when they are similar to usages in Latin; they are, indeed, often dissimilar, and the pupil should, as he proceeds, be made aware of the flexibility of the Greek language, as compared with Latin.

Constructions are covered as far as Indirect Command, Exhortations, Future Wishes, Final and Consecutive Clauses, Indirect Statement, Direct and Indirect Questions; in Grammar, Contracted Nouns and Adjectives, the Attic Declension, and Verbs in -μι, except εἰμί (*sum*), εἶμι (*ibo*), and φημί, are not included, but pupils learn some of the more common Irregular Verbs. The book should, it is hoped, be of use both in the lower forms of Secondary Schools and in Preparatory Schools.

For encouragement in preparing this volume I am grateful to many schoolmasters and to my publishers; for suggestions and corrections, to Mr. J. G. Griffith, Fellow of Jesus College, Oxford, and to Mr. F. E. Hicks, of the Dragon School.

Oxford, 1956

Introduction to the Beginner

If you have made a good beginning with Latin, you will find the beginning of Greek quite simple; a good many of your difficulties are over before you start, because you know from Latin how the endings of words are altered in Conjugations and Declensions; the same thing happens in Greek. You will also find a certain excitement in beginning Greek, because it is written in a different alphabet in different writing, and this gives an added interest. It will not be long, too, before you begin to see many Greek words which we have adopted into our own language; this will help you with English spelling and to understand more clearly the meanings of the words. It is interesting to notice that when scientists require a word to describe something new, they generally borrow from Greek to make it, though this by itself would be a poor reason for learning Greek!

When you have reached the end of this book, you will have learnt that the Greeks produced excellent story-tellers; after that, it will not take long before you are ready to read some of the finest prose and poetry that the world has ever produced and to study the life and thought of a people to whom we owe far more than these: the idea of democracy, the origins of drama, some of the best sculpture and architecture, some of the greatest philosophers, and, above all, that spirit of inquiry which has led to discoveries throughout the ages.

It is that same spirit of inquiry that leads us, by learning Greek, to discover what the Greeks have contributed to our own life and thought today.

Contents

Every chapter contains exercises. The following is a summary of the Grammar and Syntax covered by each chapter, with the titles of the pieces of continuous Greek Translation.

9

10 *Contents*

Contents 11

Illustration

MAP

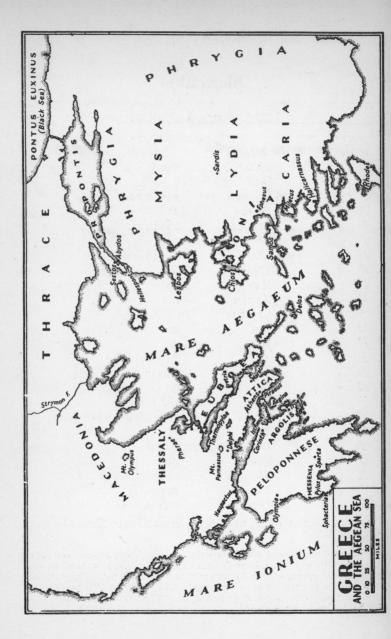

PONTUS EUXINUS
(Black Sea)

PHRYGIA

THRACE

PROPONTIS

PHRYGIA

MYSIA

·Sardis

LYDIA

CARIA

Rhodes

Sestos
Abydos
Hellespont

Lesbos

·Ephesus

IONIA

·Cnidus
Halicarnassus

Samos

Chios

MARE AEGAEUM

Delos

Strymon f.

MACEDONIA

Euboea

ATTICA
Athens·
Piraeus
·Aegina
·Megara
Marathon
Salamis
·Eleusis

Mt. Olympus

THESSALY

Pherae

Thermopylae

Delphi

Isthmus
·Corinth

ARGOLIS
Sparta
MESSENIA
Pylos

Mt. Parnassus

PELOPONNESE

Naupactus

Olympia·

Sphacteria

MARE IONIUM

GREECE
AND THE AEGEAN SEA

MILES
0 10 25   50   75   100

Chapter 1
The Greek Alphabet

Form		Name	Sound[1]
A	α	Alpha	ā or ă
B	β	Bēta	b
Γ	γ	Gamma	g as in *good*
Δ	δ	Delta	d
E	ε	Epsīlon	ĕ as in *get*
Z	ζ	Zēta	z (= δ*s*)
H	η	Ēta	ē as in *feet*
Θ	θ	Thēta	th
I	ι	Iōta	ī or ĭ
K	κ	Kappa	k
Λ	λ	Lambda	l
M	μ	Mū	m
N	ν	Nū	n
Ξ	ξ	Xī	x (= κ*s*)
O	ο	Ŏmicron	ŏ as in *got*
Π	π	Pī	p
P	ρ	Rhō	rh,[2] r
Σ	σ, ς	Sigma	s (ς only at end of word)
T	τ	Tau	t
Y	υ	Upsīlon	ū or ŭ
Φ	φ	Phī	ph
X	χ	Chī	ch as in *chorus*
Ψ	ψ	Psī	ps (= π*s*)
Ω	ω	Ōmega	ō as in *bone*

(μικρόν means *small*, and μέγα, *great*; hence Omicron and Omega).

[1] We shall never know exactly how the ancient Greeks pronounced their language: the sounds made by Greeks today when using the same words have certainly changed over the centuries and give little help. The writer of this book prefers the traditional pronunciation; some teachers may prefer to correct the vowel sounds according to the *reformed* pronunciation.

[2] At the beginning of a word.

When γ is used before γ, κ, χ, or ξ, it is sounded *ng*. So ἄγγελος, *a messenger*, is pronounced *ang-gelos*.

In Greek Proper Nouns translated into English and in English words derived from Greek c corresponds to κ, and y to υ, e.g. Περικλῆς becomes *Pericles*, and κυκλος (*a circle*) gives us the English word *cycle*.

Vowels combined in Diphthongs

αι as in *aisle*	αυ as in *pause*
ει as in *height*	ευ ⎫
οι as in *toil*	ηυ ⎭ as in *feud*
υι as *wi* in *twine*	ου as in *found*

Iota subscript. When ι follows ᾱ or η or ω, it is written underneath, and only the long vowel is sounded—ᾳ, ῃ, ῳ. This writing of the mute iota subscript only dates from about A.D. 1200, and was quite unknown to the ancient Greeks (who wrote αι, etc.). However, almost all printed Greek books have used the subscript and will no doubt continue to do so.

Breathings

When a word begins with a Vowel or Diphthong or ρ, a mark called a Breathing is written above it.

A Rough Breathing has the sound of our letter *h* and is written thus, ὁδος (pronounced *hodos*).

A Smooth Breathing has no sound and is written thus, ἐγω (pronounced *ego*).

A Breathing is always rough when a word begins with υ or ρ, e.g. ὕστερον (husteron); ῥοδον (rhodon).

Breathings are written (i) to the left of capital Vowels, unless part of a Diphthong, and (ii) over the second letter of a Diphthong, e.g. εἰρηνη, Αἴγυπτος.

Elision

Short Vowels are often cut off (elided) at the end of a word before a word beginning with another Vowel, e.g. μετ᾽ ἐμοῦ, *with me*; before another word beginning with a Vowel with a Rough Breathing, τ and π become θ and φ respectively, e.g. μεθ᾽ ἡμῶν, *with us*.

Accents

These are *grave* (ˋ), *acute* (ˊ), and *circumflex* (ˆ), and are said to have been introduced, in the third century B.C., in order to help with the correct reading of Homer.

They are inserted in this book, but the learning of their use may be put off until a later stage.

Stops and Capital letters

Full-stops and Commas are written as in English. A full-stop placed above the line (·) corresponds to an English colon or semi-colon. The Greek mark of interrogation is ;

Capital letters are used to begin proper names, and, generally, to mark a new paragraph; they are also used, for convenience, to introduce Direct Speech; apart from this, they are not used, as in English, to begin each sentence.

For the sake of clearness use is made in this book of inverted commas.

EXERCISE 1. The following English words are Greek words in origin. Write them down in Greek letters; long vowels are marked where necessary for spelling.

1. drama	9. genesis	17. calyx
2. isoscelēs	10. mētropolis	18. rhododendron
3. nectar	11. thōrax	19. iris
4. hydra	12. analysis	20. parenthesis
5. crisis	13. critērion	21. climax
6. canōn	14. basis	22. horizon
7. paralysis	15. hydrophobia	23. catastrophē
8. comma	16. cōlon	24. acropolis

18 *Alphabet Practice*

EXERCISE 2. The following persons appear in Greek legends. Write them down in English.

1. Ποσειδῶν
2. Ἄρτεμις
3. Ἑρμῆς
4. Ζεύς
5. Κύκλωψ
6. Θησεύς
7. Μίδας
8. Δημήτηρ

9. Ἀφροδίτη
10. Προμηθεύς
11. Ἥρα
12. Περσεφόνη
13. Ἡρακλῆς
14. Ἀγαμέμνων
15. Ἀνδρομάχη
16. Ἠλέκτρα

17. Ἄρης
18. Ψυχή
19. Ἀθήνη
20. Ὀδυσσεύς
21. Ὑπερίων
22. Ἕκτωρ
23. Χάρων
24. Ἄλκηστις

EXERCISE 3. The following persons and places appear in Greek history. Write them down in Greek letters; long vowels are marked where necessary for spelling.

(a) 1. Dēmosthenēs
2. Solōn
3. Leōnidas
4. Euripidēs

5. Nicias
6. Cleisthenēs
7. Pythagoras
8. Xerxēs

9. Themistoclēs
10. Alcibiadēs
11. Hippias
12. Philocratēs

(b) 1. Argos
2. Dēlos
3. Mytilēnē
4. Samos

5. Olympia
6. Naxos
7. Chios
8. Thasos

9. Eretria
10. Pylos
11. Phōcis
12. Ēlis

Do not forget Breathings.

Chapter 2

Verbs in -ω: Present Indicative Active

In Greek, as in Latin, the Verb is conjugated by adding terminations to the Stem; certain tenses also have prefixes.

Greek Verbs are divided into two Conjugations, according to whether the 1st person singular of the Present Indicative

Active ends in -ω or in μι. The -ω termination is by far the more common of the two, and except for εἰμί, *I am*, and φημί, *I say*, Verbs in μι can be left until a later stage.

Besides Singular and Plural, Greek Verbs have a third Number, called the Dual, used of two persons or things, but the Dual is not much used except in poetry, and its use may be ignored for the present.

Here is the Present Indicative Active of a Verb in -ω. Hyphens have been inserted to show the terminations which are added to the Verb-stem λυ-:

Number	Person	Part of Verb	Meaning
Sing.	1st	λύ-ω	*I loose, set free*
„	2nd	λύ-εις	*you loose*
„	3rd	λύ-ει	*he, she, or it, looses*
Plur.	1st	λύ-ομεν	*we loose*
„	2nd	λύ-ετε	*you loose*
„	3rd	λύ-ουσι(ν)	*they loose*

λύουσιν is the form used in the 3rd pers. plur. before a word beginning with a vowel, or at the end of a sentence. This use of what is called the Paragogic ν will be noticed again after certain other forms ending in ι or ε.

EXERCISE 4.

Verbs used : κωλύ-ω, *I hinder*   πέμπ-ω, *I send*
              θύ-ω, *I sacrifice*   γράφ-ω, *I write*
              φέρ-ω, *I carry*   ἄγ-ω, *I lead*

Translate into English :

1. κωλύ-εις.   6. ἄγ-ομεν.   11. γράφ-ουσι.
2. θύ-ομεν.   7. γράφ-εις.   12. ἄγ-ετε.
3. ἄγ-ει.   8. πέμπ-ουσιν.   13. πέμπ-ομεν.
4. πέμπ-ετε.   9. κωλύ-ει.   14. φέρ-εις.
5. φέρ-ουσι.   10. θύ-ετε.   15. θύ-ει.

EXERCISE 5. Hyphens should not be used.
Translate into Greek:

1. We hinder.
2. You (s.) sacrifice.
3. You (pl.) hinder.
4. He writes.
5. They hinder.
6. We carry.
7. They sacrifice.
8. You (s.) send.
9. You (pl.) write.
10. He carries.
11. You (pl.) carry.
12. He sends.
13. They lead.
14. We write.
15. You (s.) lead.

EXERCISE 6.

In this exercise various parts of new Verbs are given, with the general meaning of the Stem in brackets.

Translate, and write down the 1st pers. sing. of the Present Tense of:

1. φυλάσσομεν[1] (*guard*).
2. διώκουσι (*pursue*).
3. φεύγει (*flee*).
4. φυλάσσεις.
5. διώκετε.
6. φεύγουσιν.
7. ἔχεις (*have*).
8. πείθετε (*persuade*).
9. τοξεύομεν (*shoot*).
10. ἔχει.
11. πείθουσι.
12. τοξεύετε.

[1] -ττ- can be used instead of -σσ-, but -σσ- is used throughout this book.

EXERCISE 7.

Translate into Greek:
1. They guard.
2. We flee.
3. He persuades.
4. You (s.) pursue.
5. He shoots.
6. You (pl.) have.
7. We persuade.
8. They shoot.
9. You (pl.) guard.
10. It pursues.
11. We have.
12. You (s.) flee.

The Negative

The Negative used in direct statements is οὐ (before consonants), οὐκ (before vowels with smooth breathings), οὐχ (before vowels with rough breathings).

Common Conjunctions

καί, *and* (used as well for *also* and *even*); ἀλλά, *but*.

EXERCISE 8.

(a) 1. οὐ γράφει.
2. διώκομεν καὶ τοξεύομεν.
3. οὐ διώκει, ἀλλὰ φεύγει.
4. οὐκ ἔχομεν.

5. γράφουσι καὶ πείθουσιν.
6. ἄγει καὶ διώκει.

(b) 1. We write and persuade.
2. You do not persuade.
3. He does not shoot.
4. They do not guard, but flee.
5. We pursue and hinder.
6. You are not leading.

Chapter 3

Definite Article; the Cases; 1st Declension: Feminine Nouns; Future Indicative Active

Greek, unlike Latin, employs a **Definite Article,** corresponding to the English *the*.

The Definite Article is declined as an Adjective of three terminations, and agrees with the Noun to which it is attached in **Gender, Number,** and **Case.**

Once we have learnt the declension of the Article, we have learnt the basis of the 1st and 2nd Declensions of Nouns, and it should be learnt at once by heart:

	Singular			Plural		
	Masc.	Fem.	Neut.	Masc.	Fem.	Neut.
Nom.	ὁ	ἡ	τό	οἱ	αἱ	τά
Acc.	τόν	τήν	τό	τούς	τάς	τά
Gen.	τοῦ	τῆς	τοῦ	τῶν	τῶν	τῶν
Dat.	τῷ	τῇ	τῷ	τοῖς	ταῖς	τοῖς

The Cases

There are five Cases in Greek, Nominative, Vocative (but not found in the Declension of the Article), Accusative, Genitive, and Dative.

There is no Ablative. The **Genitive,** besides its use as a true Gen., expressing *of*, is used for expressing **Separation** (*away from, out of*), where an Abl. is used in Latin; the **Dative,** besides being used for the **Indirect Object,** is used like the Latin Abl. of the **Instrument.**

Feminine Nouns of 1st Declension

3 types: τιμή, *honour*; χώρα, *country*; Μοῦσα, *Muse*.

Sing.

Nom.	ἡ	τιμή	χώρα	Μοῦσα
Voc.	ὦ	τιμή	χώρα	Μοῦσα
Acc.	τήν	τιμήν	χώραν	Μοῦσαν
Gen.	τῆς	τιμῆς	χώρας	Μούσης
Dat.	τῇ	τιμῇ	χώρᾳ	Μούσῃ

Plur.

Nom.	αἱ	τιμαί	χῶραι	Μοῦσαι
Voc.	ὦ	τιμαί	χῶραι	Μοῦσαι
Acc.	τάς	τιμάς	χώρας	Μούσας
Gen.	τῶν	τιμῶν	χωρῶν	Μουσῶν
Dat.	ταῖς	τιμαῖς	χώραις	Μούσαις

It will be seen that τιμή is declined throughout in exactly the same way as the Fem. of the Article, and the same applies to all three types in the Plur., except that we now have a Vocative Case. The interjection ὦ, *O*, should always be placed before a Vocative. All 1st Decl. Nouns in -η and -α are Fem.

N.B. (1) If the Nom. ends in η, then η is kept throughout the Sing. (τιμή type).

(2) If the Nom. ends in α **after** ε, ι, or ρ, then α is kept throughout the Sing.; α after ε, ι, or ρ is known as α *pure.* Examples (besides χώρα, above)—θεά, *goddess*; στρατιά, **army.**

(3) If the Nom. ends in α **after any consonant except** ρ, then the Acc. Sing. ends in -αν, the Gen. in -ης, the Dat. in -ῃ (Μοῦσα type).

Rules for finding the Nom. of a 1st Decl. Noun:

(a) Case endings preceded by ε, ι, or ρ, will give us a Nom. in -α; e.g. ἀγορῶν must come from ἀγορά, *market-place*;

(b) Case endings preceded by σ, by a double consonant (ζ, ξ, ψ), or by two consonants (λλ, σσ, ττ), will give us a Nom. in -α of the Μοῦσα type; e.g. δόξης must come from δόξα, *glory*; τραπέζῃ from τράπεζα, *table*; θαλάσσαις from θάλασσα, *sea*;

(c) Case endings preceded by any other letter will give us a Nom. in -η; e.g. ἐπιστολαί must come from ἐπιστολή, *letter*.

EXERCISE 9.

1. ἡ θεὰ ἔχει τιμήν.
2. γράφει ἐπιστολάς.
3. φεύγομεν εἰς τὴν χώραν.
4. θύουσιν ἐν τῇ ἀγορᾷ.
5. θεραπεύετε τὴν θεάν.
6. τράπεζαν οὐκ ἔχομεν.
7. ἡ θεὰ φυλάσσει τὴν ἀγοράν.
8. διώκομεν τὴν στρατιὰν εἰς τὴν θάλασσαν.
9. αἱ Μοῦσαι δόξαν ἔχουσιν.
10. πιστεύεις τῇ θεᾷ.

εἰς, *to, into* (Acc.).   θεραπεύω, *I honour.*
ἐν, *in* (Dat.).   πιστεύω, *I trust* (Dat.).

EXERCISE 10.

1. They send a letter.
2. The sea hinders the army.
3. We honour the Muses.
4. The army has glory.
5. You (pl.) pursue the army into the country.
6. They flee from the sea.
7. I do not trust the letter.
8. They sacrifice to the goddesses.

9. In the market-place they are honouring the goddess.
10. We do not pursue the army, but flee.

from, ἀπό (Gen.).

EXERCISE 11. (Study the rules on pp. 22–23.)

1. Give the Acc. Sing. of—φωνή, *voice*, ἑσπέρα, *evening*, ἄμιλλα, *contest*, γῆ, *land*, σοφία, *wisdom*.

2. Give the Acc. and Gen. Sing. of—μάχη, *battle*, θύρα, *door*, πύλη, *gate*, ἅμαξα, *wagon*, ἡμέρα, *day*.

3. Give the Nom. and Dat. Sing. of—οἰκίαι, *house*, γλώσσης, *tongue*, δίψαν, *thirst*, κώμας, *village*, γεφύραις, *bridge*.

Future Indicative Active

The general rule is that -σω is added to the Verb-stem, and the Tense is conjugated like the Present; variations will be dealt with later:

Number	Person	Part of Verb	Meaning
Sing.	1st	λύ-σω	*I shall loose*
,,	2nd	λύ-σεις	*you will loose*
,,	3rd	λύ-σει	*he will loose*
Plur.	1st	λύ-σομεν	*we shall loose*
,,	2nd	λύ-σετε	*you will loose*
,,	3rd	λύ-σουσι(ν)	*they will loose*

EXERCISE 12. For some words see Ex. 11.

1. ἡ θεὰ παύσει τὴν μάχην.
2. θεραπεύσουσι τὴν θεάν.
3. ἕλκομεν τὴν ἅμαξαν εἰς τὴν κώμην.
4. ἡ θάλασσα οὐ κωλύσει τὴν στρατιάν.
5. οὐ πιστεύσομεν τῇ γεφύρᾳ.
6. στρατεύσετε εἰς τὴν γῆν.
7. αἱ ἅμαξαι κωλύσουσι τὴν μάχην.
8. θύσομεν τῇ θεᾷ ἐν τῇ κώμῃ.
9. βασιλεύσεις ἐν τῇ γῇ.
10. οὐ λύσομεν τὴν στρατιάν.

παύω, *I stop* (trans.). στρατεύω, *I march.*
ἕλκω, *I drag.* βασιλεύω, *I am king, rule*

EXERCISE 13. For some words see Ex. 11.

1. We will set free the land.
2. I shall stop the battle.
3. You will sacrifice to the goddesses.
4. They will not march into the land.
5. We shall honour the Muse.
6. He will not trust the letter.
7. They are dragging the wagons out of the market-place.
8. You will hunt in the country.
9. We shall not prevent the contest.
10. They will trust the army.

out of, ἐκ (Gen.). *I hunt*, θηρεύω. *I prevent*, κωλύω.

Chapter 4

1st Declension: Masculine Nouns; Imperfect Indicative Active

2 types: νεανίας, *young man*; κριτής, *judge*.

Sing.

Nom.	ὁ	νεανίας	κριτής
Voc.	ὦ	νεανία	κριτά
Acc.	τὸν	νεανίαν	κριτήν
Gen.	τοῦ	νεανίου	κριτοῦ
Dat.	τῷ	νεανίᾳ	κριτῇ

Plur.

Nom.	οἱ	νεανίαι	κριταί
Voc.	ὦ	νεανίαι	κριταί
Acc.	τοὺς	νεανίας	κριτάς
Gen.	τῶν	νεανιῶν	κριτῶν
Dat.	τοῖς	νεανίαις	κριταῖς

It will be noticed that the Plurals of these Nouns are declined like the Feminine Nouns of the 1st Decl. All 1st Decl. Nouns in -ας and -ης are Masc.

Like νεανίας: ταμίας, *steward*; Βορέας, *North Wind.*

Like κριτής: ναύτης, *sailor*; στρατιώτης, *soldier*; πολίτης, *citizen.*

Imperfect Indicative Active

The **Historic** Tenses of the Indicative, the Imperfect, the Aorist (see Ch. 5), and the Pluperfect, begin with a prefix known as the **Augment** (from Latin **augeo,** *I increase*); before Stems beginning with a consonant the prefix or Augment is the letter ε. All **Imperfect** Tenses are formed from the Present Stem, and the Imperfect of λύω is given here as an example:

Number	Person	Part of Verb	Meaning
Sing.	1st	ἔ-λυ-ον	*I was loosing*
„	2nd	ἔ-λυ-ες	*you were loosing*
„	3rd	ἔ-λυ-ε(ν)	*he was loosing*
Plur.	1st	ἐ-λύ-ομεν	*we were loosing*
„	2nd	ἐ-λύ-ετε	*you were loosing*
„	3rd	ἔ-λυ-ον	*they were loosing*

As in Latin, so in Greek, the **Imperfect** Tense is used of **action that is not completed** and often has the meanings of *began to, continued to, used to*:

οἱ πολῖται ἐθεράπευον τὴν θεάν.
The citizens used to worship the goddess.

EXERCISE 14.

1. οἱ στρατιῶται ἔλυον τὸν πολίτην.
2. ὁ Βορέας τὴν μάχην ἐκώλυεν.
3. οἱ νεανίαι ἐθεράπευον τὴν θεάν.
4. ἐθύετε ἐν τῇ κώμῃ.
5. ὁ κριτὴς τὴν ἅμιλλαν ἔπαυεν.
6. οἱ ναῦται ἐπαίδευον τοὺς νεανίας.
7. τῷ ταμίᾳ οὐκ ἐπιστεύομεν.

8. στρατεύσετε, ὦ νεανίαι, εἰς τὴν χώραν.
9. οἱ πολῖται ἔθυον ταῖς Μούσαις.
10. οἱ στρατιῶται ἐκώλυον τοὺς ναύτας ἀπὸ τῆς κώμης.

παιδεύω, *I train, educate.*   κωλύω ἀπό, *I keep (someone) away from.*
ὦ, *O* (with Voc.).

EXERCISE 15.

1. We were not hindering the soldiers.
2. The sailor was sacrificing to the goddess.
3. The citizens used to trust the judge.
4. You will set free the soldiers, O citizens.
5. The soldiers were not hindering the steward.
6. We were training the young men in the village.
7. You began to shoot the citizens, O soldiers.
8. The sailor was not trusting the north wind.
9. The citizens were keeping the soldiers from the houses.
10. We were honouring the Muses.

Some uses of the Article

The Article is commonly used—

(1) Instead of a Possessive Adjective when there is no emphasis, e.g. ἄγει τὴν στρατιάν, *he leads his army*;
(2) With Nouns denoting a class, e.g. οἱ ποιηταί, *poets*;
(3) With Abstract Nouns, especially when an Abstract Noun is the Subject of the sentence or the topic under discussion, e.g. ἡ δικαιοσύνη παρέχει τὴν εἰρήνην, *justice causes peace*;
(4) With names of Persons and Places (especially when first mentioned), e.g. ἡ Ἀθήνη, *Athene*; αἱ Ἀθῆναι, *Athens*.

Position of Dependent Genitive

A Possessive or Qualifying Genitive is generally placed between the Noun on which it depends and the Article of that Noun:

ἡ τοῦ κριτοῦ οἰκία, *the judge's house.*
ὁ τῆς οἰκίας ταμίας, *the steward of the house.*

But it is equally good Greek to write ἡ οἰκία ἡ τοῦ κριτοῦ (i.e. with the Article repeated before the Qualifying Genitive). Greek is a very flexible language.

EXERCISE 16.

1. οἱ ποιηταὶ θεραπεύουσι τὴν Μοῦσαν.
2. τὴν σοφίαν διώκομεν.
3. οἱ στρατιῶται ἐφύλασσον τὰς τῶν πολιτῶν οἰκίας.
4. οἱ νεανίαι εἰς τὴν Σπάρτην στρατεύσουσιν.
5. ἡ Ἀθήνη κωλύει τὸν νεανίαν.
6. ἐθεραπεύομεν τὴν τῆς χώρας θεάν.
7. ἡ στρατιὰ ἡ τοῦ Ξέρξου φεύγει.
8. οἱ κριταὶ διώκουσι τὴν δικαιοσύνην.
9. ὁ Ξέρξης παύσει τὴν μάχην τῇ φωνῇ.[1]
10. οἱ στρατιῶται ἔφευγον εἰς τὰς Ἀθήνας.

διώκω, *I pursue*, and so *seek after*.   Ξέρξης, *Xerxes* (decl. like κριτής).
Σπάρτη, *Sparta*.   δικαιοσύνη, *justice*.

[1] Dat. of Instrument.

EXERCISE 17.

1. The sailor flees to his house.
2. Athene stops the battle.
3. We were marching into the land of the Persians.
4. Young men do not always seek after wisdom.
5. Xerxes does not trust his soldiers.
6. The judge will educate the young man in justice and wisdom.
7. We will not hinder the citizen's wagon.
8. The young men began to flee to the door of the house.
9. Poets will always honour Sparta.
10. We will keep the Persians from Athens.

Persian, Πέρσης (decl. like κριτής).   to, πρός or εἰς (Acc.).   always, ἀεί

Chapter 5

2nd Declension: Masculine and Feminine Nouns; Weak Aorist Indicative Active

The Nom. of Masc. and Fem. Nouns of the 2nd Declension ends in -ος, and the Voc. in -ε; otherwise the endings are exactly the same as those of the Masc. of the Article.

1 type: λόγος, *word* (m.). νῆσος, *island* (f.).

Sing.		
Nom.	λόγος	νῆσος
Voc.	λόγε	νῆσε
Acc.	λόγον	νῆσον
Gen.	λόγου	νήσου
Dat.	λόγῳ	νήσῳ
Plur.		
Nom.	λόγοι	νῆσοι
Voc.	λόγοι	νῆσοι
Acc.	λόγους	νήσους
Gen.	λόγων	νήσων
Dat.	λόγοις	νήσοις

Like λόγος and masc.: ἵππος, *horse*; ποταμός, *river*; δοῦλος, *slave*; πόλεμος, *war*; οἱ Ἀθηναῖοι, *the Athenians*.
Like νῆσος and fem.: βίβλος, *book*; ὁδός, *road*; νόσος, *disease, plague*.

Weak Aorist Indicative Active

The **Aorist** Tense is the ordinary Past Tense used in telling of **past events,** and in this regard corresponds to the Latin Perfect without *have*.

The Aorist Tense of a Verb is called a Weak Aorist or a Strong Aorist, according to its formation. At present we will deal only with the **Weak Aorist.** This is employed by Verbs whose Stem ends in a vowel and by many others.

The Augment is prefixed to the Verb-stem and -σα is added for the 1st person. Here is the Weak Aorist of λύω :

Sing.	ἔ-λυ-σα	*I loosed*
	ἔ-λυ-σας	*you loosed,* etc.
	ἔ-λυ-σε(ν)	
Plur.	ἐ-λύ-σαμεν	
	ἐ-λύ-σατε	
	ἔ-λυ-σαν	

EXERCISE 18.

1. ὁ δοῦλος ἔλυσε τὸν ἵππον.
2. ἐπιστεύσαμεν τοῖς τοῦ νεανίου λόγοις.
3. οἱ Ἀθηναῖοι ἔθυσαν ἐν τῇ νήσῳ.
4. ὁ τῆς οἰκίας ταμίας ἐπαίδευσε τοὺς δούλους.
5. ὁ ἰατρὸς ἐθεράπευσε τὴν νόσον.
6. ἐτοξεύσαμεν τοὺς τῶν Ἀθηναίων ἵππους.
7. ἡ νόσος τὸν πόλεμον οὐκ ἔπαυσεν.
8. ὁ δοῦλος γράφει ἐν τῇ βίβλῳ.
9. ὁ ποταμὸς οὐκ ἐκώλυσε τοὺς ἵππους.
10. ὁ Ξέρξης ἄγει τὴν στρατιὰν ἐν τῇ ὁδῷ.

ἰατρός (m.), *doctor.*   θεραπεύω, *I cure, heal (illness or person).*

EXERCISE 19.

1. We set free the slaves.
2. The Athenians trained their horses.
3. We seek after wisdom in books.
4. You ran risks on the roads.
5. You healed the slave, doctor.
6. The soldiers believed the general's words.
7. We were fleeing to the island.
8. The young man trusted the words of the book.
9. The doctors did not keep the plague from Athens.
10. We are leading the horses to the river.

I run risks, κινδυνεύω.   *I believe,* πιστεύω (Dat.).
on, ἐν (Dat.).   *general,* στρατηγός (m.).

Exercises for Revision

EXERCISE 20.

1. οἱ ἰατροὶ τὰς νόσους θεραπεύουσιν.
2. ὁ δοῦλος κωλύει τοὺς ἵππους ἀπὸ τοῦ ποταμοῦ.
3. οἱ Ἀθηναῖοι τοὺς νεανίας ἐν τῇ σοφίᾳ ἐπαίδευον.
4. οἱ τῆς βίβλου λόγοι οὐ πείθουσι τοὺς Ἀθηναίους.
5. οἱ στρατιῶται ἐφύλασσον τὴν ὁδόν.
6. πέμπομεν ἐπιστολὴν εἰς τὴν νῆσον.
7. οἱ Ἀθηναῖοι ἔθυσαν τῇ θεᾷ.
8. πιστεύσομεν τῇ φωνῇ τῇ τῆς θεᾶς.
9. οἱ πόλεμοι παρέχουσι τὰς νόσους.
10. ἐφεύγομεν εἰς τὴν τῆς οἰκίας θύραν.
11. ἡ τοῦ ποιητοῦ γλῶσσα πείθει τοὺς πολίτας.
12. ἡ τοῦ Ξέρξου στρατιὰ ἐκινδύνευεν ἐν τῷ πολέμῳ.

παρέχω, I cause.

EXERCISE 21.

1. The citizens were fleeing into Athens.
2. The Persians will keep the Athenians from the island.
3. We trusted the doctor's words.
4. Thirst and illness hinder the Athenians.
5. Evening stopped the battle.
6. You did not set free the slaves.
7. The voice of the citizen began to persuade the judges.
8. The sailors are guarding the island.
9. The river will not hinder the army of the Athenians.
10. The doctor cured the young man's illness.
11. The Athenians were pursuing the sailors to the islands.
12. The soldiers were guarding the gates of the village.

Order of Words

The most important point about the order of words in Greek is that the meaning should at once be clear. We are not tied down by any rules such as the general rule in Latin that the Verb comes at the end of the clause or sentence. Sometimes emphasis will bring certain words to the beginning of the sentence; sometimes we prefer words in a certain order because the sound of the words in that order is more harmonious. The great thing is to be natural and to be clear.

Chapter 6

2nd Declension: Neuter Nouns; Perfect Indicative Active

Neuter Nouns of the 2nd Declension have the same endings as the Neuter of the Article, except that the Nom., Voc., and Acc. Sing. end in *-ον*.

1 type: *ζυγόν, yoke.*

	Sing.	*Plur.*
Nom.	ζυγόν	ζυγά
Voc.	ζυγόν	ζυγά
Acc.	ζυγόν	ζυγά
Gen.	ζυγοῦ	ζυγῶν
Dat.	ζυγῷ	ζυγοῖς

Like *ζυγόν*: *δένδρον, tree*; *δῶρον, gift*; *στρατόπεδον, camp*; *ἔργον, deed, work*; *ὅπλα* (pl.), *arms, weapons*.

Neuter Plural with Singular Verb

Neuter Nouns in the **Plural** take a **Singular Verb:**

τὰ δένδρα παρέχει καρπόν.
Trees produce fruit.

Perfect Indicative Active

With Verbs of the *λύω* type, i.e. Verbs beginning with a single consonant and having a Vowel-stem, **Reduplication** takes place in the **Perfect** Tense, i.e. the consonant is repeated (or doubled) with ε, and -κα is added as the ending of the 1st person singular; so we get λέ-λυ-κα:

Sing.	λέ-λυ-κα	*I have loosed*
	λέ-λυ-κας	*you have loosed*, etc.
	λέ-λυ-κε(ν)	
Plur.	λε-λύ-καμεν	
	λε-λύ-κατε	
	λε-λύ-κασι(ν)	

The **Perfect** Tense is used for a **past action,** the **effect** of which is still **continuing,** e.g. ἡ θάλασσα λέλυκε τὴν γέφυραν, *the sea has broken the bridge* (*and it is still broken*); ἔλυσε would mean that on a certain date the sea did break the bridge, stated as a historical fact.

EXERCISE 22.

1. οἱ δοῦλοι λελύκασι τὰ τῶν ἵππων ζυγά.
2. ὁ νεανίας κόπτει τὸ δένδρον.
3. ὁ ποιητὴς πεπαίδευκε τὰ τέκνα.
4. τὰ τῶν πολεμίων ἔργα βλάπτει τοὺς πολίτας.
5. κεκωλύκατε τοὺς πολεμίους ἀπὸ τοῦ στρατοπέδου.
6. ἐπέμπομεν δῶρα πρὸς τὸν στρατηγόν.
7. τὰ τοῦ ταμίου τέκνα ἄγει τοὺς ἵππους.
8. τὰ ὅπλα πιέζει τοὺς στρατιώτας.
9. ὁ ταμίας λέλυκε τοὺς δούλους.
10. φέρομεν τὰ ὅπλα εἰς τὸ στρατόπεδον.

κόπτω, *I cut.*	βλάπτω, *I injure.*
τέκνον, *child.*	πιέζω, *I weigh down.*
οἱ πολέμιοι, *the enemy.*	

EXERCISE 23.

1. The trees of the island provide food.
2. We have kept the horses from the river.
3. The slave has loosened the yoke.

4. Gifts do not always persuade.
5. We have educated the children.
6. The sailor's children are carrying fruit.
7. We are cutting the enemy's trees.
8. You have hindered the Persians with your weapons.
9. The trees are not bearing fruit.
10. The gifts have loosened the sailor's tongue.

> *I provide*, παρέχω. *I bear*, φέρω.
> *food*, σῖτος (m.). *fruit*, καρπός (m.).

EXERCISE 24.

1. οἱ πολέμιοι κινδυνεύουσιν ἐν τῷ στρατοπέδῳ.
2. λελύκαμεν τὸν καρπὸν ἀπὸ τῶν δένδρων.
3. οἱ στρατιῶται ἔκοπτον τὰ τῶν Ἀθηναίων δένδρα.
4. τὸ ζυγὸν βλάπτει τὸν τοῦ ταμίου ἵππον.
5. τὰ τῶν πολιτῶν ἔργα κεκώλυκε τοὺς πολεμίους.
6. οἱ ποιηταὶ τὴν δόξαν παρέχουσι τοῖς Ἀθηναίοις.
7. τὰ ὅπλα οὐ πιέζει τὸν ναύτην.
8. οἱ στρατιῶται φέρουσι δένδρα πρὸς τὸν ποταμόν.
9. ὁ ταμίας πεπαίδευκε τὸν ἵππον ζυγῷ.
10. τὸ ἔργον πιέζει τοὺς νεανίας.

EXERCISE 25.

1. The children are carrying gifts from the market-place.
2. We have prevented a battle in the island.
3. The poet was writing among the trees.
4. We were marching to the enemy's villages.
5. The glory of the contest has loosened the poet's tongue.
6. The soldiers' deeds have honour among the citizens.
7. We are sending a letter to the general.
8. The Athenians are not seeking after war, but friendship.
9. I have trained the general's horse.
10. Weapons do not produce peace.

> *among*, ἐν (Dat.). *I produce*, παρέχω.
> *friendship*, φιλία. *peace*, εἰρήνη

Chapter 7

Adjectives of 1st and 2nd Declensions, with three endings; Present Indicative of εἰμί (sum); Pluperfect Indicative Active

A very large number of Adjectives are declined in the Masc. and Neuter like Nouns of the 2nd Declension, and in the Fem. like Fem. Nouns of the 1st Declension of either the τιμή or the χώρα type.

(1) If the Masc. ending of an Adjective in -ος comes after any consonant except ρ, then the Fem. ends in -η and is declined like τιμή.

(2) If the Masc. ending of an Adjective in -ος comes after a vowel or ρ, then the Fem. ends in -α and is declined like χώρα.

(Some Adjectives, used later in this book, have the same form for the Fem. as for the Masc. They are given in the vocabulary.)

	σοφός, wise			φίλιος, friendly		
Sing.	M.	F.	N.	M.	F.	N.
N.	σοφός	σοφή	σοφόν	φίλιος	φιλία	φίλιον
V.	σοφέ	σοφή	σοφόν	φίλιε	φιλία	φίλιον
A.	σοφόν	σοφήν	σοφόν	φίλιον	φιλίαν	φίλιον
G.	σοφοῦ	σοφῆς	σοφοῦ	φιλίου	φιλίας	φιλίου
D.	σοφῷ	σοφῇ	σοφῷ	φιλίῳ	φιλίᾳ	φιλίῳ
Plur.						
N.V.	σοφοί	σοφαί	σοφά	φίλιοι	φίλιαι	φίλια
A.	σοφούς	σοφάς	σοφά	φιλίους	φιλίας	φίλια
G.	σοφῶν	σοφῶν	σοφῶν	φιλίων	φιλίων	φιλίων
D.	σοφοῖς	σοφαῖς	σοφοῖς	φιλίοις	φιλίαις	φιλίοις

Like σοφός: ἀγαθός, good; κακός, bad; καλός, beautiful, fine; δεινός, strange, terrible.

35

Like φίλιος: ἀνδρεῖος, *brave*: πλούσιος, *rich*; ἰσχυρός, *strong*; μακρός, *long*.

Position of Adjective

If the Article as well as an Adjective is used to define a Noun, then the Adjective is generally placed **between** the Article and the Noun:

ὁ ἀνδρεῖος στρατιώτης, *the brave soldier*.

But it is equally good Greek to write ὁ στρατιώτης ὁ ἀνδρεῖος; compare ἡ οἰκία ἡ τοῦ κριτοῦ in Ch. 4.

(ἀνδρεῖος στρατιώτης or στρατιώτης ἀνδρεῖος is the Greek for **a** *brave soldier*, but ὁ στρατιώτης ἀνδρεῖος or ἀνδρεῖος ὁ στρατιώτης means *the soldier is brave*, the Verb for *is* being understood.)

N.B. The Article is frequently used with Adjectives to denote a class, e.g. οἱ σοφοί, *the wise*, *wise men*.

Present Indicative of εἰμί (*sum*)

Sing.	εἰμί	*I am*
	εἶ	*you are*, etc.
	ἐστί(ν)	
Plur.	ἐσμέν	
	ἐστέ	
	εἰσί(ν)	

ἀνδρεῖοί ἐστε, *you are brave*.
τὰ δένδρα ἐστὶ καλά, *the trees are beautiful*.

The 3rd persons of εἰμί are often used with a Dative of the Possessor, e.g. τοῖς Ἀθηναίοις ἐστὶ στρατιά, *the Athenians have an army*.

EXERCISE 26.

1. ὁ σοφὸς κριτὴς πείθει τὸν νεανίαν.
2. οἱ τοῦ ποιητοῦ λόγοι εἰσὶ καλοί.
3. ἡ χώρα ἐστὶ φιλία τοῖς Ἀθηναίοις.

4. οὐ πιστεύομεν τοῖς τῶν κακῶν λόγοις.
5. δεινὰ ὅπλα ἐστὶ τοῖς Πέρσαις.
6. οἱ κίνδυνοι οὐ κωλύουσι τοὺς ἀνδρείους.
7. ἡ τῆς οἰκίας θύρα ἐστὶν ἰσχυρά.
8. ὁ μακρὸς πόλεμος πιέζει τοὺς πολίτας.
9. οἱ πολέμιοι ἔκοπτον τὰ καλὰ δένδρα.
10. οὐ πλούσιοί ἐσμεν, ὦ ᾿Αθηναῖοι.
11. ἡ σοφία ἐστὶν ἀγαθὸν δῶρον.
12. τοῖς πολεμίοις εἰσὶν ἵπποι καλοὶ καὶ ἰσχυροί.

κίνδυνος (m.), *danger.*

EXERCISE 27.

1. The strong gate hindered the soldiers.
2. The slave is a bad steward.
3. Rich men are not always wise.
4. The goddess is friendly to the Athenians.
5. You are a wise doctor.
6. The judge's letter is long.
7. The poet has a beautiful voice.
8. There are beautiful trees in the island.
9. Wise men seek after peace.
10. The Athenians have strong weapons.
11. Bad trees do not bear good fruit.
12. Terrible dangers do not hinder the brave.

Pluperfect Indicative Active, and Revision

To form the **Pluperfect,** the Reduplicated Verb-Stem is Augmented, and -κη is added as the ending of the 1st person singular:

Sing.	ἐ-λε-λύ-κη	*I had loosed*
	ἐ-λε-λύ-κης	*you had loosed,* etc.
	ἐ-λε-λύ-κει	
Plur.	ἐ-λε-λύ-κεμεν	
	ἐ-λε-λύ-κετε	
	ἐ-λε-λύ-κεσαν	

The Pluperfect Tense is not very commonly used, but it should be known; you will find that the Greek for *when they had loosed* is ἐπεὶ ἔλυσαν (Aorist).

EXERCISE 28.

1. οἱ δοῦλοι οἱ ἀγαθοὶ ἤδη ἐλελύκεσαν τοὺς ἵππους.
2. ἐθηρεύομεν δεινὰ ζῷα ἐν τῇ νήσῳ.
3. ὁ ταμίας ἐπεπαιδεύκει τοὺς δούλους.
4. οἱ τῆς κώμης πολῖται ἐχθροί εἰσι τοῖς Ἀθηναίοις.
5. οὐκ ἀεὶ πιστεύομεν τοῖς τῶν σοφῶν λόγοις.
6. ὁ νεανίας ἀγγέλλει νίκην καλήν.
7. οἱ βάρβαροι ἐκεκωλύκεσαν τοὺς Ἀθηναίους ἀπὸ τοῦ ποταμοῦ.
8. τὰ ζῷά ἐστιν ἐχθρὰ τοῖς νεανίαις.
9. ὁ τοῦ δένδρου καρπός ἐστιν ἀγαθὸς ἀνθρώποις.
10. οὐκ ἐλελύκεμεν τοὺς ἵππους ἀπὸ τῆς ἁμάξης.

ἤδη, *already.*
ζῷον, *animal.*
ἐχθρός, *hostile.*
ἀγγέλλω, *I announce.*

νίκη, *victory.*
βάρβαροι (m.), *barbarians.*
ἄνθρωπος, *man (human being).*

EXERCISE 29.

1. The river is dangerous for horses.
2. The sea had loosened the bridge.
3. The barbarians are hostile to the Athenians.
4. Good trees do not always produce fruit.
5. The long weapons weigh down the soldiers.
6. You had already set free the good slaves.
7. The general has honour on account of a fine victory.
8. The island produces strange animals.
9. Bad masters do not have good slaves.
10. The goddess of the island is friendly to the sailors.

dangerous, χαλεπός.
on account of, διά (Acc.).

master, δεσπότης.

Chapter 8

3rd Declension examples; Present Imperative and Infinitive; Connection of Sentences; μέν and δέ

The general pattern followed by Nouns of the 3rd Declension with Stems ending with a **consonant** is shown by the following:

φύλαξ (m.), *guard* (stem φυλακ-). σῶμα (n.), *body* (stem σωματ-).

Sing.

N.V.	φύλαξ	σῶμα
Acc.	φύλακα	σῶμα
Gen.	φύλακος	σώματος
Dat.	φύλακι	σώματι

Plur.

N.V.	φύλακες	σώματα
Acc.	φύλακας	σώματα
Gen.	φυλάκων	σωμάτων
Dat.	φύλαξι(ν)	σώμασι(ν)

It will be noticed that the Nom. Sing. of φύλαξ is formed from φύλακ-ς, and the Dat. Plur. from φύλακ-σι; τ is dropped before the ending -σι in the Dat. Plur. of σῶμα. Note that the paragogic ν is never added to the ι of the Dat. Sing.

Like φύλαξ: κῆρυξ (κηρυκ-), m., *herald*; θώραξ (θωρακ-), m., *breastplate*; σάλπιγξ (σαλπιγγ-), f., *trumpet*.

Like σῶμα: ὄνομα (ὀνοματ-), n., *name*; χρῆμα (χρηματ-), n., *thing*; pl. τὰ χρήματα, *money*; στράτευμα (στρατευματ-), n., *army*.

Present Imperative

The 2nd persons Sing. and Plur. of the Present Imperative of Verbs in -ω are formed by adding -ε and -ετε to the Present-stem, e.g. λῦ-ε, λύ-ετε.

The Present Imperative is used to express a **Direct Command** when the action is a **continuing** one, e.g. ἀεὶ πίστευε τοῖς ἀγαθοῖς, *always trust good men*.

Present Infinitive

The Present Infinitive is formed by adding -ειν to the Present-stem, e.g. λύ-ειν, γράφ-ειν. The Infinitive is used:

(1) as **Complement**:

χαλεπόν ἐστι διαβαίνειν τὸν ποταμόν.
It is dangerous to cross the river.

(2) **Prolatively,** after certain Verbs, exactly as in Latin:

ἐθέλομεν εὑρίσκειν τὸν φύλακα.
We wish to find the guard.

(3) In **Indirect Commands,** after all Verbs of *ordering, advising, persuading*; the Neg. before the Infinitive in an Indirect Command is μή:

ἐκελεύσαμεν τοὺς φύλακας φεύγειν
We ordered the guards to flee.

(μὴ φεύγειν, *not to flee.*)

Note the simplicity of this construction, as compared with the constructions for Indirect Command in Latin; it is the same as in English.

EXERCISE 30.

1. οἱ πολέμιοι ἐτόξευον τοὺς φύλακας.
2. οἱ στρατιῶται ὁπλίζουσι τὰ σώματα θώραξιν.
3. τὸ τοῦ ζῴου σῶμά ἐστι μικρόν.
4. διώκετε τοὺς πολεμίους, ὦ στρατιῶται.
5. ἐκέλευσα τοὺς στρατιώτας καίειν τὰς κώμας.
6. ῥᾴδιόν ἐστι λαμβάνειν τὴν νῆσον.
7. ὁ κῆρυξ ἀγγέλλει τὴν νίκην τῇ σάλπιγγι.
8. ὁ ταμίας φέρει τὰ χρήματα ἐκ τῆς οἰκίας.
9. οἱ πολέμιοι οὐκ ἐθέλουσι πιστεύειν τῷ κήρυκι.

10. ὁ στρατηγὸς ἐκέλευσε τὸν φύλακα μὴ κλείειν τὴν πύλην.
11. παίδευε τοὺς δούλους, ὦ ταμία.
12. οἱ θώρακές εἰσι χρήσιμοι τοῖς φύλαξιν.

ὁπλίζω, *I arm.*	λαμβάνω, *I take, capture.*
μικρός, *small.*	ἐθέλω, *I am willing, wish.*
κελεύω, *I order.*	κλείω, *I shut.*
καίω, *I burn.*	χρήσιμος, *useful.*
ῥᾴδιος, *easy.*	

EXERCISE 31.

1. The guards hindered the sailors.
2. The island has a beautiful name.
3. The voice of the herald announces a victory.
4. The general is leading his army to the sea.
5. The soldier is carrying his breastplate.
6. Flee from the village, citizens.
7. The general ordered the soldiers to save the children.
8. It is difficult to train horses.
9. We ordered the young men not to hunt the animals.
10. The soldier shot the general through the breastplate.
11. The general will advise the soldiers to flee.
12. Train your bodies, citizens.

Connection of Sentences, etc.

So far, the Greek exercises have consisted of separate sentences. When continuous Greek is written, every sentence is **connected** with the previous sentence by means of a **Particle,** showing how the new matter is related to what went before; these Particles need not be translated in English, unless the sense requires it.

The commonest Particles are:

(1) Coming first word in the sentence—
     καί, *and, also.* ἀλλά, *but.*
(2) Coming second word in the sentence—
     δέ, *and, but.* γάρ, *for.* οὖν, *therefore.*

τε ... καί are used as the English *both ... and*, τε coming second word, e.g. οἵ τε στρατιῶται καὶ οἱ ναῦται.

οὔτε ... οὔτε mean *neither ... nor*, e.g. τὸ δένδρον ἐστὶν οὔτε καλὸν οὔτε χρήσιμον, *the tree is neither beautiful nor useful.*

Distinguish from the above type of connecting Particle:

μέν and δέ

μέν and δέ are used to link two **corresponding** or **contrasting** clauses, each coming **second** word in its clause:

ῥᾴδιον μέν ἐστι λέγειν, χαλεπὸν δὲ πείθειν.
It is easy to speak, but difficult to persuade.

οἱ μὲν Λακεδαιμόνιοι ἐδίωκον τοὺς πολεμίους, οἱ δὲ σύμμαχοι ἔφευγον.
The Spartans began to pursue the enemy, but their allies fled.

Greek likes to express a thought in terms of such contrasts, and you will find it worth while to stop and look at every μέν and δέ that you come across in reading Greek in this book. Latin had no equivalent pair of particles and in this fact lies one of the most important differences between the two languages. Thus, in the above example Latin might most naturally have recourse to a *dum* (*while*) clause to express what is said in the μέν clause, with *fugiebant* as the main verb.

οἱ μέν ... , οἱ δέ are often used meaning *some ... , others*:

οἱ μὲν πιστεύουσι τοῖς λόγοις, οἱ δὲ τοῖς ὅπλοις.
Some put trust in words, others in weapons.

N.B. μέν does **not** serve as a link with what has gone before.

ὁ δέ, *and he*, οἱ δέ, *and they*, are often found at the beginning of a sentence, but only when picking up a preceding Noun or Pronoun in an Oblique Case; the Article was originally a Personal Pronoun:

ἐκώλυσα τὸν ἄνθρωπον· ὁ δὲ ἐθαύμαζεν.
I stopped the fellow, and he was amazed.

From this point onwards the Greek-English vocabulary at the end of the book should be used for finding out the meaning of new Greek words. There is also an English-Greek vocabulary.

For the learning of Greek Grammar, a formal 'Grammar'

should now be used. In the rest of this book, reference is made to pages in Abbott and Mansfield's 'Primer of Greek Grammar' (Duckworth), e.g. below, where A 56 refers to page 56 of that book; if other Grammars are preferred, there should be no difficulty in finding the relevant pages.

EXERCISE 32.

UNDERGROUND DWELLINGS

The Armenia referred to lay to the S.E. of the Black Sea; underground houses are still common in this district.

οἱ δὲ ᾿Αρμένιοι ἔχουσι τὰς οἰκίας κατὰ τῆς γῆς· ταῖς δὲ οἰκίαις ἐστὶ μικρὸν στόμα. καὶ τοῖς μὲν ὑποζυγίοις αἱ εἴσοδοι ὀρυκταί εἰσιν, οἱ δὲ ἄνθρωποι καταβαίνουσιν ἐπὶ κλίμακος. ἐν δὲ ταῖς οἰκίαις εἰσὶν αἶγές τε καὶ ἄλλα ζῷα· οἱ δὲ ᾿Αρμένιοι τρέφουσι τὰ ζῷα ἔνδον χιλῷ. ἐν δὲ ἀγγείοις ἐστὶν οἶνος· καὶ τὸν οἶνον εἰς τὸ στόμα μύζουσι καλάμοις.

Adapted from Xenophon, *Anabasis IV*, v, 25–27

Two uses of αὐτός (A 56)

αὐτός, αὐτή, αὐτό, declined like σοφός, except that the Nom. and Acc. of the neuter sing. ends in -ό, and there is no Vocative, is used:

(a) throughout, like **ipse**, meaning *self*, e.g. ὁ στρατηγὸς αὐτός, *the general himself* (never in this sense **between** the Article and Noun; see p. 101);

(b) in all cases except the Nom., like **eum, eam, id,** *him, her, it,* e.g. ὁ ποταμὸς ἐκώλυσεν αὐτόν (αὐτούς,) *the river hindered him (them).*

EXERCISE 33.

1. οἱ μὲν ᾿Αθηναῖοι ἐστράτευον, οἱ δὲ Λακεδαιμόνιοι ἔθυον τοῖς θεοῖς.
2. ὁ στρατηγὸς αὐτὸς ἀγγέλλει τὴν νίκην ἐν τῇ ἐκκλησίᾳ.
3. κελεύσομεν αὐτοὺς φεύγειν ἐκ τῆς κώμης.
4. οἱ μὲν φεύγουσιν, οἱ δὲ μένουσιν.

5. οἵ τε Λακεδαιμόνιοι καὶ οἱ Ἀθηναῖοι ἐστράτευον ἐπὶ
   τοὺς Πέρσας.
6. ὁ κριτὴς αὐτὸς διδάσκει τὸν νεανίαν.
7. ἡ μὲν φιλία τὴν εἰρήνην παρέχει, τὰ δὲ ὅπλα τὸν
   πόλεμον.
8. οἱ μὲν τῶν στρατιωτῶν ἐφύλασσον τὴν πύλην, οἱ δὲ
   πρὸς αὐτὴν ἔφευγον.
9. ἐδιώκομεν τὸν Ξέρξην αὐτὸν ἀπὸ τῆς χώρας
10. σοφοὶ μέν ἐστε, κακοὶ δέ.

EXERCISE 34.

1. Both the Persians and their allies were fleeing.
2. The island is small, but the guards are hostile.
3. Some of the trees are beautiful, others useful.
4. The herald is announcing the victory to the general himself.
5. We are pursuing the enemy and driving them to the
   gates.
6. They are clever, but cowardly.
7. Some trust money, others wisdom.
8. The goddess herself ordered them to sacrifice.
9. It is easy to catch the horse, but difficult to train him.
10. The young man is neither brave nor wise.

EXERCISE 35.

CYRUS IS HELPED BY CAMELS

*Croesus, king of Lydia (in Asia Minor), after conquering most
of the Greek cities to the east of the Aegean, invaded Persia in
546 B.C. in an attempt to crush the power of Cyrus the Great,
king of the Medes and Persians.*

ὁ δὲ Κροῖσος, ὅτε ἐβασίλευε τῶν Λυδῶν, ἐστράτευσεν ἐπὶ
τοὺς Πέρσας. τὸ γὰρ μαντεῖον ἔπειθεν αὐτόν, ὡς ἐνόμιζε,
καταλύειν τὴν τῶν Περσῶν ἀρχήν. πρῶτον μὲν οὖν ποταμὸν
(τὸ ὄνομά ἐστιν Ἅλυς) διαβαίνει καὶ φθείρει τὴν χώραν,
ἔπειτα δὲ τάσσει τὸ στράτευμα εἰς μάχην. (This battle was
indecisive; Croesus retired to Sardis, his capital, before which

Cyrus soon appeared). καὶ ὁ Κῦρος ἀθροίζει τὰς καμήλους καὶ
κελεύει στρατιώτας ἀναβαίνειν καὶ ἐλαύνειν αὐτὰς πρὸς τὴν
τοῦ Κροίσου ἵππον,[1] τοὺς δὲ πεζοὺς τάσσει ὄπισθε τῶν
καμήλων, τὴν δὲ ἵππον ὄπισθε τῶν πεζῶν· οἱ γὰρ ἵπποι
οὐχ οἷοί τέ εἰσι φέρειν οὔτε τὴν ἰδέαν οὔτε τὴν ὀδμὴν τῶν
καμήλων. ἐν δὲ τῇ μάχῃ αἱ κάμηλοι δεινὸν φόβον παρέχουσι
τοῖς ἵπποις. οὕτω δὲ ὁ Κῦρος ἀναγκάζει τοὺς τοῦ Κροίσου
στρατιώτας φεύγειν.[2]

Adapted from Herodotus, I, 76–80.

[1] ἡ ἵππος, Collective Noun, *cavalry.*
[2] When they had subdued Lydia, the Persians went on to reduce the
Greek cities in Asia Minor.

Chapter 9

3rd Declension : Stems in -τ, -δ, -θ (A 31) ;
Future of εἰμί (sum) (A 118)

EXERCISE 36.

1. ῥᾴδιον ἔσται λαμβάνειν τὴν ὄρνιθα.
2. οἱ σύμμαχοι ἔσονται χρήσιμοι τοῖς Ἀθηναίοις.
3. οὐκ ἐσόμεθα ἐχθροὶ τοῖς φυγάσιν.
4. οἱ παῖδες χάριν ἔχουσι τῷ δούλῳ.
5. στρατεύετε, ὦ Ἀθηναῖοι, ὑπὲρ τῆς πατρίδος.
6. ἡ Ἑλλὰς ἔσται ἐλευθέρα.
7. τοῖς ὁπλίταις εἰσὶ κόρυθές τε καὶ ἀσπίδες.
8. αἱ τῶν Περσῶν ἐλπίδες εἰσὶ κεναί.
9. οἱ φυγάδες ἀπὸ τῆς Ἑλλάδος ἔφευγον.
10. τὰ τόξα ἐστὶν ἕτοιμα τοῖς παισίν.
11. ἀνδρεῖοι ἔσεσθε, ὦ στρατιῶται, καὶ ἄξιοι τῆς τιμῆς.
12. χάριν ἔχομεν ὅτι σῴζετε τὴν πατρίδα.

Exercise 37.

1. The Athenians will not be slaves.
2. It will be useful to have shields.
3. The Persians are fleeing from Greece.
4. Greece will be both strong and free.
5. The boys are carrying torches in the market-place.
6. The enemy will be friendly to the exiles.
7. The exiles feel grateful to the Athenians.
8. We wish to drive the enemy from our country.
9. We will be faithful to the general.
10. The soldiers trust neither their shields nor their helmets.
11. The girls were sacrificing to the goddess.
12. We will not trust empty hopes.

3rd Declension: Stems in -ντ, -κτ (A 32); Imperfect of εἰμί (sum) (A 117)

Exercise 38.

1. ἀνδριὰς ἦν τοῦ γέροντος ἐν τῇ ἀγορᾷ.
2. ὁ Ἰάσων ἔσπειρε τοὺς τοῦ δράκοντος ὀδόντας ἐν τῇ γῇ.
3. χαλεπόν ἐστι θηρεύειν τοὺς λέοντας.
4. οἱ φυγάδες ἦσαν ἐν κινδύνῳ.
5. ὁ Ξενοφῶν ἔπαυσε τὴν μάχην διὰ τὴν νύκτα.
6. οἱ τοῦ γίγαντος ὀδόντες ἦσαν δεινοί.
7. οὐκ ἦσθα δίκαιος, ὦ κριτά.
8. οἱ μὲν νεανίαι εἰσὶν ἀνδρεῖοι, οἱ δὲ γέροντες σοφοί.
9. ἐμένομεν τὴν νύκτα ἐν τῇ ὕλῃ.
10. ἐν τῇ Ἑλλάδι εἰσὶ καλοὶ ἀνδριάντες.
11. οἱ Ἀθηναῖοι ἐθέλουσι σώζειν τούς τε γέροντας καὶ τοὺς παῖδας.
12. ἦν καλὰ δένδρα ἐν τῇ νήσῳ.

Exercise 39.

1. Honour old men, my sons.
2. The teeth of the lion are strong.
3. It was not easy to kill the giant.
4. We were once slaves, O Athenians.

5. There were dangerous snakes in the island.
6. The slaves will be faithful to the old man.
7. The giant himself was still in the sea.
8. Night stopped the battle.
9. The young men pursued the enemy, but the old men fled.
10. We were admiring the statues of the gods.
11. You were in danger because of the lion.
12. The nights are now long.

EXERCISE 40.

THE BATTLE OF THERMOPYLAE

In 480 B.C. three hundred Spartans with their king, Leonidas, heroically tried to defend Greece against the invading army of Xerxes, king of Persia. The battle took place at Thermopylae, a narrow pass, in the south of Thessaly.

ὅτε δὲ ὁ Ξέρξης ἐστράτευεν ἐπὶ τὴν Ἑλλάδα, οἱ Λακεδαιμόνιοι ἐφύλασσον τὴν ἐν ταῖς Θερμοπύλαις εἰσβολήν· καὶ
πρὸ τῆς μάχης λέγει τις τῶν συμμάχων, 'Τοσοῦτός ἐστιν ὁ
ἀριθμὸς τῶν βαρβάρων, ὥστε ἀποκρύπτουσι τὸν ἥλιον τοῖς
τοξεύμασιν.' 'Ἀγαθὰ ἀγγέλλεις,' λέγει Λακεδαιμόνιός τις,
ὀνόματι Διηνέκης· 'ἡ οὖν μάχη ὑπὸ σκιᾷ ἔσται, καὶ οὐκ
ἐν ἡλίῳ.' ὁ δὲ Λεωνίδας, ὁ τῶν Λακεδαιμονίων στρατηγός,
ἐκέλευσε τοὺς στρατιώτας μένειν οὗ ἦσαν.

ἐν δὲ τῇ μάχῃ αὐτῇ οἱ λοχαγοὶ ἐποτρύνουσι τοὺς Πέρσας
μάστιξιν· οἱ γὰρ βάρβαροι οὐκ ἀνδρεῖοι ἦσαν. οἱ δὲ Λακεδαιμόνιοι ἀνδρείως μὲν ἐφύλασσον τὴν εἰσβολὴν ὑπὲρ τῆς
πατρίδος, μάτην δέ· μόνον γὰρ τριακόσιοι ἦσαν. ὁ δὲ Λεωνίδας
αὐτὸς ἐν τῇ μάχῃ πίπτει· καὶ σήμερόν ἐστιν ἐπὶ τῷ τοῦ
Λεωνίδου τάφῳ λίθινος λέων.

Adapted from Herodotus, VII, 225–226.

Note on Direct Questions

Direct Questions are dealt with in Ch. 24, with the introduc-
tion of the Interrogative Pronoun. If it is so wished, however,

some experience in Direct Questions may be gained before that point is reached; many of the sentences may be turned into the form of questions with or without ἆρα, or introduced by an Interrogative word, e.g. τί; *why?* ποῦ; *where?* ποῖ; *whither?* πόθεν; *whence?* πῶς; *how?* (see the section in Ch. 24), e.g. Ex. 21, 1, could become 'Why were the citizens fleeing into Athens?'

Chapter 10

3rd Declension: Stems in -ρ (A 33); Syllabic and Temporal Augments (A 90–91)

Syllabic and Temporal Augments

Sections 123 and 125 of A may be omitted for the time being.

EXERCISE 41.

Write down the 1st person sing. of the Imperfect Indicative Active of—

1. ἀγγέλλω.	8. συμβουλεύω.	15. προπέμπω.
2. ὁπλίζω.	9. καταλύω.	16. διαβαίνω.
3. ἀναγκάζω.	10. ἄγω.	17. περιπέμπω.
4. ἐλαύνω.	11. εὑρίσκω.	18. αὐξάνω.
5. ψεύδω.	12. ἐκπέμπω.	19. ἁρπάζω.
6. οἰκίζω.	13. ἀποφεύγω.	20. αἰσχύνω.
7. ἄρχω.	14. εἰσβάλλω.	21. ἥκω

Note. If an Augmented part of a Verb begins with η, then the Verb-stem must begin with α or ε or η itself (as in ἡσυχάζω, which cannot receive an Augment).

EXERCISE 42.

1. ὁ τοῦ Ξέρξου πατὴρ ἦν Δαρεῖος.
2. οἱ παῖδες χάριν ἔχουσι τῇ μητρί.

3. οἱ ἄνδρες ἤλαυνον τοὺς θῆρας ἐκ τῆς ὕλης.
4. οἱ Ἀθηναῖοι ἐθαύμαζον τοὺς τοῦ ῥήτορος λόγους.
5. οἶνός ἐστιν ἐν τῷ κρατῆρι.
6. ὁ λέων ἤσθιε τὸν θῆρα.
7. ἐν πολέμῳ οἱ πατέρες θάπτουσι τοὺς παῖδας.
8. ὁ γέρων ἤκουε τὴν τῆς θυγατρὸς φωνήν.
9. τριακόσιοι ἄνδρες ἐφύλασσον τὴν εἰσβολήν.
10. οἱ ἀροτῆρες ὤρυσσον τὴν γῆν.
11. ὁ στρατηγὸς ὥπλιζε τοὺς ἄνδρας θώραξί τε καὶ κόρυσιν.
12. ὁ θὴρ ἥρπαζε τὸ ζῷον τοῖς ὀδοῦσιν.

EXERCISE 43.

1. We do not trust the orator.
2. The mothers were sending away their sons to the war.
3. The men were pursuing wild beasts.
4. The orator's words were foolish.
5. In peace sons bury their fathers.
6. The old man's daughter was writing a letter.
7. The mothers of the Spartans admire courage.
8. It is not always easy for fathers to educate their children.
9. The exiles were founding a colony.
10. They used to call the earth their mother.
11. The tyrant had a beautiful daughter.
12. The fathers plant the trees, but the sons eat the fruit.

3rd Declension: Stems in -ν (A 34); some Verbs with Consonant Stems (Guttural)

The conjugation of Greek Verbs with Consonant Stems is extremely irregular and it would be impossible to give a set of rules to cover them all. Much the easiest thing is to learn off the principal parts and then to study the general pattern that emerges. It will be enough at the moment to learn a few tenses of some common Verbs, and to see that in the Future and Weak Aorist the -σ that we found in λύσω, ἔλυσα, is still there, either by itself or in a double consonant, ξ or ψ:

Present	Future	Aorist	Perfect	
διώκω	διώξω	ἐδίωξα	δεδίωχα	I pursue
ἄρχω	ἄρξω	ἦρξα	ἦρχα	I rule over, am in command of (Gen.)
ἄγω	ἄξω	ἤγαγον	ἦχα	I lead
πράσσω	πράξω	ἔπραξα	πέπραχα	I do, manage, fare

πέπραχα, I have done; πέπραγα I have fared

τάσσω	τάξω	ἔταξα	τέταχα	I draw up
ταράσσω	ταράξω	ἐτάραξα	—	I confuse
φυλάσσω	φυλάξω	ἐφύλαξα	πεφύλαχα	I guard

Two important points should be noticed:—

(1) When the Stem begins with a **vowel,** as in ἄρχω and ἄγω above, the Augment, instead of Reduplication, is used with the Perfect tense (see A 91, Section 126, for this rule and others, e.g. that for Verbs beginning with χ, θ, φ, as φυλάσσω above);

(2) ἤγαγον, the Aorist of ἄγω, is our first example of a **Strong Aorist;** Strong Aorists end in -ον, and are conjugated exactly like an Imperfect tense, e.g. ἤγαγον, ἤγαγες, ἤγαγε, etc. (see p. 26 above).

EXERCISE 44.

1. ὁ Λεωνίδας ἔταξε τοὺς Ἕλληνας εἰς μάχην.
2. ὁ Ξέρξης οὐκ ἄρξει τῆς Ἑλλάδος.
3. οἱ ποιμένες ἤγαγον τοὺς αἶγας εἰς τὸν λειμῶνα.
4. οἱ Πέρσαι οὐκ ἐδίωξαν τοὺς Ἕλληνας.
5. ὁ στρατηγὸς τέταχε τοὺς συμμάχους.
6. οἱ τριακόσιοι μάτην πεφυλάχασι τὴν εἰσβολήν.
7. εὖ ἐπράξατε τὰ¹ τῆς πατρίδος.
8. αἱ κάμηλοι ἐτάραξαν τοὺς ἵππους.
9. οἱ τῶν Ἀθηναίων γείτονες οὐκ ἐστράτευον.
10. διὰ τὸν χειμῶνα ὁ ἡγεμὼν οὐχ εὑρίσκει τὴν ὁδόν.
11. οἱ νεανίαι εὖ πεπράγασιν ἐν τοῖς ἀγῶσιν.
12. τῷ γέροντί ἐστι χιτὼν μακρός.

¹ *the affairs*; Greek is fond of this general use of the neuter pl. of the Article.

Exercise 45.

1. The camels will pursue the horses.
2. The lion pursued the shepherd from the meadow.
3. Xerxes will lead his army against Greece.
4. On account of the danger we guarded the harbour.
5. Cyrus has drawn up the infantry behind the camels.
6. Xerxes ruled the country after the death of Darius.
7. The generals managed the affairs of Greece.
8. The Persians will not throw the Spartans into disorder.
9. The guides led the enemy to the pass.
10. We did not fare well in the contest.
11. You guarded your neighbour well.
12. The Athenians have pursued the Persians into the sea.

Exercise 46.

XERXES WHIPS THE SEA

The bridges referred to were built across the Hellespont be-
tween Abydos and Sestos and were nearly a mile long. This was
in preparation for Xerxes' invasion in 480 B.C.; King Darius had
died in 485.

μετὰ δὲ τὸν τοῦ πατρὸς θάνατον ὁ Ξέρξης ἦρχε τῶν Περσῶν.
ὅτι δὲ ἤθελε κολάζειν[1] τοὺς Ἕλληνας διὰ τὰς ἀδικίας, ἐβού-
λευσε διαβαίνειν τὸν Ἑλλήσποντον καὶ ἄγειν στράτευμα διὰ
τῆς Εὐρώπης ἐπὶ τὴν Ἑλλάδα· ἐκέλευσεν οὖν Φοίνικας καὶ
Αἰγυπτίους δύο γεφύρας κατασκευάζειν. ἐπεὶ δὲ ἔπραξαν τὸ
ἔργον, χειμὼν μέγιστος διέλυσε τὰς γεφύρας. ὁ οὖν Ξέρξης,
ὅτε μανθάνει, μάλιστα ἐχαλέπαινε καὶ ἐκέλευσε τοὺς ἄνδρας
οὐ μόνον τόν τε Ἑλλήσποντον τριακοσίαις πληγαῖς τύπτειν
καὶ δύο πέδας εἰς αὐτὸν βάλλειν, ἀλλὰ καὶ ἀποτέμνειν τὰς τῶν
ἐπιστατῶν κεφαλάς. ἔπειτα δὲ ἄλλους ἐπιστάτας ἐκέλευσε
κατασκευάζειν τὰς γεφύρας.

Adapted from Herodotus, VII, 34–36.

[1] Darius had wanted to punish the two Greek cities of Athens and
Eretria for having helped the Greeks of Ionia (in Asia Minor) to rebel
against the Persians in 497, and his expedition had been defeated at
Marathon in 490; Xerxes thus had a further motive for his invasion in 480.

Chapter 11

Further Notes on Word Order, and Revision

(1) When a **Prepositional phrase** is used to define a Noun, the phrase is placed **between** the Article and the Noun:

τὰ ἐν τῇ νήσῳ δένδρα ἐστὶ καλά.

The trees in the island are beautiful.

Sometimes, instead of this *sandwich* construction, the Prepositional phrase follows the Noun, with its Article repeated, e.g. τὰ δένδρα τὰ ἐν τῇ νήσῳ.

(2) Just as the Neuter plural of the Article is used without a Noun, e.g. τὰ τῆς Ἑλλάδος, *the affairs of Greece*, so the Masc. and Fem. are also used for *the men, the women*:

οἱ ἐν τῇ νήσῳ, *the men on the island.*

αἱ ἐν τῇ οἰκίᾳ, *the women in the house.*

So also, οἱ πάλαι, *the men of old*; οἱ ἐκεῖ, *the people there*, where πάλαι and ἐκεῖ are Adverbs.

EXERCISE 47.

1. ἡ ἐν τῷ λιμένι μάχη ἦν μακρά.
2. οἱ Ἀθηναῖοι ἐτάραξαν τοὺς ἐν τῇ νήσῳ.
3. ἐθέλομεν εὑρίσκειν, ὦ ἡγεμών, τὴν διὰ τῆς ὕλης ὁδόν.
4. οἱ Λακεδαιμόνιοι χάριν ἔχουσι τοῖς μετὰ τοῦ Λεωνίδου.
5. χαλεπὸν ἔσται ἀπελαύνειν τοὺς Πέρσας.
6. ὁ Λεωνίδας ἤγαγε τὴν στρατιὰν διὰ τῆς Ἀττικῆς.
7. οἱ ἐν ταῖς πύλαις φυλάξουσι τοὺς πολίτας.
8. οἱ μὲν ἔπιπτον, οἱ δὲ ἔφευγον.
9. οἱ Ἀθηναῖοι ἐθαύμαζον τοὺς πάλαι.
10. οἱ γίγαντες ἦσαν δεινοί τε καὶ ἰσχυροί.

EXERCISE 48.

1. We pursued the men on the island into the sea.
2. Some were cutting down trees, others were burning them.

3. We did not believe the words of the orator.
4. The people there were pitying the prisoners.
5. The Athenians had trained their horses.
6. Night will not stop the contest.
7. The wine in the bowl is bitter.
8. The trumpets threw the horses into confusion.
9. We ordered the women in the island to flee.
10. The general himself falls in the battle.

EXERCISE 49.

1. τὰ ἐν τῇ νήσῳ ζῷα ἦν δεινά.
2. ἡ διὰ τῆς χώρας ὁδὸς ἔσται χαλεπή.
3. ἠκούομεν τὴν τοῦ στρατηγοῦ αὐτοῦ φωνήν.
4. οἱ νῦν οὐκ ἀεὶ διώκουσι τὴν σοφίαν.
5. ὁ στρατηγὸς ἔταξε τοὺς στρατιώτας καὶ αὐτοὺς ἐκέλευσε μένειν τὴν νύκτα.
6. τοὺς μὲν χρήματα πείθει, τοὺς δὲ λόγοι.
7. οἱ Ἀθηναῖοι ἐδίωκον τοὺς πολεμίους· οἱ δὲ εὐθὺς ἔφευγον.
8. λελύκαμεν τοὺς ἐν τῇ νήσῳ.
9. ὁ Λεωνίδας ἦρχε τῶν Λακεδαιμονίων.
10. οἱ δοῦλοι οἱ ἐν τῇ οἰκίᾳ οὐ κακῶς ἔπραξαν.

EXERCISE 50.

1. Some were guarding the gate, others the arms.
2. The sailors in the harbour were announcing the enemy's victory.
3. The women here do not wish to remain.
4. The young men persuade their fathers not to remain in the village.
5. Neither the old men nor the children were able to escape.
6. The enemy's general has led the men to the river.
7. The mothers have trained their daughters.
8. The sailors from the island pursued the Athenians.
9. The general himself ordered the Greeks not to burn the village.
10. You have guarded the pass well, but in vain.

EXERCISE 51.

ADMETUS AND ALCESTIS

The following is the outline of the plot of the Alcestis, one of the best known plays of Euripides (485–406 B.C.). Pherae was a town in Thessaly.

ὁ Ἄδμητος ἐβασίλευε τῶν Φερῶν καὶ ἦν τῆς Ἀλκήστιδος
ἀνήρ· ἐπεὶ δὲ ἡ ὥρα ἧκε τῷ Ἀδμήτῳ ἀποθνῄσκειν, ὁ Ἀπόλλων λέγει ὅτι διὰ τὴν πρὶν εὔνοιαν ἔξεστιν αὐτῷ ἔτι βίον
διάγειν, εἴ τις τῶν οἰκείων ἐθέλει ὑπὲρ αὐτοῦ ἀποθνῄσκειν.
ἀλλ᾽ ὁ Ἄδμητος οὐχ οἷός τε ἦν πείθειν οὔτε τὸν πατέρα οὔτε
τὴν μητέρα· καὶ δὴ ἡ Ἄλκηστις μόνη ἤθελε σῴζειν τὸν ἄνδρα·
ἐκέλευσεν οὖν χαίρειν τόν τε υἱὸν καὶ τὴν θυγατέρα καὶ τὸν
ἄνδρα αὐτόν. μετὰ δὲ τὸν τῆς Ἀλκήστιδος θάνατον ὁ Ἡρακλῆς
πάρεστιν εἰς τὰ βασίλεια· ὁ δὲ Ἄδμητος ξενίζει μὲν αὐτόν,
κρύπτει δὲ τὴν συμφοράν. τέλος δὲ ὁ Ἡρακλῆς, ὡς μανθάνει
τὰ¹ περὶ τῆς Ἀλκήστιδος παρὰ τῆς θεραπαίνης, εἰς τὸν τάφον
τρέχει καὶ ἁρπάζει τὴν Ἀλκήστιδα πρὸς βίαν ἀπὸ τοῦ Θανά-
του· εἶτα δὲ πρὸς τὸν ἄνδρα αὐτὴν κομίζει.

¹ *the news*; see note in Exercise 44.

Chapter 12

Numerals: Cardinals and Ordinals, 1–10 (A 53–54); Time

Only Numerals up to 10 are included in the following Exercises; further Numerals should be learnt afterwards and may be substituted in the sentences.

Ways of expressing Time

Time *how long* is expressed by the **Accusative**:

οἱ πολέμιοι ἔφευγον πέντε ἡμέρας.

The enemy were fleeing for five days.

Time *when* is expressed by the **Dative** (without a Preposition):

ὁ στρατηγὸς ἔταξε τὸ στράτευμα τῇ τρίτῃ ἡμέρᾳ.
The general drew up his army on the third day.

Time *within which* is expressed by the **Genitive**:

πέμψει τοὺς στρατιώτας πέντε ἡμερῶν.
He will send the soldiers within five days.

So too, τῆς νυκτός, *in the night, by night*; χειμῶνος, *in winter*.

N.B. οὐδείς, *no one*, compound of εἷς (A 54).

EXERCISE 52.

1. ἐμένομεν ἐν τῇ νήσῳ ἓξ ἡμέρας.
2. μακρὸν χρόνον ἐθηρεύομεν τὸν λέοντα.
3. θύσομεν τῇ θεᾷ τῷ τετάρτῳ μηνί.
4. οἱ στρατιῶται παρασκευάζουσι τὰ ὅπλα τῆς νυκτός.
5. ὀκτω ἡμέρας τὸ στράτευμα ἦν ἐν κινδύνῳ.
6. τῇ πρώτῃ ἑσπέρᾳ ὁ γίγας ἐσθίει δύο ἄνδρας.
7. ἐφυλάσσομεν τὴν πύλην ἐννέα ἡμέρας.
8. δέκα ἡμερῶν παιδεύσεις τὸν ἵππον.
9. τὸ στράτευμα οὐχ οἷόν τέ ἐστι διαβαίνειν τὸν ποταμὸν
   μιᾶς ἡμέρας.
10. τῆς μὲν ἡμέρας διδάσκει τοὺς παῖδας, τῆς δὲ ἑσπέρας
    γράφει.
11. τὰ ὅπλα ἦν ἑτοῖμα τῇ δευτέρᾳ ἡμέρᾳ.
12. ὀλίγων ἡμερῶν ἡ Ἑλλὰς ἐλευθέρα ἔσται.

EXERCISE 53.

1. For five nights we were waiting for the moon.
2. I shall bring back the soldiers within three days.
3. The enemy are cutting the trees by night.
4. In the fourth month he stopped the war.
5. The doctor cured him in seven days.
6. For ten months the exiles were in danger.
7. The slave was absent for two days and one night.
8. No one crosses the river at night.
9. The citizens were in the assembly for a long time.

10. Some rest by night, others by day.
11. On the second day we pursued the enemy to the sea.
12. You will be free within a few months.

3rd Declension: Stems in -σ (A 34); some Verbs with Consonant Stems (Dental)

Present	Future	Aorist	Perfect	
ἀναγκάζω	ἀναγκάσω	ἠνάγκασα	ἠνάγκακα	I compel
πείθω	πείσω	ἔπεισα	πέπεικα	I persuade
σῴζω	σώσω	ἔσωσα	σέσωκα	I save

EXERCISE 54.

1. ὁ Δημοσθένης[1] ἔπεισε τοὺς ᾿Αθηναίους πέμπειν στράτευμα.
2. ἠναγκάσαμεν τοὺς Πέρσας ἀποφεύγειν.
3. οἱ Λακεδαιμόνιοι οὐκ ἔσωσαν τοὺς ἐν τῇ νήσῳ.
4. πείσομεν τοὺς ᾿Αθηναίους πέμπειν τὰς τριήρεις.
5. οἱ ᾿Αθηναῖοι ἐφύλασσον τὴν ὁδὸν μακροῖς τείχεσιν.
6. οἱ Πέρσαι διέβαινον τὸ ὄρος τοῦ θέρους.
7. σεσώκατε τὴν πατρίδα, ὦ πολῖται.
8. τοὺς μὲν ἐπείσαμεν φεύγειν, τοὺς δὲ ἠναγκάσαμεν.
9. ἐπιστεύσαμεν τοῖς τοῦ Σωκράτους λόγοις.
10. τὰ ὄρη ἐστὶν ὑψηλά τε καὶ χαλεπά.
11. οἱ πολῖται πεφυλάχασι τὴν πατρίδα δέκα ἔτη.
12. τῷ δεκάτῳ ἔτει οἱ στρατηγοὶ ἤγαγον τὸ στράτευμα
    οἴκαδε.

[1] A famous orator of the 4th cent. whose speeches against Philip of Macedon have given us the word *philippic*, a speech of denunciation. He should not be confused with the 5th cent. general mentioned in Ch. 27.

EXERCISE 55.

1. He compelled the sailors to remain in the harbour.
2. We persuaded the exiles to escape by night.
3. The general will save both the old men and the children.
4. The Athenians persuaded the allies to send triremes and sailors.

5. The enemy compelled the Athenians to destroy the long walls.

6. It is easy to cross the mountain in summer.

7. Within three years the triremes will be ready.

8. The Persians will not compel the Spartans to flee.

9. Admetus has not persuaded his father to die.

10. The young men were listening to the words of Socrates himself.

11. We have saved the fruit of the trees.

12. The soldiers were guarding the walls.

EXERCISE 56.

THE TEN THOUSAND REACH THE SEA

In 401 B.C. Cyrus the Younger rebels against his brother Artaxerxes, king of Persia, with the aid of Greek mercenaries. Cyrus is killed at the battle of Cunaxa, not far from Babylon. Xenophon, who is chosen as one of the leaders of the Greeks, describes their return to the sea.

μετὰ δὲ τὸν πόλεμον ὁ Ξενοφῶν ἦγε τοὺς Ἕλληνας διὰ τῆς Ἀρμενίας. ὁ δὲ τῆς χώρας ἄρχων τοῖς Ἕλλησιν ἡγεμόνα πέμπει. καὶ ὁ ἡγεμών, 'Πέντε ἡμερῶν', ἔφη, 'ἄξω τὸ στράτευμα εἰς χωρίον ὅθεν ἡ θάλασσα ἔσται φανερά.' οὐ μέντοι τῆς πρὸς τοὺς Ἕλληνας εὐνοίας ἕνεκα ἦγεν αὐτούς· ἔπεισε γὰρ τοὺς Ἕλληνας ἐν τῇ ὁδῷ αἴθειν καὶ φθείρειν τὴν χώραν, ὅτι τῷ ἄρχοντι πολεμία ἦν. καὶ τῇ πέμπτῃ ἡμέρᾳ ἄγει αὐτοὺς εἰς τὸ ὄρος· ὄνομα δὲ τῷ ὄρει ἦν Θήχης. ἐπεὶ δὲ οἱ πρῶτοι ἦσαν ἐπὶ τοῦ ὄρους, ὁ Ξενοφῶν καὶ οἱ μετ' αὐτοῦ ἤκουσαν κραυγὴν μακράν. ὡς δὲ οἱ στρατιῶται ἤδη ἔθεον πρὸς τὸ ἄκρον, ὁ Ξενοφῶν ἀναβαίνει ἐφ' ἵππον καὶ ἀκούει τὴν βοήν, 'Θάλασσα, θάλασσα.' ἐπεὶ δὲ τὸ ὅλον στράτευμα ἧκεν ἐπὶ τὸ ἄκρον, περιέβαλλον ἀλλήλους καὶ στρατηγοὺς καὶ λοχαγοὺς καὶ ἐδάκρυον. καὶ οἱ στρατιῶται ἔφερον λίθους, ὡς ἤθελον κολωνὸν παρασκευάζειν. τῷ δὲ ἡγεμόνι παρέχουσι δῶρα ἵππον καὶ φιάλην καὶ σκευὴν Περσικὴν καὶ δαρεικοὺς δέκα, καὶ ἐπεὶ ἑσπέρα ἦν, οἴκαδε αὐτὸν ἀποπέμπουσιν.

Adapted from Xenophon, *Anabasis*, IV, vii.

EXERCISE 57.

THE WOODEN WALL

Between the two Persian invasions a rich vein of silver was discovered in Attica and was used for the development of the Athenian navy, which fought, first against the people of Aegina, and then against the Persians, especially at the decisive battle of Salamis in 480.

ἦν δέ ποτε ἀνὴρ Ἀθηναῖος ὀνόματι Θεμιστοκλῆς· ὅτε δὲ ἦν χρήματα οὐκ ὀλίγα ἐκ τῶν μετάλλων τοῖς Ἀθηναίοις ἐν τῷ κοινῷ, ὁ Θεμιστοκλῆς ἔπεισεν αὐτοὺς κατασκευάζειν διακοσίας τριήρεις εἰς τὸν πρὸς τοὺς Αἰγινήτας¹ πόλεμον· οὕτως ἠνάγκασε τοὺς Ἀθηναίους ἀριστεύειν κατὰ θάλασσαν.

ἐν δὲ τῷ πρὸς τοὺς Πέρσας πολέμῳ οἱ Ἀθηναῖοι πέμπουσιν ἄνδρας εἰς Δελφούς,² ὅτι ἐν μεγίστῳ κινδύνῳ ἦσαν. καὶ ἡ Πυθία,² ‘Πιστεύετε,’ ἔφη, ‘τῷ ξυλίνῳ τείχει.’ ὁ δὲ Θεμιστοκλῆς ὧδε συμβουλεύει τοῖς πολίταις· “Ὁ θεὸς τῷ ξυλίνῳ τείχει οὐ τὴν ἀκρόπολιν σημαίνει, ἀλλὰ τὸ ναυτικόν, καὶ κελεύει τοὺς πολίτας ταῖς τριήρεσι πιστεύειν.’ οὕτω δ' ἔπεισε τοὺς Ἀθηναίους καὶ ἄλλο ναυτικὸν κατασκευάζειν.

μετὰ δὲ τὴν ἐν ταῖς Θερμοπύλαις μάχην, οἱ μὲν Πελοποννήσιοι ἐφύλασσον τὸν Ἰσθμὸν³ τείχει, οἱ δὲ Ἀθηναῖοι ἐξεκόμισαν τά τε τέκνα καὶ τοὺς οἰκέτας ἐκ τῆς Ἀττικῆς, τοὺς μὲν εἰς Τροιζῆνα,⁴ τοὺς δὲ εἰς Αἴγιναν, τοὺς δὲ εἰς Σαλαμῖνα,⁵ καὶ οὕτως ἔσωσαν αὐτούς. οἱ δὲ Πέρσαι εἰσβάλλουσιν εἰς τὴν Ἀττικὴν καὶ καταλαμβάνουσι τὰς Ἀθήνας καὶ καίουσι τὴν Ἀκρόπολιν.

Adapted from Herodotus, VII, 141–144, VIII, 41 and 53.

¹ Aegina was an island to the south of Attica, and a strong naval power.
² Delphi, situated in the centre of Greece, under the slopes of Mt. Parnassus, was the seat of the famous oracle of Apollo; the Pythian priestess uttered the answers of the god.
³ The Isthmus of Corinth.
⁴ A town in the Argolid, south of Aegina.
⁵ An island belonging to Athens, facing her harbour, the Piraeus.

Chapter 13

3rd Declension: Stems in ι and υ (A 29); Some Verbs with Consonant Stems (Labial)

Present	Future	Aorist	Perfect	
πέμπω	πέμψω	ἔπεμψα	πέπομφα	'I send
λείπω	λείψω	ἔλιπον	λέλοιπα	I leave
γράφω	γράψω	ἔγραψα	γέγραφα	I write
βλάπτω	βλάψω	ἔβλαψα	βέβλαφα	I harm
κρύπτω	κρύψω	ἔκρυψα	κέκρυφα	I hide
ῥίπτω	ῥίψω	ἔρριψα	ἔρριφα	I throw
τύπτω	τύψω	ἔτυψα	—	I strike

EXERCISE 58.

1. πέμψομεν τοὺς πρέσβεις εἰς τὴν πόλιν.
2. οἱ πολέμιοι ἔβλαψαν οὔτε τοὺς παῖδας οὔτε τοὺς γέροντας.
3. οἱ γέροντες ἔρριψαν λίθους ἐπὶ τοὺς Πέρσας.
4. οἱ λῃσταὶ κεκρύφασι τὰ χρήματα ἐν τῇ ὕλῃ.
5. ὁ ναύτης ἔτυψε τὸν ἰχθὺν πελέκει.
6 οὐ λείψομεν τὰ τέκνα ἐν τῇ πόλει.
7. ὁ στρατηγὸς ἐπιστολὴν γέγραφε περὶ τῆς νίκης.
8. πεπόμφαμεν δέκα ὗας¹ εἰς τὸ ἄστυ.
9. ἐλίπομεν τοὺς μικροὺς ἰχθῦς ἐν τῇ θαλάσσῃ.
10. ἰσχυρὰ ἦν ἡ τοῦ ναυτικοῦ δύναμις.
11. οἱ Ἀθηναῖοι ἔγραψαν τὰ τῶν στρατιωτῶν ὀνόματα ἐν λίθῳ.
12. οἱ πολέμιοι κατέλιπον τὰ ὅπλα ἐν τῷ ἄστει.

¹ ὗς (not σῦς) was the prevailing form in Attic Greek.

EXERCISE 59.

1. I will write a letter and send it to my father.
2. The lion did not harm the slave.

3. The Athenians sent their children out of the city.
4. The men on the wall will throw stones on to the enemy.
5. The enemy struck the gate with axes.
.6. We have left behind a few old men in the Acropolis.
‹7. The young man will send the fish to the market.
8. We hid the money in the tree.
9. The Athenians have sent ambassadors to the Persians.
10. The Spartans had few towns.
11. The power of the orator's words was small.
12. The Persians will not damage the city.

Exercises for Revision

EXERCISE 60.

1. φυλάξομεν τὰς τῆς πόλεως πύλας.
2. οἱ τοῦ ῥήτορος λόγοι οὐκ ἔπεισαν τοὺς πολίτας.
3. οὐ ῥᾴδιον ἦν τῷ γίγαντι διώκειν τοὺς ναύτας.
4. ὁ Θεμιστοκλῆς ἔπεισε τοὺς Ἀθηναίους τῷ ναυτικῷ
   πιστεύειν.
5. ἠναγκάσαμεν τοὺς πολεμίους διαβαίνειν τὸν ποταμόν.
6. ὁ Λεωνίδας ἦρχε τῶν Λακεδαιμονίων ἐν τῇ μάχῃ.
7. τὰ τοξεύματα ἀπέκρυψε τὸν ἥλιον.
8. οἱ πολέμιοι οὐ βεβλάφασι τοὺς ἀνδριάντας.
9. χαλεπὸν ἦν ἀναγκάζειν τοὺς ἵππους ἐν τῇ μάχῃ μένειν.
10. ὁ Ξενοφῶν αὐτὸς χάριν ἔχει τῷ ἡγεμόνι.
11. οἱ μὲν τὰ τείχη ἐφύλασσον, οἱ δὲ ἡσύχαζον.
12. οἱ ἐν τῇ νήσῳ ἔκρυψαν τὰ χρήματα ἐν τῇ γῇ.

EXERCISE 61.

1. There are high mountains in Greece.
2. The men on the wall were not in danger.
3. Pericles managed the affairs of the Athenians.
4. Ten triremes will be ready in three months.
5. His daughter was leading the old man through the
   market-place.
6. The navy is strong, but the army is small.
7. The enemy were already on the mountain.

8. The boy threw the small fish into the sea.
9. The Athenians admire wisdom, the Spartans courage.
10. Demosthenes persuaded the citizens themselves to march against the enemy.
11. I ordered the boy not to throw stones, and he escaped into the house.
12. We pursued the enemy from the walls of the city to the river.

EXERCISE 62.

1. αἱ τῶν Λακεδαιμονίων μητέρες ἀνδρεῖαι ἦσαν.
2. οἰκτείρετε·τοὺς αἰχμαλώτους, ὦ πολῖται.
3. ὁ Λεωνίδας καὶ οἱ μετ' αὐτοῦ ἔσωσαν τὴν Ἑλλάδα.
4. τριῶν ἡμερῶν τὴν πατρίδα ἀπολείψετε, ὦ παῖδες.
5. οἱ ἐν τῷ ποταμῷ ἰχθύες εἰσὶ μικροί.
6. ὁ στρατηγὸς ἐκέλευσε τοὺς στρατιώτας μὴ βλάπτειν τὸ ἄστυ.
7. αἱ ἐν τῇ πόλει ἔκρυψαν τά τε χρήματα καὶ τὰ ὅπλα.
8. ἐκκομίζομεν τοὺς παῖδας εἰς τὰς νήσους διὰ τὸν κίνδυνον.
9. ὁ παῖς ἤλαυνε τοὺς ὄνους ἐκ τῆς ἀγορᾶς.
10. οἱ βάρβαροι ἐποτρύνουσι τὰς καμήλους μάστιξιν.
11. τρεῖς μῆνας ἐμένομεν τοὺς συμμάχους· οἱ δὲ μάτην ἐστράτευσαν.
12. οὐχ οἷοί τε ἦμεν πείθειν τοὺς γέροντας μὴ μένειν ἐν τῇ ἀκροπόλει.

EXERCISE 63.

1. The general has fared well in the battle.
2. Captains, draw up the soldiers for battle.
3. The soldiers were cutting down the trees on the island.
4. The boys were carrying the fish into the house.
5. The men in the city were friendly to the enemy.
6. The rich are not always worthy of honour.
7. Owing to the general's wisdom we shall not be in danger.
8. Some threw stones, others struck the gate with axes.
9. The ambassadors did not persuade the Athenians.

10. On the tenth day I wrote a letter and sent it to my daughter.
11. Alcestis was willing to die for her husband.
12. We sent six triremes to the island.

EXERCISE 64.

HOW EGYPTIANS AVOIDED GNATS

ἐν δὲ τῇ Αἰγύπτῳ εἰσὶ κώνωπες πλεῖστοι. οἱ μὲν οὖν
Αἰγύπτιοι οἱ ἄνω τῶν λιμνῶν τῆς νυκτὸς ἀναβαίνουσιν εἰς
πύργους ὑψηλοὺς καὶ ἐκεῖ καθεύδουσιν·¹ οἱ γὰρ κώνωπες οὐχ
οἷοί τέ εἰσιν ἀναβαίνειν ἐκεῖσε διὰ τοὺς ἀνέμους· οἱ δὲ περὶ
τὰς λίμνας Αἰγύπτιοι τὰ σώματα ὧδε φυλάσσουσιν· ὅτι οὐκ
ἔχουσι πύργους, ἕκαστος ἀνὴρ ἀμφίβληστρον ἔχει· τῆς μὲν
ἡμέρας ἰχθῦς θηρεύει, τῆς δὲ νυκτὸς ὑπ᾽αὐτῷ ἐν τῇ κοίτῃ
καθεύδει. οἱ δὲ κώνωπες, εἴ τις μόνον ἐν ἱματίῳ καθεύδει, δι᾽
αὐτοῦ δάκνουσιν, ἀλλ᾽ οὔποτε διὰ τοῦ ἀμφιβλήστρου.

Adapted from Herodotus, II, 95.

¹ This custom is still found in parts of India.

Chapter 14

3rd Declension: Stems in Diphthongs (A 30); Passive of λύω, Present and Imperfect (A 74); the Agent

The Agent after a Passive Verb

This is expressed by ὑπό and the **Genitive**; this use corresponds to that of *a* or *ab* with the Ablative in Latin. The simple **Dative** is used in Greek to denote the **Instrument**. This is an interesting example of the way in which Greek uses two Cases to do the work performed by the Abl. (with or without *ab*) in Latin:

> διωκόμεθα ὑπὸ τῶν πολεμίων.
> *We are being pursued by the enemy.*
>
> ἡ θάλασσα μάστιξι τύπτεται.
> *The sea is lashed with whips.*

EXERCISE 65.

1. οἱ στρατιῶται τάσσονται ὑπὸ τοῦ βασιλέως.
2. τρεῖς βόες ἐθύοντο ἐν τῇ ἀγορᾷ.
3. ἡ τῆς πόλεως πύλη φυλάσσεται ὑπὸ τῶν πολεμίων.
4. οἱ ἱππεῖς ἔφευγον πρὸς τὸ τεῖχος.
5. ταῖς γραυσὶν ἦν μόνον εἷς ὁδοὺς καὶ εἷς ὀφθαλμος.
6. οἱ αἰχμάλωτοι λύονται ὑπὸ τῶν Ἀθηναίων.
7. πέμπεσθε εἰς τὰς νήσους, ὦ παῖδες.
8. οἱ παῖδες ἤλαυνον τοὺς βοῦς εἰς τὸν λειμῶνα.
9. τὰ τῆς πόλεως ἐπράσσετο ὑπὸ τῶν στρατηγῶν.
10. ἐδιωκόμεθα ὑπὸ τῶν βασιλέως[1] ἱππέων.
11. οἱ πολέμιοι λίθοις ἐτύπτοντο.
12. ὁ δρομεὺς ἧκεν εἰς τὴν Σπάρτην τῇ δευτέρᾳ ἡμέρᾳ.

[1] βασιλεύς without an Article refers to the king of Persia.

EXERCISE 66.

1. The oxen are being loosed by the boy.
2. An ambassador is being sent by the Persians
3. The king was being pursued by the Greeks.
4. The soldier's helmet is struck by a stone.
5. The priests were sacrificing the oxen.
6. The cavalry were being led by a guide.
7. The enemy did not harm the old women in the city.
8. The door of the house was being guarded by three soldiers.
9. Themistocles sent a letter to the king of Persia.
10. The runner is worthy of honour.
11. Two men were being eaten by the giant.
12. The oxen are being pursued by the lion.

Irregular Nouns, γυνή, ναῦς, Ζεύς, ὕδωρ (A 36, 37); **Passive of**
λύω, **Aorist and Future** (A 74)

EXERCISE 67.

1. τριῶν ἡμερῶν ἐλύθησαν ὑπὸ τῶν συμμάχων.
2. ἡ ναῦς ἐκωλύθη τῷ χειμῶνι.
3. οἱ Πέρσαι οὐκ ἐκωλύθησαν ὑπὸ τῶν Λακεδαιμονίων.
4. πέμπετε τάς τε γυναῖκας καὶ τοὺς παῖδας ἐκ τῆς
   πόλεως.
5. οἱ νεανίαι παιδευθήσονται εἰς τὸν πόλεμον.
6. οἱ ἱερεῖς ἔθυον τὸν βοῦν τῷ Διί.
7. ὁ μὲν οἶνός ἐστιν ἀγαθός, τὸ δὲ ὕδωρ ἄριστον.
8. ἡ ναυμαχία ἐπαύθη ὑπὸ βασιλέως.
9. ὁ Ἄδμητος ἔπεισε τὴν γυναῖκα ἀποθνήσκειν.
10. τῇ ἑσπέρᾳ οἱ βόες ἀπὸ τῶν ζυγῶν λυθήσονται.
11. ὁ νεανίας ἐπαιδεύθη ὑπὸ τοῦ Σωκράτους.
12. ὁ Θεμιστοκλῆς ἔπεισε τοὺς Ἀθηναίους κατασκευάζειν
    διακοσίας ναῦς.

EXERCISE 68.

1. The slave was set free by his master.
2. The women were hindered by the children on the journey.
3. The horses were trained by the cavalry.
4. The battle will be stopped by the king.
5. It is difficult for the soldiers to find water in the island.
6. The Greeks used to worship Zeus.
7. Admetus was set free from death by his wife.
8. The ships will not be hindered by the storm.
9. We were not set free by the Spartans.
10. The rowers will be trained in the ship.
11. The cities sent earth and water to the king of Persia.
12. Themistocles was trusted by the Athenians.

EXERCISE 69.

THE CUNNING OF ARTEMISIA

*The following episode took place at the battle of Salamis, where
in* 480 B.C. *the Greeks defeated the Persian fleet.*

παρῆν δὲ ἐν τῇ ναυμαχίᾳ ἡ τῶν ᾽Αλικαρνασσέων[1] βασίλεια,
ὀνόματι ᾽Αρτεμισία. ἐπεὶ δὲ αἱ τῶν Περσῶν νῆες ἐπιέζοντο
καὶ μάλιστα ἐβλάπτοντο ὑπὸ τῶν ῾Ελλήνων, ἡ τῆς ᾽Αρτε-
μισίας ναῦς ἐδιώκετο νηὶ ᾽Αττικῇ· ἡ δὲ ᾽Αρτεμισία οὐχ οἷα
τ᾽ ἦν διαφεύγειν· ἔμπροσθε γὰρ αὐτῆς ἦσαν ἄλλαι νῆες φίλιαι·
ἐκέλευσεν οὖν τοὺς ναύτας ἐμβάλλειν νηὶ φιλίᾳ καὶ αὐτὴν
κατέδυσεν. ὁ δὲ τῆς ᾽Αττικῆς νεὼς τριήραρχος οὐκέτι τὴν
τῆς ᾽Αρτεμισίας ναῦν ἐδίωκεν, ἀλλ᾽ ἐνέβαλλεν ἄλλαις· φανερῶς
γάρ, ὡς ἐνόμιζεν, ἢ ἡ τῆς ᾽Αρτεμισίας ναῦς φιλία ἦν ἢ οἱ
ναῦται αὐτόμολοι ἦσαν. οὕτως δὲ ἡ ᾽Αρτεμισία ἐκ τῆς μάχης
διαφεύγει.

τὸ δὲ τῆς βασιλείας ἔργον οὐ λανθάνει τὸν Ξέρξην· βασιλεὺς
γὰρ αὐτὸς ἐν ὑψηλῷ θρόνῳ ἐπὶ τῆς ἀκτῆς ἐκάθιζεν. λέγει δέ
τις τῶν μετ᾽ αὐτοῦ, ῾Δέσποτα, ἡ ᾽Αρτεμισία κατέδυσε ναῦν
τῶν πολεμίων.᾽ ὁ δὲ Ξέρξης πρῶτον μὲν οὐ πιστεύει αὐτῷ,
τέλος δὲ πείθεται· μάλιστα δὲ ἐθαύμασε τὴν τῆς βασιλείας
ἀρετήν. ῾Οἱ μὲν γὰρ ἄνδρες,᾽ ἔφη, ῾νῦν εἰσι γυναῖκες· αἱ δὲ
γυναῖκες ἄνδρες.᾽ τύχῃ δὲ οὐδεὶς ἐκ τῆς νεὼς περιῆν κατήγορος.

Adapted from Herodotus, VIII, 87–88.

[1] Halicarnassus was a city in Caria, in Asia Minor; it was Herodotus'
own birthplace.

Chapter 15

Regular Comparison of Adjectives in -ος
(A 50); Genitive of Comparison and use of ἤ;
Passive of λύω, Perfect and Pluperfect (A 74)

In the regular Comparison of Adjectives in -ος, -τερος is
added to the masculine Stem to form the Comparative, and
-τατος to form the Superlative, but if the last syllable but one

of the Adjective is short, then the o of the stem is lengthened to
ω:

			Comparative	Superlative
So	δεινός,	*strange*	δεινότερος	δεινότατος
	μῶρος,	*foolish*	μωρότερος	μωρότατος
But	σοφός,	*wise*	σοφώτερος	σοφώτατος
	ἄξιος,	*worthy*	ἀξιώτερος	ἀξιώτατος

Genitive of Comparison and the use of ἤ

A **Genitive** of **Comparison** may be used if two persons or
things are directly compared with each other; otherwise a
Comparative is followed by ἤ, *than*, with the same Case after
it as before it; compare the equivalent uses in Latin of the Abl.
of Comparison and of *quam*:

> ὁ Σωκράτης σοφώτερος ἦν τῶν ἄλλων.
> *Socrates was wiser than the others.*

> οἱ Ἕλληνες ἔχουσι μικρότερον ναυτικὸν ἢ οἱ βάρβαροι.
> *The Greeks have a smaller fleet than the barbarians.*

EXERCISE 70.

1. οἱ Λακεδαιμόνιοι ἀνδρειότεροί εἰσι τῶν Περσῶν.
2. ὁ δοῦλος ὑπὸ τοῦ δεσπότου λέλυται.
3. ὁ Ἡρακλῆς ἦν ἰσχυρότατος τῶν τότε.
4. οἱ νεανίαι πεπαίδευνται ἐν ταῖς Ἀθήναις.
5. οἱ κάμηλοι δεινότεροι ἦσαν τοῖς στρατιώταις τῶν
   ὅπλων.
6. αἱ τριήρεις τρεῖς ἡμέρας ἐκεκώλυντο τῷ χειμῶνι.
7. ὁ χειμὼν ἦν χαλεπώτερος τοῖς Πέρσαις ἢ τοῖς
   Ἀθηναίοις.
8. ἡ μάχη ἐπέπαυτο τῇ νυκτί.
9. ἡ Ἄλκηστίς ἐστιν ἡ ἀξιωτάτη γυναικῶν.
10. οὔπω λελύμεθα ἐκ τοῦ δεσμωτηρίου.

EXERCISE 71.

1. We have been trained by the general.
2. Heracles was stronger than the lion.
3. The yokes of the oxen have been loosed.
4. We are not wiser than Socrates.
5. Odysseus and those with him had been hindered by the giant.
6. We are hurrying by a more difficult road than the enemy.
7. The prisoners had not yet been set free.
8. The navy was very useful in the war.
9. The war has been stopped by the winter.
10. The city itself was more ancient than the walls.

EXERCISE 72.

1. οἱ Ἀθηναῖοι ἐλευθερώτεροι ἦσαν τῶν Λακεδαιμονίων.
2. οἱ νεανίαι ἐπεπαίδευντο εἰς χαλεπώτατον ἀγῶνα.
3. οὐδένα φίλον ἔχομεν δικαιότερον ἢ τὸν Σωκράτη.
4. οἱ ἐν τῇ νήσῳ οὐ λέλυνται ὑπὸ τῶν Λακεδαιμονίων.
5. αἱ νῆες βεβαιότεραι ἦσαν ἢ τὸ τεῖχος.
6. δέκα βόες τέθυνται τῷ θεῷ.
7. νομίζομεν τοὺς Λακεδαιμονίους ἀνδρειοτέρους ἢ τοὺς Πέρσας.
8. αἱ Ἀθῆναι κατελέλυντο ὑπὸ τῶν Περσῶν.
9. ἐλευθερώτατοί ἐσμεν τῶν Ἑλλήνων.
10. κεκωλύμεθα ὑψηλοτάτῳ ὄρει.

EXERCISE 73.

1. Socrates was the wisest of the Athenians.
2. The women have been hindered by the children.
3. Some men are wiser, others are stronger.
4. The river was more dangerous than the mountain.
5. An ox had been sacrificed to the goddess.
6. A stronger army has been trained by the Spartans than by the Athenians.
7. The judges think her wiser than the others.
8. Alcestis was more worthy of honour than her husband.

9. Socrates has not been set free from the prison.
10. The richest are not always the wisest.

Chapter 16

Indicative Middle of λύω (A 74 and 76)

Besides the Active and Passive, many Greek Verbs have a third Voice, called the **Middle Voice**; its Tenses are formed in the same way as those of the Passive, except for the Future, e.g. λύσομαι, the Weak Aorist, e.g. ἐλυσάμην, and the Strong Aorist (with certain Verbs), e.g. ἐπιθόμην (from πείθομαι, *I obey*), which is conjugated like the Imperfect Passive (ἐλυόμην).

(1) The Middle Voice is often used for actions which in some way affect the subject:

λύομαι τους αἰχμαλώτους, *I ransom the prisoners (I get the prisoners loosed for myself)*.
διδάσκομαι τὸν υἱόν, *I get my son taught*.
φέρομαι ἆθλον, *I win (carry away for myself) a prize*.

(2) Many Verbs in the Middle Voice may be regarded as similar in function to Latin Deponent Verbs:

αὐλίζομαι, *I encamp*	παύομαι, *I cease (from*, Gen.)
βουλεύομαι, *I deliberate*	πείθομαι, *I obey* (Dat.)
μάχομαι, *I fight*	πορεύομαι, *I march, journey*
ὀργίζομαι, *I grow angry*	στρατοπεδεύομαι, *I encamp*

Note. αὐλίζομαι and μάχομαι are not found in the Active; παύω is Transitive in the Active, *I stop*, and so is πείθω, *I persuade*.

EXERCISE 74.

1. λυσόμεθα τοὺς ἐν τῇ νήσῳ.
2. οἱ Πέρσαι ἐβουλεύοντο περὶ τῆς εἰρήνης.
3. τὸ τῶν Ἑλλήνων στράτευμα πρὸς τὴν θάλασσαν ἐπορεύετο.
4. ἡ μάχη οὐ παύσεται πρὸ τῆς ἑσπέρας.
5. ὁ Ξέρξης ὠργίζετο διὰ τὴν τῶν ναυτῶν δειλίαν.
6. οἱ παῖδες ἐπαύσαντο τοῦ ἔργου.
7. οὐκ ἐπιθόμεθα τοῖς τοῦ ῥήτορος λόγοις.
8. οἱ Ἕλληνες ἐστρατοπεδεύσαντο παρὰ τῷ ποταμῷ.
9. οἱ Ἀθηναῖοι ἐμάχοντο ὑπὲρ τῆς πατρίδος.
10. οἱ στρατιῶται ηὐλίζοντο ἐγγὺς τῆς κώμης.
11. ὁ νεανίας φέρεται καλὰ ἆθλα ἐν τοῖς ἀγῶσιν.
12. οἱ πολέμιοι ἐλύσαντο τοὺς αἰχμαλώτους δέκα ἡμερῶν.

EXERCISE 75.

1. We ransomed the general.
2. The soldiers were marching to the gates of the city.
3. Wise men obey the laws.
4. The old men deliberated about the war for three days.
5. We shall cease from the battle before night.
6. Some obey Socrates, others grow angry.
7. The Persians were fighting against the Greeks.
8. We encamped outside the walls of the city.
9. The general ransomed the prisoners after the battle.
10. The Athenian poet is winning the prize.
11. The Greeks were marching through the enemy's country.
12. We get our sons taught in Athens.

Infinitives of λύω (A 73, 75, 77) and εἰμί (A 117, 118)

The Infinitives are used in Greek, as in Latin, in Indirect Statement (which is dealt with later in this book); it should be noticed that in other constructions the Present Infinitive (learnt in Ch. 8) and the Aorist Infinitive may both refer to Present Time, but with this difference, that the Aorist Infinitive generally refers to a **single act**:

ἐκέλευσε τοὺς στρατιώτας καταλῦσαι τὴν πόλιν.
He ordered the soldiers to destroy the city.

At this stage, there is no need for the beginner to mark this difference in writing Greek sentences, but he should learn the grammatical forms, so that he may recognize them.

The Perfect Infinitive is used for a completed action; it is formed by changing the -α of the 1st person sing. of the Indicative into -έναι in the Active, e.g. λελυκέναι, and by changing the -ε of the 2nd person plur. of the Indicative into -αι in the Passive, e.g. λελύσθαι:

ἀγαθόν ἐστι πεπαῦσθαι τοῦ ἔργου.
It is good to have ceased from work.

A Strong Aorist Infin., like a Present Infin., ends in -εῖν in the Active, e.g. λιπεῖν, *to leave*; in -έσθαι in the Middle, e.g. πιθέσθαι, *to obey*.

Note. A Future Infin. is used after μέλλω, *I am about to*, *I intend*, and also after ἐλπίζω, *I hope*, when it refers to the Future, e.g. μέλλομεν στρατεύσειν, *we are about to march*; ἐλπίζω εὖ πράξειν, *I hope to fare well*.

EXERCISE 76.

1. ἐθέλομεν λῦσαι τοὺς αἰχμαλώτους.
2. ὁ νεανίας μέλλει λύσειν τὸν βοῦν.
3. ὁ Ξέρξης ἐκέλευσε τοὺς λοχαγοὺς παρασκευάζειν τὰς ναῦς.
4. ὁ ποιητὴς ἄξιός ἐστι δέχεσθαι τὸ ἆθλον.
5. ἐπείσαμεν τοὺς Λακεδαιμονίους πέμψαι τὸ στράτευμα.
6. ἡ Ἄλκηστις ἔμελλε σώσειν τὸν ἄνδρα.
7. ἐλπίζομεν λυθήσεσθαι ὑπὸ τῶν συμμάχων.
8. καλὸν ἦν τοῖς Ἀθηναίοις σεσωκέναι τὴν πατρίδα.
9. οὐχ οἷοί τ᾽ ἐσόμεθα παύσασθαι τῆς ναυμαχίας πρὸ τῆς νυκτός.
10. ὁ Σωκράτης ἐφαίνετο εἶναι σοφώτατος.
11. οἱ μετὰ τοῦ Ξενοφῶντος ἔμελλον πορεύσεσθαι πρὸς τὴν θάλασσαν.

12. οἱ Ἀθηναῖοι ἤλπισαν λύσεσθαι τοὺς αἰχμαλώτους.
13. αἰσχρὸν ἦν τῷ Κροίσῳ κωλυθῆναι ὑπὸ τῶν καμήλων.
14. ὁ ταμίας ἐλπίζει ἔσεσθαι πλούσιος.
15. κακόν ἐστι μὴ πείθεσθαι τοῖς νόμοις.

EXERCISE 77.

1. The general ordered the soldiers to save both the women and the children.
2. We are not able to send the army at once.
3. The enemy intended to ransom the general.
4. It was fine for the young men to have been educated by Socrates.
5. We hoped to persuade the old man to stay.
6. The citizens appeared to be friendly.
7. The men in the city were about to be saved by the allies.
8. It was difficult to encamp on the hill.
9. The enemy were not willing to ransom the prisoners.
10. The soldiers hoped to be saved.
11. It was shameful to leave the old men behind.
12. We persuaded the Armenians to send a guide.
13. It will be good to have set free the country.
14. The Spartans were about to pursue the enemy.
15. It will be difficult to cease from work before night.

Imperatives of λύω (A 72, 74, 76) and εἰμί (A 117)

As stated in Ch. 8, the 2nd persons of the **Present** Imperative are used to express **Direct Commands** when the action is a **continuing** one, e.g. ἀεὶ πίστευε τοῖς ἀγαθοῖς.

When the action is a **single** one on a particular occasion, Greek uses the **Aorist** Imperative, λῦσον, λύσατε; e.g. λῦσον τὸν βοῦν, *loose the ox*.

A Direct Command referring to the 3rd person is regularly expressed by the 3rd persons of the Present or Aorist Imperatives in the same way:

> μενόντων οἱ ναῦται ἐν τῷ λιμένι.
> *Let the sailors remain in the harbour* (continuing action).

λυσάτω ὁ γέρων τοὺς βοῦς.
Let the old man loose the oxen (single action).

EXERCISE 78.

1. σῴζετε τὴν πατρίδα, ὦ στρατιῶται.
2. πιστευόντων οἱ νεανίαι τοῖς τοῦ Σωκράτους λόγοις
3. πεμψάτω ὁ στρατηγὸς τοὺς ἱππέας εἰς τὴν μάχην.
4. εὐθὺς λυθέντων οἱ αἰχμάλωτοι.
5. σῶσον τὸν γέροντα, ὦ νεανία.
6. μενέτω ἡ εἰρήνη, ὦ πολῖται.
7. βουλευέσθων οἱ σύμμαχοι περὶ τοῦ πολέμου.
8. ἀνδρεῖοι ἔστε ἐν τῷ κινδύνῳ, ὦ νεανίαι.
9. πιθέσθων οἱ πολῖται τῷ ῥήτορι.
10. παιδευέσθω ὁ παῖς ἐν ταῖς Ἀθήναις.
11. πέμψατε πέντε ναῦς πρὸς τὴν νῆσον.
12. λυσάσθω ὁ στρατηγὸς τοὺς συμμάχους

EXERCISE 79.

1. Persuade the allies to remain.
2. Trust the ships, O citizens.
3. Let the soldiers guard the camp.
4. Let there be peace in the city.
5. Fight for your country, citizens.
6. Let the prisoners stay in the camp.
7. Order him not to say foolish things.
8. Let the people be set free.
9. Send home the allies today.
10. Let the Persians ransom the prisoners.
11. Lead the army to the sea.
12. Let them encamp near the village.

EXERCISE 80.

VICTORY IN BAD WEATHER

Here are further episodes in the march of the Ten Thousand.

ἕως δὲ οἱ Ἕλληνες ἐστρατοπεδεύοντο, χιὼν πλείστη ἐπι-
πίπτει τῆς νυκτὸς καὶ ἀποκρύπτει τά θ' ὅπλα καὶ τοὺς ἀνθρώ-

πους καὶ τὰ ὑποζύγια· οἱ δὲ στρατιῶται ἐν ἀθυμίᾳ ἦσαν. ἐπεὶ δὲ ὁ Ξενοφῶν γυμνὸς ἔσχιζε ξύλα, εὐθὺς καὶ ἄλλοι ἔσχιζον καὶ πῦρ ἔκαιον. ἔπειτα δὲ ὁ Ξενοφῶν ἐκέλευσε τοὺς στρατιώτας ἀπολιπεῖν τὸ χωρίον, οὗ ἐστρατοπεδεύοντο, καὶ σπεύδειν εἰς τὰς κώμας εἰς στέγας.[1]

ἀγγέλλει δὲ αὐτοῖς αἰχμάλωτός τις ὅτι οἱ πολέμιοι ἐγγύς εἰσι καὶ μέλλουσιν αὐτοῖς προσβαλεῖν ἐν τῇ τοῦ ὄρους εἰσβολῇ. οἱ οὖν στρατηγοὶ συνήγαγον τὸ στράτευμα ἀπὸ τῶν κωμῶν καὶ ἐκέλευσαν τοὺς μὲν φυλάσσειν τὸ στρατόπεδον, τοὺς δὲ πορεύεσθαι ἐπὶ τοὺς βαρβάρους· ὁ δὲ αἰχμάλωτος ἡγεμὼν ἦν αὐτοῖς. ἐπεὶ δὲ ὑπερέβαλλον τὸ ὄρος, οἱ πελτασταὶ οὐκ ἔμενον τοὺς ὁπλίτας, ἀλλὰ κραυγῇ ἔθεον ἐπὶ τὸ τῶν βαρβάρων στρατόπεδον. οἱ δὲ βάρβαροι, ὡς ἤκουσαν τὸν θόρυβον, οὐχ ὑπέμενον, ἀλλ' ἔφευγον. οἱ δὲ Ἕλληνες ὀλίγους τῶν βαρβάρων ἀποκτείνουσι καὶ λαμβάνουσιν εἴκοσιν ἵππους καὶ τὴν τοῦ ἄρχοντος σκηνὴν καὶ ἐν αὐτῇ κλίνας ἀργυρᾶς[2] καὶ ἐκπώματα. οἱ δὲ τῶν ὁπλιτῶν στρατηγοὶ τῇ σάλπιγγι ἐκέλευσαν τοὺς πελταστὰς παύσασθαι τῆς μάχης καὶ πορεύεσθαι πάλιν εἰς τὸ τῶν Ἑλλήνων στρατόπεδον.

Adapted from Xenophon, *Anabasis*, IV, iv.

[1] *to roofs*, i.e. *so as to get under cover.*
[2] This is a contracted Adjective (see A 39).

Chapter 17

Personal Pronouns : 1st and 2nd Persons (A 55)

ἐγώ, *I*, and σύ, *thou* (and their plurals) are not used in the Nom. Case as the Subject of a Verb, except to call **special attention** to the **Subject,** or for the sake of **contrast** between two Persons :

ἡμεῖς ἐλυσάμεθα τοὺς αἰχμαλώτους.
It was we who ransomed the prisoners.

ἐγὼ μὲν κελεύω, σὺ δὲ πείθει.

I give orders, but you obey.

Note. με, μου, μοι, σέ, σοῦ, σοί should never be used at the beginning of a sentence, and the words με, μου, μοι should not be used after a Preposition.

EXERCISE 81.

1. ὁ στρατηγὸς ἐκέλευσεν ἐμὲ φέρειν τὴν ἐπιστολήν.
2. ὑμεῖς μὲν ἀνδρεῖοί ἐστε, ἐγὼ δὲ δειλός.
3. οὐδείς ἐστι σοφώτερος σοῦ.
4. ὁ δοῦλος οὐκ ἤθελε μένειν μετ᾽ ἐμοῦ.
5. ὁ θεὸς κελεύει ὑμᾶς πιστεύειν τῷ ξυλίνῳ τείχει.
6. ἡμεῖς μὲν εἰς τὰς νήσους ἐκομιζόμεθα, οἱ δὲ γέροντες ἐν τῇ πόλει ἔμενον.
7. ἡ Ἄλκηστίς σε σώσει, ὦ Ἄδμητε.
8. ὁ βασιλεὺς ἐπιστολὴν πρὸς ἐμὲ ἔπεμψεν.
9. ὑμεῖς φέρεσθε τὸ ἆθλον, ὦ Λακεδαιμόνιοι.
10. ἀεὶ πεισόμεθά σοι, ὦ στρατηγέ.

EXERCISE 82.

1. The Persians compelled us to flee.
2. We shall never persuade you to fight.
3. You are wise, but Socrates is wiser.
4. It is difficult for me to trust him.
5. The allies are not willing to fight for us.
6. I am a sailor, you are a soldier.
7. We will obey you, Socrates.
8. The general ordered you not to remain on the wall.
9. It was you who saved the city.
10. I ordered the slaves to escape with me.

Possessive Pronouns of the 1st and 2nd Persons (A 56)

The Possessive Pronouns of the 1st and 2nd Persons, ἐμός, ἡμέτερος, σός, ὑμέτερος, are not used unless they are needed to make the sense clear; they are always **preceded by the Article**, e.g. ὁ ἐμὸς πατὴρ ἐπορεύετο, *my father was travelling.*

If the sense is clear, the Article alone is used, e.g. ἐπορευόμην μετὰ τοῦ πατρός, *I was travelling with my father*.

αὐτοῦ, αὐτῆς, αὐτοῦ

There is no Possessive Pronoun of the 3rd Person in Attic Greek; it uses the Gen. of αὐτός,—αὐτοῦ, αὐτῆς, αὐτοῦ (pl. αὐτῶν), for *his, her, its* (*their*), when these are **not** reflexive; **this Gen. always follows the Noun** to which it refers. Compare the equivalent use in Latin of *eius, eorum*, etc., and see Ch. 8 for use of αὐτός in oblique Cases:

ἔλυσα τὸν δοῦλον αὐτοῦ.
I set free his slave.

EXERCISE 83.

1. ὁ ἐμὸς υἱὸς οὐκ ἀεὶ πείθεται τῷ διδασκάλῳ.
2. οἱ πολέμιοι οὐ καταλύσουσι τὴν ἡμετέραν πόλιν.
3. βουλευσόμεθα περὶ τῆς ὑμετέρας σωτηρίας.
4. ὁ Ἡρακλῆς οἰκτείρει τὸν Ἄδμητον καὶ σῴζει τὴν γυναῖκα αὐτοῦ.
5. ἔπεμψα τὸν υἱὸν εἰς τὴν ἀγοράν.
6. τὸ ἡμέτερον ναυτικόν ἐστι μικρόν.
7. θαυμάζομεν τὴν σὴν θυγατέρα καὶ τὴν σοφίαν αὐτῆς.
8. οἱ ὑμέτεροι σύμμαχοι φεύγουσιν ἐκ τοῦ στρατοπέδου.
9. ἡ ἐμὴ γυνὴ καὶ ἐγὼ ἐβαδίζομεν μετὰ τῆς θυγατρός.
10. οὐδεμία πόλις ἐστὶ τιμῆς ἀξιωτέρα τῆς ἡμετέρας.
11. πιστεύομεν τῷ Δημοσθένει καὶ πειθόμεθα τοῖς λόγοις αὐτοῦ.
12. ἡ Ἀρτεμισία παρῆν ἐν τῇ ναυμαχίᾳ· ὁ δὲ Ξέρξης ἐθαύμαζε τὴν ἀνδρείαν αὐτῆς.

EXERCISE 84.

1. Our city will always be free.
2. My son was running with me.
3. Your fleet is smaller than ours.
4. I ransomed my son from the enemy.
5. The Athenians sacrifice to the goddess and guard her temple.

6. I persuaded your father not to remain.
7. The Persians admired the Spartans' general and his army.
8. Our fleet was fighting in a narrow place.
9. My slave is wiser than yours.
10. We are fleeing with our children.
11. Your country is worthy of honour, citizens.
12. We admire his wisdom.

EXERCISE 85.

DOUBLE DEALINGS OF THEMISTOCLES

Although the Greeks had won a decisive naval victory at Salamis, the Persian army was not yet defeated, and this accounts for the attitude of the Spartans shown in this piece. When later in his life Themistocles lost his countrymen's trust and was exiled, he claimed credit from the Persians for having tried to help them.

μετὰ δὲ τὴν ἐν Σαλαμῖνι ναυμαχίαν ὁ Θεμιστοκλῆς πρῶτον συνεβούλευε τοῖς Ἕλλησι διώκειν τὸ τῶν Περσῶν ναυτικὸν καὶ καταλύειν τὰς ἐν τῷ Ἑλλησπόντῳ γεφύρας. ὁ δὲ Εὐρυβιάδης, ὁ τῶν Λακεδαιμονίων στρατηγός, ἔπεισε τοὺς Ἕλληνας μὴ καταλύειν τὰς γεφύρας. 'Ἄλλως γὰρ,' λέγει, 'ἀναγκαῖον ἔσται τῷ Πέρσῃ ἐνθάδε μένειν· οὕτως δὲ οἷός τ' ἔσται καταστρέφεσθαι τὴν ὅλην Εὐρώπην· οὐ γὰρ μέλλει ἡσυχάσειν.' καὶ οὕτως ὁ Εὐρυβιάδης ἔπεισε τοὺς ἄλλους στρατηγούς.

ὁ δὲ Θεμιστοκλῆς, ὡς μανθάνει ὅτι οὐ πείθει τοὺς Ἕλληνας ἐπείγεσθαι εἰς τὸν Ἑλλήσποντον, λέγει ὧδε· 'Οὐχ ἡμεῖς, ἀλλ' οἱ θεοὶ σεσώκασιν οὐ μόνον ἡμᾶς αὐτοὺς ἀλλὰ καὶ τὴν Ἑλλάδα· οἱ γὰρ θεοὶ οὐκ ἤθελον ἕνα ἄνδρα τῆς τε Ἀσίας καὶ τῆς Εὐρώπης βασιλεῦσαι· δεῖ οὖν ἡμᾶς ἐν τῇ Ἑλλάδι καταμένειν καὶ θεραπεύειν τοὺς ἡμετέρους.' Θεμιστοκλῆς μὲν οὕτως ἔλεγεν, ὡς ἐβούλετο χαρίζεσθαι βασιλεῖ, οἱ δὲ Ἀθηναῖοι ἐπείθοντο· ἐφαίνετο γὰρ αὐτοῖς εἶναι σοφώτατος ὁ ἀνήρ.

ὁ δὲ Θεμιστοκλῆς ἔπεμψεν ἀγγέλους ὡς βασιλέα· ἐν δὲ τοῖς ἀγγέλοις ἦν οἰκέτης τις, ὀνόματι Σίκιννος· καὶ ἔλεγεν ὧδε· 'Ἔπεμψέ με ὁ Θεμιστοκλῆς, στρατηγὸς μὲν Ἀθηναίων, ἀνὴρ

Personal Pronouns

δὲ τῶν συμμάχων σοφώτατος· ὡς βούλεται εὐεργέτης σοι
εἶναι, ἔπεισε τοὺς Ἕλληνας μήτε διώκειν τὰς σὰς ναῦς μήτε
τὰς ἐν τῷ Ἑλλησπόντῳ γεφύρας καταλύειν. καὶ νῦν οἷός τ'
ἔσει σῴζεσθαι εἰς τὴν σὴν χώραν.'

Adapted from Herodotus, VIII, 108–110.

EXERCISE 86.

XERXES AND THE HELMSMAN

*Xerxes, says Herodotus, actually returned by land to the
Hellespont and was ferried across, as the bridges had been
destroyed by a storm. He writes that the following alternative
account 'seems quite unworthy of belief'.*

ἐπεὶ δὲ ὁ Ξέρξης ἐκ τῶν Ἀθηνῶν ἧκεν ἐπὶ τὸν Στρυμόνα,¹
ἐντεῦθεν οὐκέτι κατὰ γῆν ἐπορεύετο, ἀλλὰ τὴν μὲν στρατιὰν
τῷ στρατηγῷ ἐπέτρεψε καὶ ἐκέλευσεν αὐτὸν πορεύεσθαι εἰς
τὸν Ἑλλήσποντον, αὐτὸς δ' ἐπὶ νεὼς Φοινίσσης² ἐκομίζετο
εἰς τὴν Ἀσίαν. ἡ δὲ ναῦς μάλιστα ἐπιέζετο ἀνέμῳ τε καὶ
χειμῶνι καὶ ἔμελλε καταδύσεσθαι· συχνοὶ γὰρ Πέρσαι μετὰ
βασιλέως ἐκομίζοντο καὶ ἐπὶ τοῦ καταστρώματος ἐπῆσαν. ὁ
οὖν Ξέρξης καὶ ὁ κυβερνήτης περὶ τοῦ κινδύνου ἐβουλεύοντο·
καὶ ὁ κυβερνήτης λέγει, 'Δέσποτα, εἰ βούλει σῴζειν τὴν σὴν
ψυχήν, ἀναγκαῖόν ἐστι ἀπαλλάσσεσθαι τῶν ἐπιβατῶν.' ὁ δὲ
Ξέρξης λέγει τοῖς Πέρσαις, '῎Ανδρες Πέρσαι, νῦν καιρός³
ἐστιν ὑμῖν ἀποφαίνειν τὴν ὑμετέραν πρὸς ἐμὲ φιλίαν· ἐν ὑμῖν
γάρ ἐστιν ἡ ἐμὴ σωτηρία.' οἱ δὲ εὐθὺς ἐξάλλονται εἰς τὴν
θάλασσαν· καὶ οὕτως ἔσωσαν βασιλέα, ἐπεὶ ἡ ναῦς νῦν ἦν
κουφοτέρα. ὁ δὲ Ξέρξης, ὡς ἀποβαίνει εἰς γῆν, ὅτι μὲν ἔσωσε
τὴν βασιλέως ψυχήν, παρέχει τῷ κυβερνήτῃ χρυσοῦν⁴ στέφα-
νον, ὅτι δὲ ἠνάγκασε συχνοὺς Πέρσας ἀποβάλλεσθαι, ἀποτέμνει
τὴν κεφαλὴν αὐτοῦ.

Adapted from Herodotus, VIII, 118.

¹ A river in Macedonia.
² A Phoenician squadron had fought at Salamis.
³ καιρός, *precise moment* or *opportunity*, as opposed to χρόνος, *time*.
⁴ Another contracted Adjective (A 39).

Chapter 18

Verbs in -αω, Indicative, Imperatives, and Infinitives Active (A 84–85)

In order to learn the Contracted Verbs, it is far easier to learn the **rules** of Contraction first, and then to apply them, than to learn off the Tenses mechanically.

EXERCISE 87.

(a)
1. νικῶσι.
2. ἐτιμῶμεν.
3. ὁρᾷ.
4. ἐνίκων.
5. νικᾶτε.
6. βοᾶν.
7. ὁρῶμεν.
8. νικήσει.
9. ἐτίμησας.
10. τίμα.
11. νικήσετε.
12. ἐβόα.
13. ὁρᾷς.
14. νενικήκαμεν.
15. ἐτιμᾶτε.

(b)
1. We conquer.
2. They see.
3. You (s.) honour.
4. You (pl.) see.
5. They were shouting.
6. I will conquer.
7. He shouts.
8. He was honouring.
9. They will conquer.
10. To honour.
11. He conquered.
12. You (pl.) have honoured.
13. You (s.) conquered.
14. Honour (pl.).
15. Shout (s.).

EXERCISE 88.

1. ἀεὶ τιμῶμεν τοὺς ἀνδρείους.
2. οἱ Πέρσαι νικῶσι τοὺς Λακεδαιμονίους.
3. οἱ στρατιῶται ἐβόων, Θάλασσα, θάλασσα.
4. ὁ Ξέρξης ὁρᾷ τὴν ναυμαχίαν.
5. οἱ πολέμιοι οὔποτε νικήσουσιν ἡμᾶς.
6. ἐτιμήσαμεν τὸν στρατηγὸν μετὰ τὴν ναυμαχίαν.
7. οἱ Ἀθηναῖοι ἐνίκων ἐν τῇ πρὸς τοὺς Πέρσας μάχῃ.
8. ἐτιμᾶτε τὸν σοφώτατον τῶν Ἀθηναίων.
9. οἱ ἡμέτεροι σύμμαχοι οὐ νενικήκασι τοὺς πολεμίους.

10. ἐτίμας τὴν θεάν, ὦ θύγατερ.
11. τιμᾶτε τούς τε πατέρας καὶ τὰς μητέρας, ὦ παῖδες.
12. χαλεπὸν ἦν τοῖς Ἕλλησι νικᾶν τοὺς Πέρσας.

EXERCISE 89.

1. The Athenians were honouring the young men after the contest.
2. You do not honour the cowardly.
3. The Greeks are honouring the guide with gifts.
4. Death did not overcome Alcestis.
5. After the victory the Athenians were shouting.
6. We see the sea from the mountain.
7. It will be easy to overcome the men in the island.
8. Conquer or die, my son.
9. The barbarians did not honour the goddess.
10. At last we have overcome the enemy.
11. The poet was honouring Athens by his words.
12. We shall conquer the enemy's army within a few days.

**Verbs in -αω, Indicative, Imperatives, and Infinitives Passive
(A 84-85)**

EXERCISE 90.

1. οἱ δειλοὶ οὐ τιμῶνται ὑπὸ τῶν πολιτῶν.
2. ὁ Σοφοκλῆς τιμᾶται ὑπὸ τῶν Ἀθηναίων.
3. νικᾶσθε, ὦ πολῖται, διὰ τὴν ὑμετέραν βραδυτῆτα.
4. οἱ νεανίαι ἐτιμῶντο ἐν τοῖς ἀγῶσιν.
5. οὐ νικηθήσεσθε ὑπὸ τῶν ἱππέων.
6. τιμάσθω ὁ Λεωνίδας διὰ τὴν ἀνδρείαν.
7. αἰσχρόν ἐστι νικᾶσθαι ὑπὸ τῶν βαρβάρων.
8. ὁ ποιητὴς τετίμηται ἐν τῇ ἑορτῇ.
9. οἱ πολέμιοι ὁρῶνται ἐπὶ τῶν ὀρῶν.
10. ἐνικήθημεν τοῦ θέρους τῇ νόσῳ.
11. τιμᾶσθε ὑπὸ τῶν παίδων, ὦ γέροντες.
12. ἀγαθόν ἐστι τιμᾶσθαι ὑπὸ τοῦ δήμου.

EXERCISE 91.

1. The poet is honoured by the people.
2. Wise men were not always honoured by the Athenians.
3. The Persians are being conquered in the sea-battle.
4. The generals have been honoured on account of the victory.
5. Let the young man be honoured with gifts.
6. The captain and those with him were being overcome by the cavalry.
7. The Spartans will always be honoured for their bravery.
8. Nobody is seen in the market-place by night.
9. Demosthenes wished to be honoured by the citizens.
10. We hope to be honoured.
11. We were not conquered by the enemy.
12. Leonidas was being overcome by the Persians.

Verbs in -εω, Indicative, Imperatives and Infinitives Active
(A 86-87)

EXERCISE 92.

(a)
1. φιλοῦμεν.
2. ζητεῖς.
3. βοηθεῖτε.
4. ἐποίει.
5. ζητοῦσι.
6. ἐβοηθοῦμεν.
7. ἐμισεῖτε.
8. ἐβοηθήσαμεν.
9. βοηθεῖν.
10. ποιήσετε.
11. ἐβοήθουν.
12. ἐφίλησε.
13. ζητεῖ.
14. πεποίηκα.
15. ἐζήτεις.

(b)
1. They hate.
2. You (pl.) make.
3. We were seeking.
4. He loves.
5. You (s.) are helping.
6. I was seeking.
7. Love (pl.).
8. He was helping.
9. They will make.
10. You (s.) helped.
11. They have made.
12. He hated.
13. To seek.
14. You (s.) will help.
15. They loved.

EXERCISE 93.

1. φιλοῦμεν τὴν πατρίδα, ὦ Λακεδαιμόνιοι.
2. οἱ φυγάδες φιλοῦσι τὴν Ἑλλάδα.

3. οἱ ἱππεῖς ἐζήτουν τοὺς πολεμίους.
4. οἱ Ἀθηναῖοι ἐποίουν ναῦς εἰς τὸν πόλεμον.
5. εὖ ποιεῖτε τοὺς αἰχμαλώτους, ὦ σύμμαχοι.
6. βοηθοῦμεν τοῖς Ἀθηναίοις τοῖς χρήμασιν.
7. οἱ βάρβαροι ἡμᾶς κακῶς ἐποίησαν.
8. ὁ Σωκράτης ἔπεισε τοὺς νεανίας φιλεῖν τὴν δικαιοσύνην.
9. ζητεῖτε καὶ διώκετε τὸ τῶν πολεμίων ναυτικόν.
10. ῥᾴδιον μέν ἐστι ζητεῖν, χαλεπὸν δὲ εὑρίσκειν.
11. ἡ Ἄλκηστις ἀποθνήσκει ὑπὲρ τοῦ ἀνδρός, ὡς αὐτὸν φιλεῖ.
12. οἱ πολέμιοι εὖ πεποιήκασι τάς τε γυναῖκας καὶ τὰ τέκνα.

EXERCISE 94.

1. The young man loves his father and mother.
2. The Greeks were seeking freedom.
3. It is not easy for us to love enemies.
4. You are helping us with your fleet.
5. Always love your country, citizens.
6. Xerxes did not treat the captains well.
7. The cavalry were seeking the general of the allies.
8. Some masters treat slaves well, others badly.
9. We have sought for the river in vain.
10. Socrates persuaded us to seek wisdom.
11. We will help the king with our army.
12. You were treating your friends well.

Verbs in -εω, Indicative, Imperatives, and Infinitives Passive
(A 86-87)

EXERCISE 95.

1. τὰ χρήματα ἐζητεῖτο ὑπὸ τοῦ δούλου.
2. πρότερον μὲν ὁ Θεμιστοκλῆς ἐφιλεῖτο, νῦν δὲ μισεῖται.
3. βοηθούμεθα ὑπὸ τῶν ἐν τῇ πόλει.
4. τὸ ναυτικὸν ἤδη ποιεῖται.
5. τέσσαρας ἡμέρας ἐζήτησθε.
6. καλόν ἐστι φιλεῖσθαι ὑπὸ τῶν τέκνων.
7. φιλεῖ ὑπὸ τῶν δούλων, ὦ δέσποτα.

8. ὁ Δαρεῖος ἐποιήθη βασιλεύς.
9. ἡ σοφία ζητεῖται ὑπὸ τοῦ Σωκράτους.
10. ἀεὶ φιληθήσεται ἡ ἡμετέρα πατρίς.
11. ὁ λέων ἐζητεῖτο ἐξ ἡμέρας.
12. ὁ Μιλτιάδης ἐπεποίητο στρατηγός.

EXERCISE 96.

1. The general is loved by the soldiers.
2. The oxen are being sought by the old man.
3. Ships were being made in the harbour.
4. The king ordered his son to be sought.
5. Peace was made in the tenth year.
6. You will always be loved, because you saved your city.
7. We were being helped by the Athenians.
8. The traitor was being sought in the camp.
9. The ship has at last been made.
10. Miltiades will be made general.
11. The arms had not yet been made.
12. I shall be helped by my slaves.

Verbs in -οω, Indicative, Imperatives, and Infinitives, Active and Passive (A 88-89)

EXERCISE 97.

(*a*)
1. δηλοῖ.
2. ἐδήλους.
3. ἠλευθέρουν.
4. ἐδουλοῦμεν.
5. δηλοῖς.
6. ἐλευθεροῦμεν.
7. δήλου.
8. δουλοῦτε.
9. ἐδήλου.
10. ἐδήλωσας.
11. δουλώσετε.
12. δηλοῦν.
13. ἐλευθεροῦται.
14. δεδηλώκασι.
15. ἐδουλώθη.

(*b*)
1. We show.
2. They were enslaving.
3. You (pl.) are freeing.
4. He enslaves.
5. You (pl.) were showing.
6. You (s.) show.
7. To enslave.
8. I was showing.
9. He was freeing.
10. We shall show.
11. They enslaved.
12. Show (pl.).
13. He has shown.
14. They were being freed.
15. It is being shown.

EXERCISE 98.

1. οἱ ᾿Αθηναῖοι δουλοῦσι τὰς νήσους.
2. ὁ ἡγεμὼν δηλοῖ τὴν ὁδὸν τοῖς ῞Ελλησιν.
3. χαλεπὸν ἔσται ἐλευθεροῦν τὴν ῾Ελλάδα ἀπὸ τῶν βαρβάρων.
4. οὐ δουλοῦμεν ὑμᾶς, ὦ ἄνδρες.
5. δηλώσομεν τῷ στρατηγῷ τὸ τῶν πολεμίων στρατόπεδον.
6. ὁ νεανίας ἐδήλου τὰ ἆθλα τῷ πατρί.
7. ἡ ῾Ελλὰς οὔποτε δουλωθήσεται ὑπὸ τῶν βαρβάρων.
8. τὸ ναυτικὸν ἐδηλοῦτο βασιλεῖ.
9. αἱ νῆσοι δεδούλωνται ὑπὸ τῶν ᾿Αθηναίων.
10. ὁ στρατηγὸς δηλοῖ τὴν βουλὴν τοῖς συμμάχοις.
11. κακόν ἐστι δουλοῦν συμμάχους πιστούς.
12. ἡ πόλις ἐλευθεροῦται ὑπὸ τοῦ στρατηγοῦ.
13. δήλου ἡμῖν τὴν σὴν βουλήν, ὦ Δημόσθενες.
14. ἡ ἡμετέρα πατρὶς ἠλευθερώθη ἀπὸ τῶν Περσῶν.
15. δηλούτω τις ἡμῖν τὴν ὁδόν.

EXERCISE 99.

1. The general is enslaving the citizens.
2. We do not show the way to traitors.
3. The soldiers are freeing the country from the enemy.
4. The citizen was showing to me the house of Socrates.
5. Show me the road to the harbour.
6. We shall free the citizens in five days.
7. The city was enslaved by the barbarians.
8. It is not easy to free the island.
9. The general's plan has been shown to the soldiers.
10. Free your city from the Persians, citizens.
11. It was disgraceful to be enslaved by barbarians.
12. The Athenians enslaved those on the island.
13. We shall be freed by our allies.
14. Themistocles did not show his plan to the Athenians.
15. It is good to be freed at last.

Adjectives of the ἡδύς type (A 39)

It is worth noting some common Adjectives declined like ἡδύς :

βαθύς, *deep.* γλυκύς, *sweet.*
βαρύς, *heavy.* εὐρύς, *wide.*
βραδύς, *slow.* ὀξύς, *sharp.*
βραχύς, *short.* ταχύς, *swift.*

EXERCISE 100.

1. ἡδύ ἐστιν ἀκούειν τὴν τοῦ ποιητοῦ φωνήν.
2. διεβαίνομεν ποταμὸν εὐρύν τε καὶ βαθύν.
3. τὰ τῶν στρατιωτῶν ὅπλα ἦν βαρέα.
4. οἱ Ἀθηναῖοι ἔπεμψαν πέντε ταχείας τριήρεις.
5. ἡ διὰ τῆς ὕλης ὁδὸς ἦν βραδεῖα.
6. βραχεῖς μὲν ἦσαν οἱ τοῦ ῥήτορος λόγοι, ἡδεῖς δέ.
7. ἐδιώξαμεν τοὺς θῆρας ὅπλοις ὀξέσιν.
8. ἐνικήσαμεν τοὺς πολεμίους, ὅτι αἱ νῆες αὐτῶν ἦσαν βραδεῖαι.
9. ἡδεῖα ἦν ἡ τοῦ ὄρνιθος φωνή.
10. ἐν τοῖς βαρβάροις ἐπίνομεν οἶνον γλυκύν.

EXERCISE 101.

1. Short is the life of man.
2. We sent a swift ship to the island.
3. It was pleasant to be honoured by the citizens.
4. The snow on the mountain was deep.
5. The young man was sharp and clever.
6. We were marching by a short and quick way to the sea.
7. The guide showed us the wide and deep river.
8. The shields of the barbarians were not heavy.
9. The enemy's cavalry are slow.
10. The water on the island was not sweet.

EXERCISE 102.

POLYCRATES AND THE RING

Polycrates was tyrant of Samos, an island off the coast of Ionia, from 532 to 523 B.C. He grew so prosperous that Amasis,

*king of Egypt, warned him that his success would provoke the
jealousy of the gods and suggested that he should appease them
by throwing away his most valuable possession.*

(1) ὁ Πολυκράτης, ὁ τῆς Σάμου τύραννος,[1] ἦν δυνατώ-
τατος· φιλίαν δὲ ἐποιήσατο πρὸς Ἄμασιν τὸν Αἰγύπτου
βασιλέα καὶ ἔπεμψε δῶρα πρὸς αὐτόν· καὶ ὁ Ἄμασις αὐτὸς
ἔπεμψε δῶρα πρὸς τὸν Πολυκράτη. καὶ ὁ Πολυκράτης ἐσύλα
πανταχοῦ καὶ ἐκράτησε συχνῶν τῶν τε νήσων καὶ τῶν ἐν τῇ
ἠπείρῳ πόλεων· ἦσαν γὰρ αὐτῷ πεντηκόντεροί θ' ἑκατὸν καὶ
χίλιοι τοξόται· ἐπεὶ δὲ τοὺς Λεσβίους[2] ναυμαχίᾳ ἐνίκησε, τοὺς
αἰχμαλώτους καὶ ἠνάγκασε ὀρύσσειν τάφρον περὶ τὴν τῶν
Σαμίων πόλιν. ὡς δὲ ὁ Ἄμασις ἤκουσε περὶ τῆς τοῦ Πολυκράτους εὐτυχίας, ἔγραψεν ἐπιστολὴν καὶ ἔπεμψεν εἰς Σάμον.

'Ἄμασις Πολυκράτει ὧδε λέγει. Ἡδὺ μέν ἐστιν, ὦ φίλε,
εὖ πράσσειν· ἐμοὶ δὲ ἡ σὴ εὐτυχία οὐκ ἀρέσκει. εἰ γάρ τις
ἀεὶ εὐτυχεῖ, οἱ θεοὶ φθονοῦσιν. πείθου οὖν ἐμοὶ καὶ ὧδε ποίει·
τῶν σῶν κτημάτων ἀπόβαλε[3] τὸ πλείστου ἀξιώτατον.' ὁ δὲ
Πολυκράτης δέχεται τὴν ἐπιστολὴν καὶ ἀναγιγνώσκει. ἔδοξε
δὲ αὐτῷ ἀποβαλεῖν σφραγῖδα χρυσῆν. πληροῖ οὖν πεντη-
κόντερον καὶ αὐτὸς εἰσβαίνει· εἶτα δὲ τοὺς ναύτας κελεύει
ἀνάγεσθαι· ὡς δὲ ἀπὸ τῆς νήσου ἑκὰς ἦσαν, ῥίπτει τὴν
σφραγῖδα εἰς τὸ πέλαγος.

[1] A tyrant was an unconstitutional ruler, but not necessarily *tyrannical.*
[2] Lesbos was another Greek island, well to the north of Samos.
[3] Strong Aorist Imperatives follow the pattern of the Present Imperative.

(2) τῇ δὲ πέμπτῃ ἢ τῇ ἕκτῃ ἡμέρᾳ ἁλιεύς τις ἰχθὺν μέγιστον λαμβάνει καὶ οὐκ ἀξιοῖ φέρειν αὐτὸν εἰς τὴν ἀγοράν·
φέρει οὖν εἰς τὰ βασίλεια εἰς ὄψιν Πολυκράτει καὶ λέγει·
'Δοκεῖ ἐμοὶ ὁ ἰχθὺς σοῦ τε εἶναι ἄξιος καὶ τῆς σῆς ἀρχῆς·
αἰτῶ σε αὐτὸν δέχεσθαι.' ὁ δὲ ἥδεται τοῖς λόγοις· ''Ἡδύ ἐστιν
ἀκούειν τε τοὺς σοὺς λόγους καὶ δέχεσθαι τὸ δῶρον· ὅτι δὲ
εὖ ἐποίησας, καλοῦμέν σε ἐπὶ δεῖπνον.' ὁ μὲν οὖν ἁλιεὺς
μάλιστα ἥδεται, ὅτι οὕτως τιμᾶται, καὶ οἴκαδε ἀποχωρεῖ· οἱ δὲ
θεράποντες, ὡς τέμνουσι τὸν ἰχθύν, ἐν τῇ γαστρὶ εὑρίσκουσι

τὴν σφραγῖδα. ὡς δὲ ὁρῶσιν αὐτήν, εὐθὺς παρὰ τὸν Πολυκράτη φέρουσι καὶ τὸ πρᾶγμα ἐξηγοῦνται. ὁ δὲ Ἄμασις, ἐπεὶ ἤκουσε περὶ τοῦ θαύματος, ἠπόρει καὶ κήρυκα ἔπεμψεν εἰς Σάμον καὶ διελύσατο τὴν πρὸς αὐτὸν φιλίαν· οὐκέτι γὰρ ἤθελε ξένος εἶναι τοῦ Πολυκράτους, εἰ ἀεὶ εὐτυχεῖ.

Adapted from Herodotus, III, 39–43.

Chapter 19

Adjectives of the εὔφρων and εὐγενής types
(A 44)

Like εὔφρων, *kindly*.
  εὐδαίμων, *happy*.
  σώφρων, *prudent*.

Like εὐγενής, *well-born*.
  ἀληθής, *true*.

ἀσθενής, *weak*.
ἀσφαλής, *safe*.
εὐτυχής, *fortunate*.
σαφής, *clear*.
ψευδής, *false*.

N.B. τὸ ἀληθές or τὰ ἀληθῆ, *the truth*.

EXERCISE 103.

1. οἱ πλούσιοι οὐκ ἀεὶ εὐδαίμονές εἰσιν.
2. ὁ Ἄδμητος ἐφαίνετο εἶναι εὐτυχής.
3. ἐπιτρέπομεν τὴν ἀρχὴν τοῖς εὐγενέσιν.
4. ὁ Θεμιστοκλῆς οὐκ ἔγραψε τὰ ἀληθῆ.
5. ἡ πρὸς τὴν θάλασσαν ὁδὸς οὐκ ἦν σαφής.
6. οὐκ ἀσφαλές ἐστι πιστεύειν τοῖς τείχεσιν.
7. ὁ Ἄμασις οὐκ ἐνόμισε τὸν Πολυκράτη εἶναι σώφρονα.
8. πιθανὸς μέν ἐστιν ὁ ῥήτωρ, ψευδὴς δέ.
9. οἱ Ἀθηναῖοι ἔπεμψαν τοὺς ἀσθενεῖς εἰς τὰς νήσους.
10. σῶφρόν ἐστι τὰ ἀληθῆ λέγειν.

EXERCISE 104.

1. The orator's words were not clear.
2. The Greeks were being led by a false guide.
3. The walls of the city were weak.
4. Few men are always fortunate.
5. The rule of the well-born was sometimes harsh.
6. Citizens, I am telling you the truth.
7. The Athenians will be safe on account of their fleet.
8. Socrates was both wise and prudent.
9. The words of the messenger were false.
10. The soldiers were being led by a prudent general.

μέγας, πολύς, **and Adjectives of the** τάλας **type (A 42)**

EXERCISE 105.

1. ὁ Πολυκράτης ἐσύλα πολλὰς τῶν νήσων.
2. ἐπίνομεν οἶνον μέλανά τε καὶ γλυκύν.
3. ὁ Περικλῆς ἐβούλετο ποιεῖν τὴν πόλιν μεγάλην καὶ καλήν.
4. πολλαὶ τῶν νεῶν κατεδύθησαν ἐν τῇ Σαλαμῖνι.
5. ὁ γίγας μεγάλῃ φωνῇ ἐβόα.
6. οἱ θεράποντες εὑρίσκουσι σφραγῖδα ἐν ἰχθύι μεγάλῳ.
7. οἱ Ἀθηναῖοι ἔμενον τοὺς Λακεδαιμονίους πολὺν χρόνον.
8. οἱ ἐκεῖ βάρβαροι μέλανες ἦσαν.
9. ὁ τύραννος ἐν πολλῇ ἀπορίᾳ ἦν.
10. οἱ Ἀθηναῖοι ᾠκοδόμουν τεῖχος μέγα.
11. οἱ Κορίνθιοι ᾤκισαν πολλὰς ἀποικίας ἐν τῇ Σικελίᾳ.
12. πολλὰ ἔλεγεν ὁ Δημοσθένης.

EXERCISE 106.

1. Many of the ships were black.
2. We were crossing a big and broad river.
3. The Athenians sent many soldiers against the Persians.
4. There was a large ship outside the harbour.
5. Many of the trees were being cut down by the Spartans.
6. The fisherman was carrying the big fish to Polycrates.
7. The Spartans remained in the island for many days.

8. Xerxes was leading a large army into Greece.
9. We ransomed the prisoners with much money.
10. There was not much water in the river.
11. We were listening to the voice of the black bird.
12. The Athenians were preparing a large fleet in the harbour.

Chapter 20

Present Participle in -ων (A 73)

As in Latin, so in Greek, the Present Participle is used when the time of the action (or state) represented by the Participle is the same as the time of the action of the Verb with which it is used, e.g. in English, *I hear you calling*, where the *calling* and the *hearing* happen at the same time; all uncontracted Participles in -ων are declined like ἑκών (A 41), which should now be learnt; Contracted Present Participles will be found on the same page.

A participle is often used for a *when*, *while* or *since* Clause.

ὁ στρατηγὸς πίπτει φεύγων.
The general falls while fleeing.

οὐκ ἔχοντες χρήματα, ἀποροῦμεν.
Since we have no money, we are at a loss.

The Article and the Participle

The Article and the Participle (in any Tense) are often used where in English we would use a **Relative Clause**:

οὐ τιμῶμεν τοὺς ἐκ τῆς μάχης φεύγοντας.
We do not honour those who flee from battle.

The position of ἐκ τῆς μάχης between the Article and the Participle should be carefully noticed.

We often find a Participle **after** a Noun, with the Article repeated:

> οὐ τιμῶμεν τοὺς στρατιώτας τοὺς ἀποφεύγοντας.
> *We do not honour soldiers who run away.*

EXERCISE 107.

1. οἱ πολέμιοι διώκοντες ἐκωλύθησαν τῷ χειμῶνι.
2. οἱ τὸν ποταμὸν διαβαίνοντες ὁρῶνται ὑπὸ τῶν πολεμίων.
3. ὁρῶμεν τὰς καμήλους διωκούσας τοὺς ἵππους.
4. οἱ ἐν τῇ πόλει μένοντές εἰσι μῶροι.
5. ὁ Λεωνίδας πίπτει ἐν τῇ μάχῃ ἄγων τοὺς Λακεδαιμονίους.
6. τιμᾶτε τοὺς πολίτας τοὺς ὑπὲρ τῆς πατρίδος κινδυ-
   νεύοντας.
7. πιστεύομεν τοῖς τὴν πύλην φυλάσσουσιν.
8. ἀκούω τὰς τῶν θυόντων φωνάς.
9. οἱ τοῖς Ἀθηναίοις πιστεύοντες λυθήσονται.
10. ὁ Ὀδυσσεὺς ἐκάθιζε πίνων οἶνον γλυκύν.
11. τιμῶμεν τοὺς ἐπὶ τοὺς Λακεδαιμονίους στρατεύοντας.
12. οἱ νεανίαι οἱ ἐν τοῖς ἀγῶσι νικῶντες τιμηθήσονται.

EXERCISE 108.

1. We see the enemy cutting down the trees.
2. Those who are fleeing are not worthy of honour.
3. The Athenians honour those who are willing to fight.
4. While crossing the mountain we were hindered by the enemy.
5. Those who trust the orator are wise.
6. Honour those who write beautiful poems.
7. We can see the Persians fleeing.
8. Those who were pursuing could not cross the river.
9. You will honour the soldiers who are saving the city.
10. While fleeing from the city, we were hindered by the river.
11. Orators who speak well do not always persuade.
12. Since we have no allies, we shall not conquer easily.

Future, Aorist, and Perfect Participles Active (A 40, 41, 73)

All Aorist Participles in -ας are declined like πᾶς, πᾶσα, πᾶν
(A 40), which should now be learnt.

The Perfect Participle is only used to express a *state* or *continued action*, e.g. οἱ κατατεθνηκότες (from καταθνήσκω), *those who have died, the dead*; for a single past action, Greek always uses the Aorist Participle:

> τοὺς πολεμίους εἰς τὸν ποταμὸν διώξαντες, ἐπαυσάμεθα
> τῆς μάχης.
>
> *Having pursued the enemy to the river, we ceased fighting*
> (or, *When we had pursued, after pursuing*, etc.).

Notice that owing to the full range of Active Participles, a Greek sentence is often very different in construction from a Latin one.

EXERCISE 109.

1. ἀποπέμψας τοὺς συμμάχους, ὁ στρατηγὸς ἔταξε τὸν
   στρατόν.
2. τιμήσομεν τοὺς τὴν πόλιν σώσαντας.
3. λύσας τοὺς βοῦς, ὁ γέρων ἔμενεν ἐν τῷ λειμῶνι.
4. οἱ ἐν τῇ πόλει ἐφύλασσον τὰς πύλας πᾶσαν τὴν νύκτα.
5. κολάσομεν τοὺς παῖδας τοὺς τὰ δένδρα βλάψαντας.
6. ὁ στρατηγὸς ἔλυσε πάντας τοὺς αἰχμαλώτους.
7. οὐ πιστεύομεν τοῖς τὸν ἄγγελον πέμψασιν.
8. χάριν ἔχομεν τοῖς τὴν πατρίδα σεσωκόσιν.
9. οἱ τὰ χρήματα πέμψαντες ἄξιοί εἰσι τῆς τιμῆς.
10. ἦν ἡδὺ πᾶσι τοῖς μετὰ τοῦ Ξενοφῶντος ὁρᾶν τὴν
    θάλασσαν.
11. πείσας τὴν γυναῖκα ἀποθνήσκειν, ὁ Ἄδμητος ἔτι
    ἐβασίλευεν.
12. οἱ Ἀθηναῖοι χάριν ἔχουσι τοῖς βοήθειαν πέμψουσιν.
13. οἱ ἐν τοῖς ἀγῶσι νικῶντες ἆθλα φέρονται.
14. τιμῶμεν τοὺς ἡμᾶς εὖ πεποιηκότας.
15. ἀπεπέμψαμεν πάσας τὰς γυναῖκας τὰς ἔτι μενούσας εἰς
    τὰς νήσους.

EXERCISE 110.

1. Having persuaded the allies to send help, the general began to march.
2. Those who sent help are fighting in the harbour.
3. When he had punished the boy, he sent him home.
4. After sending away all the women and children, the Athenians trusted their ships.
5. It is wise to trust those who trust us.
6. Those who have conquered in the sea-battle are worthy of honour.
7. The general sent away those who were not willing to fight.
8. Socrates was the wisest of all the Greeks.
9. We shall guard the ships that remain in the harbour.
10. Xerxes ordered all the cities to send earth and water.
11. Few are those who will send help.
12. Those who have fared well will help the rest.
13. When he had saved his country, Themistocles helped the Persians.
14. All the prisoners will be set free in three days.
15. After conquering the Persians, the allies are marching home.

Middle and Passive Participles (A 40, 75, 77)

EXERCISE 111.

1. οἱ ᾿Αθηναῖοι λυσάμενοι τοὺς αἰχμαλώτους εἰρήνην ἐποιήσαντο.
2. διωκόμενοι ὑπὸ τῶν ᾿Αθηναίων, οἱ Πέρσαι φεύγουσιν εἰς τὴν θάλασσαν.
3. τῷ ποταμῷ κωλυθείς, ὁ στρατηγὸς ἐκέλευσεν ἡμᾶς στρατοπεδεύεσθαι.
4. οἱ ἡμᾶς λυσόμενοι οὐ σπεύδουσιν.
5. οἰκτείρομεν τοὺς ἐν τῇ μάχῃ νικηθέντας.
6. οἱ λυθέντες οἴκαδε ἀπεχώρησαν.
7. ὁ Μιλτιάδης στρατηγὸς ποιηθεὶς ἐνίκησε τοὺς Πέρσας.

8. πολὺν χρόνον βουλευσάμενοι, οἱ στρατηγοὶ ἐκέλευσαν
   τὴν στρατίαν προχωρεῖν.
9. σώσομεν τοὺς δεδουλωμένους.
10. ἡ ναῦς ἡ τῷ χειμῶνι κωλυθεῖσα ἔμενεν ἐγγὺς τῆς
    νήσου.

EXERCISE 112.

1. Having been hindered by the broad river, the enemy
   went away.
2. The general ordered those who had been set free to
   encamp.
3. Those who have been conquered are hurrying home.
4. We are willing to wait for those who will ransom us.
5. The women who had been set free were rejoicing.
6. Leonidas falls while fighting against the Persians.
7. Those who have been made generals will manage the
   affairs of the city.
8. Obeying the god, the Athenians trusted not the wooden
   walls themselves, but their ships.
9. While marching through Armenia, the Greeks were in
   great danger.
10. Those who are taught are sometimes wiser than those
    who teach.

EXERCISE 113.

THE INGENUITY OF CYRUS

*Cyrus the Great, who reigned from 549 to 529, after conquer-
ing Lydia and Ionia, turned east and captured Babylon in 538;
his campaigns had extended as far as India.*

οἱ δὲ Βαβυλώνιοι, νικηθέντες μάχῃ ἔξω τῶν τειχῶν, εἰς τὴν
πόλιν ἀπεχώρησαν. ὁ δὲ Κῦρος μάλιστα ἠπόρει, ὅτι τοῖς
Βαβυλωνίοις ἦν εὐπορία σίτου. βουλευσάμενος οὖν πολὺν
χρόνον ἐποίησεν ὧδε. τάξας μέρος τοῦ στρατοῦ, ᾗ ὁ Εὐφράτης
εἰς τὴν πόλιν εἰσρεῖ, καὶ ἑτέρους στρατιώτας τάξας ὄπισθε τῆς
πόλεως, ᾗ ὁ ποταμὸς ἀπορρεῖ ἐκ τῆς πόλεως, ἐκέλευσεν
αὐτοὺς ἐκεῖ μένειν.

ἔπειτα δὲ ὁ Κῦρος ἤγαγε τοὺς λοιποὺς τοῦ στρατοῦ πρὸς
τὸν τόπον, οὗ ἡ τῶν Βαβυλωνίων βασίλεια, ὀνόματι Νίτωκρις,
ἐν τῷ πρὶν χρόνῳ ἔλυτρον ὤρυξε λίμνῃ (*for a lake*) ἐγγὺς
τοῦ ποταμοῦ· ὁ δὲ Κῦρος τὸν ποταμὸν διώρυχι εἰσήγαγεν εἰς
τὴν λίμνην (νῦν γὰρ ἔλος ἦν) καὶ ἐποίησεν αὐτὸν διαβατὸν
εἶναι. καὶ οὕτως οἱ ἔξω τῆς πόλεως οἷοί τ᾽ ἦσαν πορεύεσθαι
ἐν τῷ ποταμῷ, ὥσπερ ἐν ὁδῷ, καὶ αἱρεῖν τὴν Βαβυλῶνα. καὶ
οὐκ ἔξεστι τοῖς Βαβυλωνίοις προσβάλλειν τοῖς Πέρσαις, ὅτι
οὐχ ὁρῶσιν αὐτοὺς προχωροῦντας εἰς τὴν πόλιν· διὰ δὲ τὸ τῆς
Βαβυλῶνος μέγεθος οἱ τὸ μέσον οἰκοῦντες μόνον μετὰ πολὺν
χρόνον περὶ τῆς συμφορᾶς ἀκούουσιν· καὶ τύχῃ ἐχόρευον, ὅτι
ἦν τότε ἑορτή.

Adapted from Herodotus, I, 190–191.

Chapter 21

Perfect, Aorist, and Future Passive Tenses
of some Verbs with Consonant Stems (A 81)

(1) Perfect Passive Tenses. The first three examples on page
81 of A should be learnt by heart, πέπλεγμαι, πέπεισμαι,
τέτυμμαι. Note the formation of the 3rd pers. plural (Participle
with εἰσί).

The corresponding Pluperfect Tenses are formed on the same
principle, e.g. from τάσσω, *I draw up* (Perfect τέταγμαι):

ἐτετάγμην   *I had been drawn up.*
ἐτέταξο
ἐτέτακτο
ἐτετάγμεθα
ἐτέταχθε
τεταγμένοι ἦσαν

(2) Aorist Passive Tenses end in -ην, if Strong; in -θην, if Weak; in either case, they are conjugated like ἐλύθην.

(3) Future Passive Tenses end in -ήσομαι, if Strong; in -θήσομαι, if Weak; in either case, they are conjugated like λυθήσομαι.

The following Tenses of common Verbs should be learnt:

A. Guttural Verbs (πέπλεγμαι type)

Verb	Meaning	Perf. Pass.	Aor. Pass.	Fut. Pass.
διώκω	I pursue	δεδίωγμαι	ἐδιώχθην	διωχθήσομαι
ἄγω	I lead	ἦγμαι	ἤχθην	ἀχθήσομαι
πράσσω	I do	πέπραγμαι	ἐπράχθην	πραχθήσομαι
τάσσω	I draw up	τέταγμαι	ἐτάχθην	ταχθήσομαι
φυλάσσω	I guard	πεφύλαγμαι	ἐφυλάχθην	φυλαχθήσομαι

B. Dental Verbs (πέπεισμαι type)

ἀναγκάζω	I compel	ἠνάγκασμαι	ἠναγκάσθην	ἀναγκασθήσομαι
πείθω	I persuade	πέπεισμαι	ἐπείσθην	πεισθήσομαι
σῴζω	I save	σέσωσμαι	ἐσώθην	σωθήσομαι

C. Labial Verbs (τέτυμμαι type)

πέμπω	I send	πέπεμμαι	ἐπέμφθην	πεμφθήσομαι
λείπω	I leave	λέλειμμαι	ἐλείφθην	λειφθήσομαι
γράφω	I write	γέγραμμαι	ἐγράφην	γραφήσομαι
βλάπτω	I harm	βέβλαμμαι	ἐβλάβην	βλαβήσομαι
κρύπτω	I hide	κέκρυμμαι	ἐκρύφθην	—
τύπτω	I strike	τέτυμμαι	ἐτύπην	—

EXERCISE 114.

1. τὸ στράτευμα εἰς τὴν μάχην τέτακται.
2. οἱ πολέμιοι ἐδιώχθησαν εἰς τὴν θάλασσαν.
3. ἡ πόλις αὑτὴ οὐ βέβλαπται ὑπὸ τῶν πολεμίων.
4. οἱ Ἕλληνες ἐπείσθησαν μὴ καταλῦσαι τὴν γέφυραν.
5. αἱ Ἀθῆναι σωθήσονται τῷ ξυλίνῳ τείχει.
6. οἱ Πέρσαι ἠναγκάσθησαν ἀποφεύγειν ἐκ τῆς Ἀττικῆς.
7. πολλὰ χρήματα ἐπέμφθη ὑπὸ τῶν συμμάχων.
8. οἱ ἐν τῇ νήσῳ σεσωσμένοι εἰσίν.

9. τὸ ἔργον τριῶν ἡμερῶν ἐπέπρακτο.
10. ὁ στρατὸς ἐτάχθη ὑπὸ τοῦ Κύρου.
11. λελείμμεθα, ὦ ἄνδρες, ὑπὸ τῶν συμμάχων.
12. πολλοὶ πεισθήσονται τοῖς τοῦ Δημοσθένους λόγοις

EXERCISE 115.

1. We have been saved by Miltiades.
2. Only a few men have been left in Athens.
3. The cavalry were pursued by the camels.
4. The work has now been accomplished.
5. The Greeks were led to the sea by a guide.
6. Much money had been hidden in the tomb.
7. The women and children will not be left in the city.
8. Not many allies had been sent.
9. Citizens, you have been harmed by the orator's words.
10. You have been drawn up near your allies, soldiers.
11. A letter has been written and will be sent to the king.
12. We have been persuaded to fight for our country.

EXERCISE 116.

1. ἀναγκασθησόμεθα ἀναλίσκειν πολλὰ χρήματα.
2. ἥ τε γῆ καὶ τὸ ὕδωρ ἐπέμφθησαν ὡς βασιλέα.
3. πολλοὶ πολῖται τετυμμένοι ἦσαν λίθοις.
4. τετάγμεθα εἰς μεγάλην μάχην.
5. φυλαχθήσεσθε ταῖς ναυσίν, ὦ πολῖται.
6. πολλὰ δένδρα ἐβλάβη ὑπὸ τῶν Λακεδαιμονίων.
7. οὐ πολλοὶ ἐλείφθησαν ἐν τῇ πόλει.
8. πάντα τὰ ἀναγκαῖα πραχθήσεται ὑπὲρ τῆς πατρίδος.
9. οἱ Ἕλληνες πεπεισμένοι ἦσαν μὴ διώκειν τὰς τῶν Περσῶν ναῦς.
10. οὐ βέβλαψαι ὑπὸ τῶν Ἑλλήνων, ὦ βασιλεῦ.

EXERCISE 117.

1. The allies had been persuaded to go away.
2. We were saved by the Spartans.
3. A large army was led by Xerxes.
4. The ring of Polycrates had been saved.

5. You have not been persuaded, citizens.
6. The island will be saved within a few days.
7. Many soldiers have been hidden in the wood.
8. Not much money has been left in the city.
9. The city's affairs will be managed by the generals
10. The letter had already been written.

EXERCISE 118.

VAIN APPEAL TO SPARTA

The expedition sent by Darius in 490 to punish Athens and Eretria sailed up the west coast of Euboea and sacked Eretria. The Persians then landed in Attica in the bay of Marathon.

οἱ δὲ ᾿Αθηναῖοι ἦσαν ἐν μεγάλῳ κινδύνῳ· ὁ οὖν Φιλιππίδης ἐπέμφθη κῆρυξ εἰς Σπάρτην ὑπὸ τῶν στρατηγῶν· καὶ δευτεραῖος[1] ἐκ τῶν ᾿Αθηνῶν ἦν ἐν Σπάρτῃ καὶ ἔλεγε τοῖς ἄρχουσιν· "Ὦ Λακεδαιμόνιοι, οἱ ᾿Αθηναῖοι αἰτοῦσιν ὑμᾶς αὐτοῖς βοηθῆσαι μηδὲ ἐᾶν τὴν ἐν τοῖς Ἕλλησιν ἀρχαιοτάτην πόλιν δουλοῦσθαι ὑπὸ τῶν βαρβάρων· ἤδη γὰρ ᾿Ερέτρια[2] ἠνδραπόδισται.᾿ οἱ δὲ Λακεδαιμόνιοι ἤθελον μὲν βοηθεῖν τοῖς ᾿Αθηναίοις, ἀδύνατον δὲ ἦν αὐτοῖς, οὐ βουλομένοις λύειν τὸν νόμον· ἔδει γὰρ αὐτοὺς τὴν πανσέληνον μένειν.

Adapted from Herodotus, VI, 105.

[1] The distance was 140 miles.
[2] This city lies on the west coast of Euboea

EXERCISE 119.

THE BATTLE OF MARATHON

ἐν δὲ τῷ μεταξὺ οἱ μὲν βάρβαροι εἰς τὸν Μαραθῶνα ἤχθησαν ὑπὸ τοῦ ῾Ιππίου,[1] τοῦ πρὶν ἐν ταῖς ᾿Αθήναις τυράννου, οἱ δὲ ᾿Αθηναῖοι ἐκεῖ τεταγμένοι ἦσαν. τῶν δὲ ᾿Αθηναίων στρατηγῶν οἱ μὲν οὐκ ἤθελον εὐθὺς μάχεσθαι (ὅτι οἱ μὲν ᾿Αθηναῖοι ἦσαν ὀλίγοι, οἱ δὲ Πέρσαι πολλοί), οἱ δὲ ἐβούλοντο· καὶ ἐν αὐτοῖς ἦν ὁ Μιλτιάδης. τέλος δὲ ὁ Καλλίμαχος, ὁ πολέμαρχος.[2]

[1] Son of Peisistratus, also tyrant of Athens, and expelled in 510 B.C.
[2] The Polemarch, as commander-in-chief, had a casting vote.

ἐπείσθη ὑπὸ τοῦ Μιλτιάδου μάχην ψηφίζεσθαι. οἱ δὲ 'Αθηναῖοι δρόμῳ προὐχώρησαν εἰς τὴν μάχην καὶ ἀνδρείως ἐμάχοντο. καὶ τὸ μὲν μέσον[3] ἐνικῶντο οἱ 'Αθηναῖοι καὶ ἐδιώχθησαν εἰς τὴν μεσόγαιαν· τὸ δὲ κέρας ἑκάτερον[3] οἱ 'Αθηναῖοι ἐνίκων. ἔπειτα δὲ οἱ 'Αθηναῖοι συναγαγόντες ἀμφότερα τὰ κέρατα προσέβαλον τοῖς τὸ μέσον τρέψασιν, καὶ ἐνίκων. καὶ οὕτως οἱ Πέρσαι ἐδιώχθησαν εἰς τὴν θάλασσαν.

Adapted from Herodotus, VI, 107–113.

[3] *in the centre*; *on each wing* (Accusatives of Respect).

Chapter 22

Further Comparison of Adjectives (1)
(A 50–51); Declension of μείζων (A 44)

The Adjectives will be found in Sections 82 and 83; less common ones should be omitted.

N.B. All Comparatives in -ων are declined like μείζων.

EXERCISE 120.

1. οἱ τοῦ θεοῦ λόγοι ἦσαν ἀληθέστατοι.
2. ὁ οἶνος γλυκύτερός ἐστι τοῦ ὕδατος.
3. ὁ Πολυκράτης ἦν πάντων ἀνθρώπων ὁ εὐτυχέστατος.
4. αἱ τῶν πολεμίων νῆές εἰσι θάσσονες τῶν ἡμετέρων.
5. ἦν μεγίστη ναυμαχία ἐν τῷ λιμένι.
6. οἱ ἀποφεύγοντες ἐχθίονες ἡμῖν εἰσι τῶν πολεμίων αὐτῶν.
7. τὸ τῶν Περσῶν ναυτικὸν ἦν μεῖζον ἢ τὸ τῶν 'Αθηναίων.
8. ἀσφαλέστερόν ἐστι μὴ πιστεύειν τῷ ῥήτορι.
9. ὁ τῶν βαρβάρων οἶνος ἦν μελάντατος.
10. αἴσχιστον ἔσται καταλείπειν τοὺς γέροντας.
11. ἡ "Αλκηστις ἦν γυνὴ πιστοτάτη.
12. ἀσθενέστεροί ἐσμεν ἢ οἱ πολέμιοι.

98 *Further Comparison of Adjectives. Adverbs*

EXERCISE 121.

1. We shall be safer in the islands.
2. Socrates was a very prudent man.
3. The water from the spring was very sweet.
4. The swiftest ships are not always the safest.
5. We think Socrates greater than his enemies.
6. I never heard truer words.
7. The men in the village were very hostile to Xenophon's army.
8. Cyrus captures Babylon, a very big city.
9. The son was more fortunate than his father.
10. It is more shameful to flee than to be conquered.
11. Xerxes was leading a bigger army (στρατία) than Leonidas.
12. The plan of the enemy was now very clear.

Further Comparison of Adjectives (2) (A 51); Formation and Comparison of Adverbs (A 52)

The Adjectives will be found in Section 84; πέπων and πίων should be omitted.

Note. For present use, remember μικρότερος, μικρότατος, *smaller, smallest,* μείων being rare; ἐλάσσονες, *fewer.*

Of the Adjectives of the ἡδύς type, βαθύς, βαρύς, βραδύς, εὐρύς, ὀξύς are compared like γλυκύς; βραχύς is compared either like γλυκύς or like ἡδύς.

EXERCISE 122.

1. ἐλάσσονές εἰσιν ἡμῖν ἱππεῖς ἢ τοῖς πολεμίοις.
2. ἄμεινόν ἐστιν ἀποχωρεῖν ἢ ἐν τῇ πόλει μένειν.
3. ὁ Πραξιτέλης ἐποίησεν ἀνδριάντας καλλίστους.
4. κατεδύσαμεν πλείους ναῦς ἢ οἱ πολέμιοι.
5. ῥᾷόν ἐστι λέγειν ἢ πείθειν.
6. κάκιστα πάσχομεν ἐν τῷ πολέμῳ.
7. ταχέως ἔτρεχον οἱ Πέρσαι πρὸς τὴν θάλασσαν.
8. οἱ ἀνδρείως μαχόμενοι τιμῶνται ὑπὸ τῶν Λακεδαιμονίων.

9. οἱ ᾿Αθηναῖοι μάλιστα μισοῦσι τοὺς τυράννους.
10. ῥᾳδίως νικήσομεν τοὺς ἐφ᾽ ἡμᾶς στρατεύοντας.
11. προαιρούμεθα τὴν εἰρήνην μᾶλλον ἢ τὸν πόλεμον.
12. οἱ ῞Ελληνες βραδύτερον ἐπορεύοντο διὰ τὴν χιόνα.
13. ἡδέως ἀκούομεν τῶν εὖ λεγόντων.[1]
14. ἡ τῆς ᾿Αρτεμισίας ναῦς τάχιστα ἐδιώκετο.
15. οἱ ἄριστα λέγοντες οὐκ ἀεὶ ἡμᾶς πείθουσιν.

[1] ἀκούω takes the Acc. of a *thing*, but the Gen. of a *person*.

EXERCISE 123.

1. The army of the Spartans was very small.
2. It will be very easy to cross the river.
3. Most of the enemy retreated at once.
4. Even the worst men have friends.
5. Few cities are more beautiful than Athens.
6. We have more ships than the enemy.
7. The best of the ships were sunk.
8. The Spartans were fewer than the Persians.
9. The giant was shouting terribly.
10. Pericles managed the affairs of the city more wisely than Cleon.
11. My sword is sharper than yours.
12. Themistocles did not always act wisely.
13. The allies began to march very quickly.
14. Our army was drawn up more slowly.
15. We shall conquer the enemy more easily by sea than by land.

EXERCISE 124.

CROCODILES

Cambyses, son of Cyrus the Great, invades Egypt, and Herodotus with his typical thoroughness devotes a whole book to an account of the country—including the crocodiles of the Nile.

(1) ὁ δὲ κροκόδειλος τέσσαρας μῆνας τοῦ χειμῶνος ἐσθίει οὐδέν. ἡ δὲ θήλεια τίκτει μὲν ᾠὰ καὶ ἐκλέπει ἐν τῇ γῇ καὶ ἐκεῖ διατρίβει τὸ πολὺ[1] τῆς ἡμέρας, τὴν δὲ νύκτα πᾶσαν ἐν τῷ

[1] *most.*

ποταμῷ· θερμότερον γάρ ἐστι τὸ ὕδωρ τῆς δρόσου. πάντων δὲ ζῴων ὁ κροκόδειλος ἐξ ἐλαχίστου μέγιστον γίγνεται· τὰ μὲν γὰρ ᾠὰ οὐ πολλῷ μείζονά ἐστι τῶν χηνός· αὐξανόμενος δὲ ὁ κροκόδειλος γίγνεται (reaches) καὶ εἰς ἑπτακαίδεκα πήχεις καὶ μείζων ἔτι. ἔχει δὲ ὀφθαλμοὺς μὲν ὑός, ὀδόντας δὲ μεγάλους· γλῶσσαν δὲ μόνον θηρίων οὐκ ἔχει, οὐδὲ τὴν κάτω γνάθον κινεῖ, ἀλλὰ τὴν ἄνω γνάθον προσάγει τῇ κάτω.

(2) τοῖς μὲν δὴ τῶν Αἰγυπτίων ἱεροί εἰσιν οἱ κροκόδειλοι, τοῖς δὲ οὔ. οἱ δὲ περὶ Θήβας[1] οἰκοῦντες ἕνα κροκόδειλον ἐκ πάντων τιμῶσιν· τρέφουσιν αὐτὸν σίτῳ καὶ τά τ᾽ ὦτα καὶ τοὺς πόδας κοσμοῦσι χρυσῷ. οἱ δὲ περὶ Ἐλεφαντίνην[1] οἰκοῦντες καὶ ἐσθίουσιν αὐτούς. ὁ δὲ βουλόμενος κροκόδειλον αἱρεῖν δελεάζει (puts as a bait) νῶτον ὑὸς περὶ ἄγκιστρον καὶ εἰσβάλλει εἰς μέσον τὸν ποταμόν·[2] αὐτὸς δὲ ἐν τῇ γῇ ἔχων ὗν ζωόν, αὐτὸν τύπτει. ἀκούσας δὲ τὴν φωνήν, ὁ κροκόδειλος σπεύδει πρὸς τὴν φωνὴν καὶ τὸ νῶτον καταπίνει (swallows down)· οἱ δὲ ἐν τῇ γῇ ἕλκουσιν. πρῶτον δὲ πάντων ὁ θηρευτὴς πηλῷ καλύπτει τοὺς ὀφθαλμοὺς αὐτοῦ· ἔπειτα αὐτὸν ῥᾷστα ἀποκτείνει.

Adapted from Herodotus, II, 68–70.

[1] *Egyptian Thebes (modern Luxor), with its hundred gates, was destroyed by Cambyses; it lay some 550 miles upstream; Elephantine was about 120 miles beyond it.*
[2] Notice the position of the Article: τὸν μέσον ποταμόν would mean *the middle river (of three).*

Chapter 23

Further uses of Pronouns : ὁ αὐτός ; Reflexive Pronouns ; ὅδε, οὗτος, ἐκεῖνος.

We have already met the following uses of αὐτός :

(1) αὐτός meaning *self* in all its Cases, ὁ ἀνὴρ αὐτός, *the man himself* (Ch. 8).

(2) αὐτός **in any Case except the Nom.,** meaning *him, her, it, them* (Ch. 8).

(3) αὐτός in the Gen., meaning *his, her, its, their*, when these Pronouns are not Reflexive (Ch. 17).

ὁ αὐτός, 'the same' (A 56)

When αὐτός is **preceded** by the Article, it means *the same*, e.g. ἡ αὐτὴ γυνή, *the same woman*; τὸ αὐτό, *the same thing*.

Reflexive Pronouns (A 57)

These correspond to **me ipsum, te ipsum, se** in Latin, e.g. φιλοῦμεν ἡμᾶς αὐτούς, *we love ourselves*; φιλεῖ ἑαυτόν, *he loves himself*. Notice that in the plural the forms ἑαυτούς, etc., are more common than σφᾶς αὐτούς, etc.

The Gen. sing. and Gen. plur. of ἑαυτόν, ἑαυτήν, ἑαυτό, **are** used in Greek for the Reflexive Possessive Pronoun of the 3rd Person, *his own, her own, its own, their own*, corresponding in meaning and use to the Latin **suus** (there being no commonly used equivalent Adjective in Greek); these Genitives are always placed **between the Article and the Noun:**

οἱ βάρβαροι ἀπεχώρησαν εἰς τὴν ἑαυτῶν χώραν.
The barbarians retreated to their own country.

(εἰς τὴν χώραν αὐτῶν would mean *to their country*, i.e. *someone else's country*.)

ἡ 'Αθήνη φυλάσσει τοὺς ἑαυτῆς πολίτας.
Athene protects her own citizens.

EXERCISE 125.

1. ἔγραψα πολλὰς ἐπιστολὰς τῇ αὐτῇ ἡμέρᾳ.
2. ἡ "Αλκηστις αὐτὴ ἐθέλει ἀποθνήσκειν ὑπὲρ τοῦ ἀνδρός.
3. ὁ "Αδμητος ᾤκτειρεν ἑαυτόν.
4. ὁ 'Αγαμέμνων ἔθυσε τὴν ἑαυτοῦ θυγατέρα.
5. ὁ ῥήτωρ ἀεὶ τὰ αὐτὰ ἔλεγεν.
6. ἡ 'Αρτεμισία ἔσωσεν ἑαυτὴν ἐν τῇ ναυμαχίᾳ.

7. ὁ Θεμιστοκλῆς οὐ διώκει βασιλέα, ἀλλ' ἀγγέλους ὡς
　　αὐτὸν πέμπει.

8. οἱ ἵπποι οὐχ οἷοί τέ εἰσι φέρειν οὔτε τὰς καμήλους
　　οὔτε τὴν ὀδμὴν αὐτῶν.

9. οἱ σοφοὶ οὐ θαυμάζουσιν ἑαυτούς.

10. οἱ τύραννοι οὐκ ἐπίστευον τοῖς ἑαυτῶν.

11. ἡ αὐτὴ λίμνη ἦν χρησίμη τῷ Κύρῳ.

12. ἐπεὶ ἡ ναῦς κουφοτέρα ἐστίν, οἷός τ' εἶ σῴζειν σεαυτόν.

Exercise 126.

1. Polycrates himself throws away the ring.
2. The fisherman finds the same ring in the fish.
3. Most men are willing to fight for their own native land.
4. Good men love others more than themselves.
5. The Athenians feared Xerxes and his army.
6. The queen saved her own ship.
7. It is difficult for me to save myself.
8. The same queen made Babylon more beautiful.
9. Many of the Athenians admired Socrates and his wisdom.
10. In the same year the Greeks conquered both by land and
　　　by sea.
11. Flee at once and save yourselves.
12. Xerxes did not trust his own soldiers.

ὅδε, οὗτος, ἐκεῖνος (A 57)

ὅδε and οὗτος both mean this, ὅδε being used for something
actually present, like *hic* in Latin; ἐκεῖνος means *that*
(yonder), corresponding to *ille*; ὅδε is declined like the
Article, with the addition of the suffix -δε; ἐκεῖνος, -η, -ο, is
also declined like the Article.

ὅδε, οὗτος, ἐκεῖνος may be used:

(1) Adjectivally, the Article coming **between** the Pronoun and
the Noun, e.g. ἥδε ἡ γυνή, *this woman*; ταῦτα τὰ δένδρα, *these
trees*; ἐκείνη ἡ νῆσος, *that island*;

(2) Substantivally, without the Article, e.g. τόδε, *this*; οὗτοι,
these men; ἐκείνη, *she* (Latin, *illa*).

Notice in Section 95 of A τοιοῦτος, *such*, and τοσοῦτος, *so great* (in plur. *so many*); with both of these the Article **precedes** the Pronoun, e.g. ὁ τοιοῦτος ἀνήρ, *such a man*; cf. *un tel homme* in French.

EXERCISE 127.

1. οἵδε οἱ στρατιῶται ἀνδρειότατα ἐμάχοντο.
2. ἡ σφραγὶς ἦν ἐν τῷδε τῷ ἰχθύι.
3. μετὰ τοῦτο ὁ Ξέρξης ἐκ τῆς Ἀττικῆς ἀπεχώρησεν.
4. ἐκείνη ἡ ναῦς κατεδύθη ὑπὸ τῆς Ἀρτεμισίας.
5. οὗτοί εἰσιν ἀξιώτεροι τῆς τιμῆς ἢ ἐκεῖνοι.
6. ὁ Θεμιστοκλῆς πέμπει τὴν τοιαύτην ἐπιστολὴν ὡς βασιλέα.
7. ἥδε ἐστὶν ἡ τοῦ Ἀδμήτου γυνή.
8. αὕτη ἡ λίμνη ὠρύχθη ὑπὸ τῆς βασιλείας.
9. ἐκείνῳ τῷ ἔτει οἱ Πέρσαι ἐνικήθησαν ὑπὸ τῶν Ἑλλήνων.
10. ταῦτα τὰ δένδρα βέβλαπται ὑπὸ τῶν Λακεδαιμονίων.
11. ἐκείνη ἀνδρειότερον ἐμάχετο ἢ οἱ ναῦται.
12. ὁ Θεμιστοκλῆς οὐκ ἐδήλωσε ταύτην τὴν βουλὴν τοῖς Ἀθηναίοις.

EXERCISE 128.

1. This city is very beautiful.
2. That tyrant is always fortunate.
3. These gifts were sent to Apollo by Croesus.
4. On account of this we shall march towards the river.
5. She has been saved by the friend of Admetus.
6. This sword is better than that.
7. These men have been persuaded by Demosthenes to fight.
8. This is the son of Socrates.
9. We cannot conquer such an army.
10. The general ordered us to cross that mountain before night.
11. In that month we were in very great danger.
12. This has never been done before by the Spartans.

EXERCISE 129.

A STRANGE RESCUE

*This interesting story is a mere digression of Herodotus.
Periander was tyrant of Corinth about 600 B.C.; he promoted both
commerce and the arts; Arion is said to have invented a new form
of poetry.*

(1) ἦν δέ ποτε ἐν Κορίνθῳ κιθαρῳδός τις, ὀνόματι Ἀρίων·
καὶ οὗτος ὁ Ἀρίων, ὡς λέγουσι, πολὺν χρόνον διατρίψας παρὰ
τῷ Περιάνδρῳ, τῷ Κορίνθου τυράννῳ, τέλος ἔπλευσεν εἰς
Ἰταλίαν τε καὶ Σικελίαν· ἐπεὶ δὲ διὰ τὴν τέχνην ἐδέξατο ἐκεῖ
πολλὰ χρήματα, ἠθέλησεν πάλιν εἰς Κόρινθον πλεῦσαι.
πιστεύων δὲ οὐδενὶ μᾶλλον ἢ τοῖς Κορινθίοις, ἐμισθώσατο
πλοῖον ἀνδρῶν Κορινθίων. ὡς δὲ ὡρμήσαντο ἐκ Τάραντος,[1]
οἱ ναῦται ἐπεβούλευσαν ἐκβαλεῖν τὸν Ἀρίονα καὶ κλέψαι τὰ
χρήματα· ὁ δέ, τοῦτο μαθών, ᾔτησεν αὐτοὺς χρήματα μὲν
λαβεῖν, ἑαυτὸν δὲ σῶσαι. ἀλλ᾽ οὐ πεισθέντες οἱ ναῦται ἐκέλευσαν αὐτὸν ἢ ἑαυτὸν ἀποκτείνειν ἢ ἐκπηδᾶν εἰς τὴν θάλασσαν.
ὁ δὲ Ἀρίων εἶπεν αὐτοῖς· "Ἐᾶτέ με πρῶτον ἀείδειν.' οἱ δὲ
ἀνεχώρησαν ἐκ τῆς πρύμνης εἰς μέσην τὴν ναῦν. ἔπειτα δὲ ὁ
μὲν Ἀρίων, φορῶν πᾶσαν τὴν σκευήν, λαβὼν τὴν κιθάραν
καὶ ἀείσας, ἔρριψεν ἑαυτὸν εἰς τὴν θάλασσαν, οἱ δὲ ναῦται
ἀπέπλευσαν εἰς Κόρινθον.

[1] Taras or Tarentum, in south Italy, was the only colony founded by
Sparta.

(2) καὶ τότε δὴ μέγιστον θαῦμα ἐγένετο· δελφὶς γὰρ αὐτὸν
ὑπολαβὼν ἐκόμισεν οἴκαδε. ὁ μὲν οὖν Ἀρίων πᾶν τὸ πρᾶγμα
ἐξηγεῖται τῷ Περιάνδρῳ· ὁ δὲ διὰ τὴν ἀπιστίαν ἔχει αὐτὸν
ἐν φυλακῇ. ἐπεὶ δὲ τέλος οἱ ναῦται εἰς Κόρινθον ἀφίκοντο,
ἠρώτησεν αὐτοὺς περὶ τοῦ Ἀρίονος· οἱ δὲ ἀπεκρίναντο ὅτι
ἔλιπον αὐτὸν εὖ πράσσοντα ἐν Τάραντι. ἕως δὲ ἔτι τοῦτο
λέγουσιν, ἐπιφαίνεται αὐτοῖς ὁ Ἀρίων αὐτός, φορῶν τὴν
αὐτὴν σκευήν, ὥσπερ πρότερον· οἱ δὲ ναῦται τῷδε τῷ τρόπῳ
ἐλέγχονται.

Adapted from Herodotus, I, 23–24.

Chapter 24

Exhortations and Prohibitions; Relative and Interrogative Pronouns; Direct Questions; Indefinite Pronoun

Exhortations

(1) The 1st person plur. of the **Subjunctive** (A 73, 75, 77, 84–89) is used to express an Exhortation (Neg. μή); the **Aorist** Subjunctive is preferred for **single** acts, the **Present** for **continuous** acts:

θαυμάζωμεν τοὺς ἀγαθούς, *let us admire the good.*

λύσωμεν τὴν βοῦν, *let us loose the cow.*

μὴ παυσώμεθα τοῦδε τοῦ πολέμου.
Let us not cease from this war.

Prohibitions with 2nd Person

(2) (*a*) The 2nd persons of the **Aorist Subjunctive,** introduced by μή, are used to express a **Prohibition,** when a **particular** occasion is referred to:

μὴ ἀποπέμψῃς τοὺς συμμάχους.
Do not send away the allies.

(*b*) The 2nd persons of the **Present Imperative,** introduced by μή, are used to express a **general Prohibition,** e.g. μὴ κλέπτε, *don't steal (ever).*

N.B. μή is **never** used with the 2nd persons of the **Aorist Imperative.**

Prohibitions with 3rd Person

(3) μή (μηδείς, *no one*) is used with the 3rd person of the **Present Imperative** to express a **general Prohibition**; with the **Aorist Subjunctive** for **particular** acts:

μὴ οἱ γέροντες βλαπτέσθων.
Let not the old men be hurt.

μηδεὶς πιστεύσῃ τῷ ῥήτορι.
Let no one believe the orator.

(μή with the 3rd persons of the Aorist Imperative is also found occasionally.)

It will be noticed that the rules for Prohibitions with the 2nd and 3rd persons are generally the same.

EXERCISE 130.

1. ἀεὶ τὰ ἀληθῆ λέγωμεν.
2. μὴ πιστεύετε τοῖς τοιαῦτα λέγουσιν.
3. φύγωμεν[1] εἰς τὰ ὄρη.
4. μὴ κωλύσῃς τοὺς τῇ πόλει βοηθοῦντας.
5. μὴ λυθῶσιν οἱ αἰχμάλωτοι.
6. ἀεὶ πράσσωμεν ἀξίως τῆς πόλεως.
7. μὴ παύσησθε τοῦ ἔργου, ὦ νεανίαι.
8. μηδεὶς βοηθείτω τοῖς πολεμίοις.
9. μήτε διώξητε τοὺς Πέρσας, ὦ ἄνδρες, μήτε αὐτοὺς
   κωλύσητε.
10. μὴ πέμψωμεν ἀγγέλους ὡς βασιλέα.
11. ἀνδρείως φυλάσσωμεν τοὺς ἐν τῇ πόλει.
12. μὴ ἀπολίπητε τὴν πατρίδα, ὦ πολῖται.

[1] Strong Aorist Subjunctives follow the pattern of the Present Subjunctive.

EXERCISE 131.

1. Let us educate our children.
2. Do not cut down these trees.
3. Let no one be persuaded by money.
4. Let us not cease from the sea-battle.

5. Do not draw up the cavalry on the mountain.
6. Let us neither hinder nor pursue the enemy.
7. Let us always fight worthily of our country.
8. Do not treat prisoners badly.
9. Let not the general escape.
10. Do not be enslaved by the king, O citizens.
11. Let the soldiers not attack the city before night.
12. Do not be hindered by the high mountain.

Relative Pronoun (A 58)

The **Relative** Pronoun is rarer in Greek than in Latin, for the Article used with the Participle so often takes the place of a Relative Clause; nevertheless there are occasions when the Relative Pronoun must be used:

ἐπορεύοντο πρὸς τὸν ποταμόν, ὃς ἦν τῆς χώρας ὁ ὅρος.
They were marching to the river, which was the boundary of the country.

Interrogative Pronoun; Direct Questions (A 58)

τίς; τί; **Interrogative** Pronouns, are used exactly like *quis? quid? who? what?* in Latin, e.g. τίς πάρεστιν; *who is here?*

A semi-colon in Greek corresponds to a question mark in English. Other common Interrogative words are ποῦ; *where?* ποῖ; *whither?* πόθεν; *whence?* πῶς; *how?*

Questions are often introduced by the Interrogative Particle, ἆρα, which corresponds to -*ne* in Latin (though ἆρα is often omitted); ἆρ' οὐ generally corresponds to *nonne*; both ἆρα and ἆρ' οὐ can also do the work of *num*; ἆρα μή is rare:

ἆρα πιστεύεις αὐτῷ; *do you trust him?*
ἆρ' οὐ πιστεύεις αὐτῷ; *surely you trust him, don't you?*
ἆρα (μή) πιστεύεις αὐτῷ; *surely you don't trust him?*

Indefinite Pronoun (A 58)

τις, τι (without an accent) are used as **Indefinite** Pronouns, *anyone* or *anything*, *someone* or *something*, and also as an Adjective, *any* or *some*; this Pronoun is often equivalent to

quidam, *a certain* ; it should never be used as the first word of a sentence or clause :

κόπτει τις τὰ δένδρα.

Someone is cutting down the trees.

ἁλιεύς τις ἰχθὺν μέγιστον λαμβάνει.

A certain fisherman catches a very large fish.

EXERCISE 132.

1. ὁ ῎Αμασις, ὃς ἦν Αἰγύπτου βασιλεύς, ἔγραψεν ἐπιστολήν.
2. ἦν ᾿Αθηναῖός τις, ὀνόματι Θεμιστοκλῆς.
3. ἆρα πιστεύετε τῷ ὑμετέρῳ στρατηγῷ;
4. τίς εὗρε τὸν ἰχθύν;
5. ποῦ ᾤκισαν οἱ Λακεδαιμόνιοι τὴν ἀποικίαν;
6. ἦν βασίλειά τις, ἣ ἐναυμάχησεν ὑπὲρ τῶν Περσῶν.
7. τῶν ᾿Αθηναίων τινὲς ἐμίσουν τὸν Δημοσθένη.
8. οἱ ῞Ελληνες ἀπέπεμψαν τὸν ἄνδρα ὃς αὐτοὺς ἤγαγεν πρὸς τὸ ὄρος.
9. ἆρ᾿ οὐ μάλιστα ἐφίλησε τὸν ῎Αδμητον ἡ ῎Αλκηστις;
10. ποῖ καὶ διὰ τί πορεύονται οἱ Πέρσαι;
11. οἱ Λακεδαιμόνιοι, οἳ μόνον τριακόσιοι ἦσαν, τὴν εἰσβολὴν μάτην ἐφύλαξαν.
12. ἆρα ἀπολείψετε τοὺς ὑμετέρους συμμάχους;

EXERCISE 133.

1. We reached a river which was both wide and deep.
2. Where did you hide the money?
3. A certain messenger, Sicinnus by name, was sent to the king.
4. The captain whose ship the queen was pursuing was not a Greek.
5. Some of the allies were not willing to help the Athenians.
6. Surely you do not admire this traitor?
7. Why are you marching through our country?
8. Did you pursue those who were fleeing from the battle?
9. What do you intend to do in this danger, O citizens?

10. Someone was announcing the victory of the Athenians.
11. The cavalry whom we were pursuing hid themselves in the wood.
12. From where were the enemy marching?

EXERCISE 134.

ARISTAGORAS AND HIS MAP

The Greeks in Ionia, as has already been said, had been subjected in turn to Lydia and Persia. In 499 B.C. Aristagoras resigned his position as tyrant in Miletus and headed the revolt against Persia. He attempted to get help from Sparta, before going to Athens and Eretria.

(1) ὁ δὲ ᾿Αρισταγόρας, ὃς ἦν πρότερον τῆς Μιλήτου[1] τύραννος, ἐβούλετο ἐλευθεροῦν τοὺς ῎Ιωνας ἀπὸ τῆς τῶν Περσῶν ἀρχῆς. ἔπλευσεν οὖν εἰς τὴν Σπάρτην καὶ διελέγετο τῷ Κλεομένει, τῷ τὴν ἀρχὴν ἔχοντι· καὶ ἔφερεν, ὡς οἱ Λακεδαιμόνιοι λέγουσι, χαλκοῦν πίνακα, ἐν ᾧ περίοδος τῆς πάσης γῆς ἐγέγραπτο, καὶ θάλασσά τε πᾶσα καὶ ποταμοὶ πάντες. 'Μὴ θαυμάσῃς,' ἔφη, 'ὦ Κλεόμενες, ὅτι δεῦρο ἀφῖγμαι· μέγιστον μὲν γὰρ ἄλγος ἐστὶν ἡμῖν, ὅτι οἱ τῶν ᾿Ιώνων παῖδές εἰσι δοῦλοι ἀντ' ἐλευθέρων, μεῖζον δὲ ὑμῖν, οἳ πρωτεύετε ἐν τῇ ῾Ελλάδι. νῦν οὖν σώσατε τοὺς ῎Ιωνας ἐκ δουλοσύνης, ἄνδρας ὁμαίμονας ὄντας. ῥᾴδιον δέ ἐστι τοῦτο ποιεῖν· οἱ γὰρ βάρβαροι οὐκ ἀνδρεῖοί εἰσιν· χρῶνται δὲ τόξοις καὶ αἰχμαῖς βραχείαις, καὶ μάχονται ἀναξυρίδας ἔχοντες καὶ κυρβασίας ἐπὶ ταῖς κεφαλαῖς. τοῖς δὲ ἐκείνην τὴν ἤπειρον οἰκοῦσίν ἐστι πλείω ἀγαθὰ ἢ οὐδενί[2] ἄλλῳ, χρυσός τε καὶ ἄργυρος, καὶ ὑποζύγιά τε καὶ ἀνδράποδα· πάντα ταῦτα ὑμῖν αὐτοῖς ἔξεστιν ἔχειν, εἰ βούλεσθε.'

[1] A city in Ionia, S.E. of Samos.
[2] The negative is seemingly superfluous, but the Greek use of it emphasizes that no one else had such wealth.

(2) καὶ ταῦτα λέγων ἐδήλωσεν ἐν τῇ τῆς γῆς περιόδῳ, ἣν ἐν τῷ πίνακι γεγραμμένην ἔφερε, τὰς χώρας πάντων τῶν βαρ-

βάρων, ἐξηγούμενος τὸν πλοῦτον ἑκάστης, καὶ τὰ Σοῦσα¹ αὐτά, ἐν οἷς οἱ βασιλέως μεγάλου θησαυροὶ ἐνῆσαν. 'Λαβόντες ταύτην τὴν πόλιν', ἔφη, 'πλουσιώτατοι γενήσεσθε· μὴ πολεμήσητε τοὺς ὑμετέρους γείτονας, τούς τε Μεσσηνίους² καὶ τοὺς Ἀργείους,² οἷς οὔτε χρυσός ἐστιν οὔτε ἄργυρος.' ὁ δὲ Κλεομένης εἶπεν, "Ὦ ξένε Μιλήσιε, τριῶν ἡμερῶν ἀποκρινοῦμαι.' ἐπεὶ δὲ ἡ κυρία ἡμέρα ἐγένετο, ὁ Κλεομένης ἠρώτησε, 'Πόσων ἡμερῶν ἐστιν ἡ ὁδὸς ἀπὸ τῆς τῶν Ἰώνων θαλάσσης παρὰ βασιλέα;' ὁ δὲ Ἀρισταγόρας εἶπεν, 'Τριῶν μηνῶν.' ὁ δὲ Κλεομένης εὐθὺς ἀπεκρίνατο· "Ὦ ξένε Μιλήσιε, ἀποχώρησον ἐκ Σπάρτης πρὸ ἡλίου δυσμῶν· οὐ γὰρ εὖ συμβουλεύεις τοῖς Λακεδαιμονίοις, βουλόμενος αὐτοὺς τριῶν μηνῶν ὁδὸν στρατεύειν.'

Adapted from Herodotus, V, 49–50.

¹ The capital of the Persian empire, N. of the Persian Gulf; the Royal Road, regularly maintained, ran all the way there from Ephesus in Ionia.

² Sparta's neighbours in the Peloponnese, to the west and north-east respectively.

Chapter 25
Wishes for the Future: Optative Mood

The **Optative** Mood (from Latin **optare**, *to wish*) is used to express a wish for the Future, generally introduced by εἴθε or εἰ γάρ (*Would that! O if*), though these may be omitted; the **Present** Optative is used for a **continuous** act, the **Aorist** for a **single** act, the Neg. in each case being μή (A 73, 75, 77; see also Optatives of Contracted Verbs and εἰμί); no exclamation mark is used in Greek:

εἰ γὰρ ἡ θεὰ ἀεὶ ἡμᾶς φυλάσσοι.
May the goddess always protect us!

εἴθε μὴ νικήσαιεν ἡμᾶς οἱ πολέμιοι.
May the enemy not conquer us!

EXERCISE 135. Miscellaneous Wishes, Exhortations, Commands, and Prohibitions.

1. εἰ γὰρ ὁ στρατηγὸς λύσαι τοὺς αἰχμαλώτους.
2. εἴθε ἄξιοι εἶμεν τῆς πόλεως.
3. μὴ τοῦτο γένοιτο.
4. εἴθε ὁ Δημοσθένης πείσαι τοὺς πολίτας.
5. ἀνδρειότερον μαχώμεθα ὑπὲρ τῆς πατρίδος.
6. εἰ γὰρ ἀφικοίμεθα εἰς τὴν πόλιν πρὸ τῆς νυκτός.
7. εἴθε οἱ στρατιῶται εὖ φυλάσσοιεν τὰς πύλας.
8. εὐθὺς λυθέντων οἱ αἰχμάλωτοι.
9. μὴ νικηθείη τὸ στράτευμα.
10. εἴθε φέροιο πολλὰ ἆθλα ἐν τοῖς ἀγῶσιν.
11. μὴ βλαπτέσθω τὰ ἱερά.
12. μὴ γράψῃς ἐπιστολὴν σήμερον.

EXERCISE 136.

1. Would that we might set free our friends!
2. May he be wiser than his father!
3. May the orator always speak the truth!
4. May the enemy not reach the river!
5. Let us build a big wall round the city.
6. Would that some guide would show us the way!
7. Let the ox be loosed at once.
8. Do not order the allies to go away.
9. May we be set free from this danger!
10. Let the young men listen to Socrates.
11. I wish I might become a sailor!
12. May the women and children not be harmed.

Genitive Absolute

A **Genitive Absolute** is used in Greek exactly as the Ablative Absolute in Latin, i.e. when a Noun or Pronoun with a Participle in agreement cannot be made the Subject or Object of the Main Verb; this is a normal Greek construction, but note that Greek has more freedom of choice in the ways it can use its Participles than Latin (p. 90):

τοῦ στρατηγοῦ κελεύσαντος, ἀπεχωρήσαμεν.

After the general had given the order, we withdrew.

(lit. *the general having ordered.*)

ἔρχομαι is used in Present Indicative for *I come, go*. εἶμι (A 118) supplies its Future (εἶμι), its Imperfect (ᾔειν or ᾖα), Present Imperative, Subjunctive, Optative, Infinitive, and Participle. The Opt., Infin., and Partic. of εἶμι are also used with reference to the Future. The Aorist of both ἔρχομαι and εἶμι is supplied by ἦλθον (Partic. ἐλθών).

EXERCISE 137. Various uses of Participles.

1. τῶν πολεμίων ἀπελθόντων, ἐστρατοπεδευσάμεθα.
2. ἰδόντες τὴν θάλασσαν, πάντες ἐβοῶμεν.
3. τοῦ ναυτικοῦ νικηθέντος, ὁ Ξέρξης ἠπόρει.
4. οἱ πολέμιοι ἡμῖν προσέβαλον τὸν ποταμὸν διαβαίνουσιν.
5. ἡμῶν εἰς τὴν Βαβυλῶνα εἰσιόντων, οἱ πολῖται ἔφυγον.
6. οἱ τοῦτο ποιήσοντες κολασθήσονται.
7. κελεύσαντος τοῦ Κύρου, τῶν στρατιωτῶν τινες ἐτάχθησαν ὄπισθε τῆς πόλεως.
8. λαβόντες τοὺς ἐν τῇ νήσῳ, οἱ Ἀθηναῖοι ἔχαιρον.
9. οἱ δοῦλοι, τοὺς βοῦς λύσαντες, οἴκαδε ἐπανῆλθον.
10. τῆς γυναικὸς ἀποθανούσης, ὁ Ἄδμητος ἐδάκρυεν.
11. ἐπιφαινομένου τοῦ Ἀρίονος, οἱ ναῦται μάλιστα ἀποροῦσιν.
12. τοῦ Ξενοφῶντος ἄρχοντος, οἱ Ἕλληνες εἰς τὴν θάλασσαν ἀφίκοντο.

EXERCISE 138. Various uses of Participles.

1. When the Greeks had reached the sea, the guide went away.
2. After conquering him in a sea-battle, the Greeks did not pursue Xerxes.
3. While this general was in command, the Athenians fared well.
4. When Darius died, Xerxes became king.
5. There being few citizens in the city, it was easy to take it.

6. When they had been defeated, the Persians went away from Attica.

7. As the enemy were very many, Leonidas was easily defeated.

8. After Socrates had died, his friends began to weep.

9. When the enemy had ransomed the prisoners, we went away.

10. As the enemy are not here, we will return to the camp.

11. Since my father is wiser, I will obey him.

12. When the fleet had sailed away, we went home.

EXERCISE 139.

BORN TO BE KING

Astyages, the last king of the Medes, dreamt that he would be overthrown by his grandson, Cyrus, whose father, Cambyses, was a Persian; as soon as he was born, he ordered him to be put to death, but a herdsman to whom the deed was entrusted, substituted his own dead baby, and brought up Cyrus as his own son. Years afterwards, Cyrus, later known as Cyrus the Great, organized a rebellion and became king of the Medes and Persians in 549. The empire of Media, founded in about 700, had stretched from the Caspian to the Persian Gulf and included Assyria and Persia.

(1) ὁ δὲ Κῦρος, ὅτε ἦν δεκαετὴς καὶ ἔτι ἐνομίζετο εἶναι υἱὸς τοῦ βουκόλου, ἔπαιζεν ἐν τῇ κώμῃ μετ' ἄλλων τινῶν παίδων· οἱ δὲ παῖδες ἐποίησαν αὐτὸν εἶναι ἑαυτῶν βασιλέα. τοῦ δὲ Κύρου κελεύσαντος, οἱ μὲν αὐτῶν οἰκίας ᾠκοδόμουν, οἱ δὲ δορυφόροι ἦσαν, οἱ δὲ ἄλλα ἔργα ἐποίουν. εἷς δὲ τούτων τῶν παίδων, υἱὸς ὢν Ἀρτεμβάρους, ἀνδρὸς ἐν Μήδοις δοκίμου, οὐκ ἔπρασσεν ἃ ὁ Κῦρος προσέταξεν· ἐκέλευσεν οὖν ὁ Κῦρος τοὺς ἄλλους παῖδας αὐτὸν λαβεῖν. πειθομένων δὲ τῶν παίδων, ὁ Κῦρος τὸν παῖδα μάστιγι ἐκόλασεν· ὁ δὲ, ἐπεὶ ἀπέφυγεν, μάλιστα ὀργιζόμενος δι' ἃ ἔπαθεν, ἤγγειλε τὸ γενόμενον τῷ πατρί. ὁ δὲ Ἀρτεμβάρης, ἐλθὼν παρὰ τὸν Ἀστυάγην καὶ ἅμα ἄγων τὸν παῖδα, εἶπεν, "Ὦ βασιλεῦ, ὑπὸ τοῦ σοῦ δούλου, υἱοῦ ὄντος βουκόλου, ὧδε ὑβρίσμεθα.' καὶ ἐδήλωσε τοὺς τοῦ

παιδὸς ὤμους. ἀκούσας δὲ καὶ ἰδών, ὁ ᾿Αστυάγης μετεπέμψατο τόν τε βουκόλον καὶ τὸν παῖδα.

(2) τούτων δὲ παρόντων, βλέψας πρὸς τὸν Κῦρον, ὁ ᾿Αστυάγης ἔφη, 'Σὺ δὴ, ὤν υἱὸς βουκόλου, ἐτόλμησας τὸν τοῦδε υἱὸν ὧδε ὑβρίζειν;' ὁ δὲ ἀπεκρίνατο· ῞Ω δέσποτα, ἐγὼ ταῦτα δικαίως ἐποίησα. οἱ γὰρ ἐκ τῆς κώμης παῖδες, ὧν καὶ ὅδε ἦν, παίζοντες ἐποίησαν ἐμὲ ἑαυτῶν βασιλέα. ἐδόκουν γὰρ αὐτοῖς εἶναι εἰς τοῦτο ἐπιτηδειότατος. οἱ μὲν οὖν ἄλλοι παῖδες ἃ ἐκέλευσα ἔπραξαν, οὗτος δὲ οὐκ ἐπείθετο, ἕως ἐκολάσθη. εἰ οὖν ἄξιός εἰμι κολάζεσθαι, ἐνθάδε πάρειμι.' ταῦτα δὲ λέγοντος τοῦ παιδός, ὁ ᾿Αστυάγης ἐδόκει ἀναγνωρίζειν τὸ πρόσωπον αὐτοῦ καὶ πολὺν χρόνον ἄφθογγος ἦν. τοῦ δὲ ᾿Αρτεμβάρους ἀποπεμφθέντος, ἐκέλευσε τοὺς θεράποντας ἔσω ἄγειν τὸν Κῦρον. ἐπεὶ δὲ ὁ βουκόλος ὑπελέλειπτο μόνος, ὁ ᾿Αστυάγης αὐτὸν ἠρώτησεν πόθεν ἔλαβε τὸν παῖδα. ὁ δὲ ἀπεκρίνατο ὅτι ἐστὶν ὁ ἑαυτοῦ υἱός. ὁ δὲ ᾿Αστυάγης ἐσήμαινε τοῖς δορυφόροις συλλαμβάνειν καὶ τύπτειν αὐτόν. ὁ δὲ ἐν μεγίστῃ ἀπορίᾳ ὤν, ἀληθῶς πάντα ἐξηγεῖτο καὶ ᾔτησε τὸν βασιλέα ἑαυτῷ συγγιγνώσκειν.

Adapted from Herodotus, I, 114–116.

Chapter 26
Final Clauses

The most common way of expressing a **Final** or **Purpose** Clause in Greek is by using ἵνα, ὡς, or ὅπως with the **Subjunctive,** if the Main Verb is **Primary** (Present, Future, or Perfect); with the **Optative,** if the Main Verb is **Historic** (Imperfect, Aorist, or Pluperfect).

It should be carefully noticed that, whereas in Latin we observe a Sequence of Tense, in **Greek** we observe a **Sequence of Mood.** The Tense of the Subjunctive or Optative depends

Final Clauses 115

upon whether a continuous act is being expressed, in which case we use the Present, or a single act, in which case we use the Aorist; the Negative with this construction is always μή:

πορευόμεθα ἐκεῖσε, ἵνα τοὺς αἰχμαλώτους λύσωμεν.
We are marching there in order that we may set free the prisoners.

τοῦ Σωκράτους ἠκούομεν, ὅπως σοφώτεροι γιγνοίμεθα.
We were listening to Socrates to become wiser.

οἱ σύμμαχοι ἀφίκοντο, ὅπως μὴ νικηθεῖμεν.
The allies arrived so that we might not be defeated.

But Greek often uses the Subjunctive Mood even after a Historic Main Verb; this is commonly known as the **Graphic** or **Vivid Construction**; the reader is vividly transported into the **time** when the events occurred; thus, in the last example above, ὅπως μὴ νικηθῶμεν would be equally good Greek.

(Sometimes Greek uses the Future Participle (Neg. οὐ) to express purpose, e.g. ἔπεμψα τὸν παῖδα τὴν βοῦν λύσοντα, *I sent the boy to loose the cow.* When ὡς is used with this Participle, it generally expresses a presumed intention, e.g. ἦλθον ὡς ἡμᾶς βλάψοντες, *they came as though to injure us.* This construction is mentioned here for recognition purposes only, and it is suggested that it should not be used in the English-Greek sentences that follow.)

EXERCISE 140.

1. οἱ Λακεδαιμόνιοι ἐπέμφθησαν ἵνα τὰ δένδρα κόψαιεν.
2. πάρεσμεν ὅπως τῷ θεῷ θύωμεν.
3. ὁ Ξέρξης ἦγε στράτευμα, ἵνα τοὺς Ἀθηναίους κολάσῃ.
4. οἱ πολέμιοι ἔμενον ἐπὶ τοῦ ὄρους, ὡς προσβάλοιεν τοῖς Ἕλλησιν.
5. ἵνα μὴ ληφθεῖεν, οἱ Πέρσαι πρὸς τὴν θάλασσαν ἔφευγον.
6. ἐπέμψαμεν κήρυκα τοὺς στρατιώτας λυσόμενον.
7. οἱ Ἀθηναῖοι ἀπέπεμψαν τὰς γυναῖκας, ὅπως ἀσφαλεῖς εἶεν.

8. οὐκ ἀεὶ τρέχομεν ἵνα ἆθλα φερώμεθα. ⏟

9. ἡ Ἀρτεμισία κατέδυσε τὴν ναῦν, ὅπως ἑαυτὴν σώσῃ.

10. ὁ Ἀρίων ἐκπηδᾷ εἰς τὴν θάλασσαν, ἵνα μὴ ἀποθάνῃ.

EXERCISE 141.

1. The general is sending cavalry in order that he may hinder the enemy.
2. We are fighting to save our country.
3. Flee out of the city that you may not be captured.
4. We sent many soldiers to guard the bridge.
5. The Athenians sent for the general that they might honour him.
6. A guide arrived, to lead the Greeks to the sea.
7. The king waited for three days, so that he might deliberate.
8. So that they might not be defeated, the Athenians asked for help.
9. We are crossing the river to escape from danger.
10. Themistocles persuaded the citizens to build ships to save their country.

EXERCISE 142.

1. ὁ Ἀρισταγόρας ἦλθεν εἰς Σπάρτην, ἵνα πείσαι τοὺς Λακεδαιμονίους βοηθεῖν τοῖς Ἴωσιν.

2. οἱ κροκόδειλοι νυκτὸς ἀποβαίνουσιν εἰς τὴν γῆν, ὅπως καθεύδωσιν.

3. βοηθεῖτε ἡμῖν, ὦ πολῖται, ἵνα μὴ ἀνδραποδισθῶμεν ὑπὸ τῶν βαρβάρων.

4. ὁ Κῦρος εἰσήγαγε τὸν ποταμὸν εἰς τὴν λίμνην, ὡς οἱ στρατιῶται λάβωσι τὴν Βαβυλῶνα.

5. ὁ ἁλιεὺς φέρει τὸν ἰχθὺν εἰς τὰ βασίλεια, ἵνα τῷ Πολυκράτει ἀρέσκῃ.

6. ὁ Πολυκράτης ἀπέπλευσεν, ὅπως ἀποβάλοι τὴν σφραγῖδα.

7. ἴμεν Ἀθήναζε τοὺς στρατηγοὺς τιμήσοντες.

8. οἱ Πέρσαι εἰς τὴν θάλασσαν ἐξεπήδησαν, ἵνα ἡ ναῦς μὴ καταδυθῇ.

9. δεῖ ἡμᾶς ἡγεμόνα ἔχειν, ἵνα δηλοῖ ἡμῖν τὴν ὁδόν.
10. οἱ Λακεδαιμόνιοι εἰσῆλθον εἰς τὴν Ἀττικήν, ὡς ἡμῖν προσβαλοῦντες.[1]

[1] Most Active Futures without σ are conjugated like φιλέω.

EXERCISE 143.

1. The Egyptians use nets in order to protect their bodies from gnats.
2. Let us advance to the mountain to attack the enemy.
3. Cyrus sent for the boy to punish him.
4. We went to the temple to honour the goddess.
5. So that he might not die himself, Admetus persuaded his wife to die for him.
6. Arion begged the sailors to take his money, in order to save himself.
7. Croesus sends these gifts to honour the god.
8. Tell the truth in order that you may be trusted.
9. To save ourselves, we were compelled to retreat.
10. Flee to your ships that you may not be captured.

EXERCISE 144.

AN ARGUMENT ABOUT COMMAND

In the autumn of 481 B.C. *a congress of Greeks was held at the Isthmus of Corinth to decide upon measures for resisting the threatened invasion by Xerxes. Ambassadors were sent to ask for help from various states, including Syracuse, which was at this time ruled by the tyrant Gelon. Syracuse had been founded by Corinth.*

(1) Ὡς δὲ οἱ ἄγγελοι ἀφίκοντο εἰς τὰς Συρακούσας τῷ Γέλωνι ἔλεγον τάδε· "Ἔπεμψαν ἡμᾶς οἵ τε Λακεδαιμόνιοι καὶ οἱ Ἀθηναῖοι, καὶ οἱ τούτων σύμμαχοι, ἵνα αἰτήσαιμέν σε μάχεσθαι μεθ' ἡμῶν πρὸς τοὺς βαρβάρους· Πέρσης γὰρ ἀνὴρ μέλλει διαβήσεσθαι τὸν Ἑλλήσποντον καὶ ἐπάξειν πάντα τὸν στρατὸν ἐκ τῆς Ἀσίας, ἵνα στρατεύσῃ ἐπὶ τὴν Ἑλλάδα. ὡς δέ σοι, τῷ τῆς Σικελίας ἄρχοντι, μοῖρά ἐστιν οὐκ ἐλαχίστη

τῆς Ἑλλάδος, βοήθει τοῖς τὴν Ἑλλάδα ἐλευθεροῦσι καὶ ἅμα ἐλευθέρου σεαυτόν· νικηθέντων γὰρ ἡμῶν, καὶ σὺ νικηθήσει.'

Ὁ δὲ Γέλων ἀπεκρίνατο· "Ἄνδρες Ἕλληνες, ἐτολμήσατε μὲν δεῦρο ἐλθεῖν, ὅπως ἐμὲ σύμμαχον ἐπὶ τὸν βάρβαρον παρακαλέσαιτε· αὐτοὶ δέ, ὅτε ἐμοὶ πρὸς τοὺς Καρχηδονίους¹ πόλεμος ἦν, οὐκ ἤλθετε ὡς βοηθήσοντες. νῦν δέ, ἐπεὶ ὁ πόλεμος ἀφῖκται εἰς ὑμᾶς, Γέλωνος μέμνησθε. ἀτιμηθεὶς δὲ ὑφ' ὑμῶν, οὐχ ὑμᾶς ἀτιμήσω, ἀλλ' ἑτοῖμός εἰμι βοηθεῖν καὶ παρέχειν διακοσίας τριήρεις καὶ δισμυρίους ὁπλίτας καὶ δισχιλίους ἱππέας, αὐτὸς ὢν στρατηγός τε καὶ ἡγεμὼν τῶν Ἑλλήνων πρὸς τὸν βάρβαρον· ἐπὶ τούτῳ τάδε ὑπισχνοῦμαι.'

---

¹ No details are known of this war, but in 480 the Carthaginians invaded Sicily and were decisively defeated at the battle of Himera, said to have been fought on the same day as Salamis.

(2) ἄγγελος δέ τις Λακεδαιμόνιος, ταῦτα ἀκούσας, εἶπε τάδε· 'Οὔ σοι ἐπιτρέψομεν τὴν ἡγεμονίαν· ἀλλ' εἰ μὲν βούλει βοηθεῖν τῇ Ἑλλάδι, ἄρξουσιν οἱ Λακεδαιμόνιοι· εἰ δὲ μὴ βούλει ἄρχεσθαι, μὴ βοήθει.' καὶ πρὸς τάδε ὁ Γέλων ἀπεκρίνατο· 'Ὦ ξένε Λακεδαιμόνιε, ὧδ' ἐμὲ ὑβρίσας, οὔ με ἔπεισας ὑβρίζειν σε. εἰ δὲ καί μοί ἐστι πολλῷ μὲν μείζων ἡ στρατιά, πολλῷ δὲ πλείονες αἱ νῆες, ὑπείξομέν τι. ἐᾶτέ με ἡγεμονεύειν ἢ τῆς στρατιᾶς ἢ τοῦ ναυτικοῦ. καὶ δεῖ ὑμᾶς ἢ τόδε ἐᾶν ἢ ἀπιέναι ἄνευ συμμάχων.'

(3) ὁ δὲ τῶν Ἀθηναίων ἄγγελος εὐθὺς εἶπε τάδε· 'Ὦ βασιλεῦ Συρακοσίων, ἡ Ἑλλὰς ἀπέπεμψεν ἡμᾶς πρός σε οὐχ ἵνα ἡγεμόνα αἰτήσαιμεν, ἀλλὰ στρατιάν· εἰ δὲ καὶ ὁ Λακεδαιμόνιος βούλεταί σοι ἐπιτρέπειν τὴν τοῦ ναυτικοῦ ἀρχήν, ἡμεῖς οὐ βουλόμεθα· ἡμετέρα γάρ ἐστιν αὕτη, εἰ μὴ οἱ Λακεδαιμόνιοι αὐτοὶ βούλονται αὐτὴν ἔχειν.' ἀπεκρίνατο δὲ Γέλων· 'Ξένε Ἀθηναῖε, ὑμεῖς δοκεῖτε τοὺς μὲν ἄρχοντας ἔχειν, τοὺς δὲ ἀρχομένους οὔ. ἐπεὶ τοίνυν, οὐδὲν ὑπείκοντες, ἔχειν πάντα ἐθέλετε, ἀποχωρήσατε ὡς τάχιστα εἰς τὴν Ἑλλάδα.'

Adapted from Herodotus, VII, 157–162.

Chapter 27
Consecutive Clauses

Consecutive Clauses (or Adverbial Clauses of Result) are introduced by ὥστε, *so that* (sometimes, *as to*), and may be expressed in two ways : (*a*) with the Present or Aorist **Infinitive,** whether the Consequence happens or not (Neg. μή), the Subject of the Infinitive being in the Acc., if it is different from the Subject of the Main Verb; (*b*) with the **Indicative** only if the Consequence did **actually** happen (Neg. οὐ).

(*a*) may **always** be used; (*b*) only when stress is laid on what actually happened.

(*a*) οὐχ οὕτω μῶρός εἰμι ὥστε τοῦτο ποιεῖν.
  I am not so foolish as to do this.

  οὕτω μῶρός ἐστιν ὥστε ἡμᾶς αὐτῷ μὴ πιστεύειν.
  He is so foolish that we do not believe him.

(*b*) οἱ ᾿Αθηναῖοι οὕτως ἀνδρείως ἐμάχοντο, ὥστε οἱ Πέρσαι
  ἔφυγον.
  The Athenians fought so bravely that the Persians (actually)
  fled.

 ἢ ὥστε is used after the Comparative of an Adjective :
  ὁ Σωκράτης σοφώτερός ἐστιν ἢ ὥστε τοῦτο λέγειν.
  Socrates is too wise to say this (lit. *wiser than so as to say*;
  cf. Latin, *sapientior quam ut dicat*).

EXERCISE 145.
 1. οἱ Λακεδαιμόνιοι οὕτως ἀνδρεῖοί εἰσιν, ὥστε ἀεὶ εὖ
  μάχεσθαι.
 2. ὁ Σωκράτης ἦν οὕτω σοφὸς ὥστε πολλοὶ αὐτοῦ ἤκουον.
 3. τοσοῦτός ἐστιν ὁ κίνδυνος ὥστε δεῖ ἡμᾶς εὐθὺς ἀποφυγεῖν.

119

4. ὁ ποταμός ἐστιν οὕτω χαλεπός, ὥστε μηδένα αὐτὸν διαβαίνειν.

5. ὁ Ξέρξης οὐκ ἦν οὕτω μῶρος ὥστε μένειν ἐν τῇ Ἑλλάδι.

6. ὁ Θεμιστοκλῆς ἦν οὕτω δεινὸς ὥστε ἐνίκησε τοὺς Πέρσας.

7. οἱ βάρβαροι δειλότεροι ἦσαν ἢ ὥστε μάχεσθαι.

8. τοσαύτη ἦν ἡ χιὼν ὥστε τοὺς στρατιώτας ἀθυμῆσαι.

9. οἱ τριακόσιοι οὕτως ἀνδρείως ἐμαχέσαντο, ὥστε ἀεὶ ἐτιμῶντο ὑπὸ τῶν Ἑλλήνων.

10. τὸ τεῖχός ἐστιν οὕτως ὑψηλὸν ὥστε μηδένα οἷόν τε εἶναι αὐτὸ ὑπερβῆναι.

11. οὕτως εὐτυχὴς ἦν ὁ Πολυκράτης, ὥστε ὁ Ἄμασις διελύσατο τὴν πρὸς αὐτὸν φιλίαν.

12. τοσοῦτοι ἦσαν οἱ Πέρσαι ὥστε οἱ Ἀθηναῖοι οὐκέτι ἔμειναν ἐν τῇ πόλει.

13. ὁ δοῦλος ἀσθενέστερος ἦν ἢ ὥστε ἐργάζεσθαι.

14. ὀλίγοι εἰσὶν οὕτω πλούσιοι ὥστε μὴ βούλεσθαι εἶναι πλουσιώτεροι.

15. ἡ Ἄλκηστις ἐς τοσοῦτον[1] ἐφίλησε τὸν ἄνδρα ὥστε ἠθέλησεν ἀποθανεῖν ὑπὲρ αὐτοῦ.

16. ὁ Δημοσθένης οὕτως εὖ εἶπεν ὥστε τοὺς Ἀθηναίους αὐτῷ πιθέσθαι.

[1] Used with Verbs for *so, so much*.

EXERCISE 146.

1. The orator is so clever that he always persuades us.

2. The enemy were so few that we quickly overcame them.

3. The Persians were so many that nobody hindered them.

4. He is so foolish that nobody listens to him.

5. The Athenians attacked the enemy so bravely that they pursued them into the sea.

6. The storm was so great that we could not advance.

7. The general was too prudent to cross the mountain by night.

8. So many were the enemy that we were compelled to retreat.

9. Few men are so foolish as not to honour their country.

10. The ship sailed away so quickly that we did not catch it.

11. We were too few to attack the enemy.

12. The horses were so[1] afraid of the camels that they fled at once.

13. The storm is so dangerous that the ships cannot sail from the harbour.

14. The river is too difficult to cross.

15. The Athenians were not so foolish as to believe the orator.

16. The fish was so big that the fisherman carried it to the palace.

[1] See note on previous exercise.

EXERCISE 147.

PYLOS AND SPHACTERIA: (1) AN ILL WIND

In the year 425 B.C., *during the Peloponnesian War, when Athens had to face both Sparta and Corinth, an Athenian fleet on its way to Sicily was overtaken by a storm off the coast of Messenia in the Peloponnese.*

Τοσοῦτος δὲ ἦν ὁ χειμών, ὥστε αἱ νῆες ἠναγκάσθησαν καταφυγεῖν εἰς τὴν Πύλον.[1] ἔδοξε δὲ τῷ Δημοσθένει, ὃς ἦν στρατηγός, τειχίζειν τὸ χωρίον· εὐπορία γὰρ ἦν ξύλων τε καὶ λίθων. οἱ δὲ στρατιῶται οὕτω ταχέως εἰργάζοντο, ὥστε ἐξ ἡμερῶν τὸ χωρίον ἐτείχισαν· οἱ δὲ Ἀθηναῖοι τὸν μὲν Δημοσθένη ἐνταῦθα καταλείπουσι φύλακα μετὰ νεῶν πέντε, ταῖς δὲ ἄλλαις ναυσὶ εἰς Σικελίαν ἀπέπλευσαν. οἱ δὲ Λακεδαιμόνιοι εὐθὺς ἐπορεύοντο ἐπὶ τὴν Πύλον, καὶ ἐκέλευσαν τοὺς συμμάχους πέμψαι ἐκεῖσε ἑξήκοντα ναῦς· ἐν δὲ τούτῳ ὁ Δημοσθένης μεταπέμπεται ἄλλας ναῦς. οἱ δὲ Λακεδαιμόνιοι παρεσκευάζοντο ὡς τῷ τειχίσματι προσβαλοῦντες κατά τε γῆν καὶ κατὰ θάλασσαν, ἐλπίζοντες ῥᾳδίως αἱρήσειν τὸ χωρίον, ἀνθρώπων ὀλίγων ἐνόντων· διεβίβασαν δὲ ὁπλίτας εἰς τὴν νῆσον Σφακτη-

[1] The promontory of Pylos, running N. to S., is less than a mile long.

ρίαν,² ἣ ἐπίκειται τῇ Πύλῳ, καὶ εἰς τὴν ἤπειρον. μετὰ δὲ
τοῦτο προσέβαλον μὲν τῷ τειχίσματι τῷ τε κατὰ γῆν στρατῷ
καὶ ναυσὶν ἅμα, μάτην δέ.

ἐπεὶ δὲ πεντήκοντα ἄλλαι νῆες ἀφίκοντο, οἱ Ἀθηναῖοι
προσέπεσον τῷ τῶν Λακεδαιμονίων ναυτικῷ, ὥστε ἔκοψαν
μὲν πολλὰς ναῦς, πέντε δὲ ἔλαβον καὶ μίαν τούτων αὐτοῖς
ναύταις,³ καὶ ἀπέλαβον πολλοὺς ἄνδρας ἐν τῇ νήσῳ. μετὰ δὲ
τὴν ναυμαχίαν ἔδοξε τοῖς Ἀθηναίοις εὐθὺς τὴν νῆσον περι-
πλεῖν καὶ ἐν φυλακῇ ἔχειν. ὡς δὲ εἰς τὴν Σπάρτην ἠγγέλθη
τὰ περὶ Πύλον γενόμενα, ἔδοξε τοῖς Λακεδαιμονίοις σπονδὰς
ποιήσασθαι καὶ πέμψαι εἰς τὰς Ἀθήνας πρέσβεις, ὅπως τοὺς
ἄνδρας ὡς τάχιστα κομίσαιντο.

Adapted from Thucydides, IV, 3–15.

² Sphacteria, nearly 3 m. long, lies immediately to the S. of Pylos, sepa-
rated by a narrow stretch of water; to the east is the modern bay of
Navarino, where a famous naval engagement took place in 1827.

³ *crew and all* (often expressed with the Article: αὐτοῖς τοῖς ναύταις).

Chapter 28

Indirect Statement

1. Verbs of 'saying' and 'thinking'

The Verb of an **Indirect Statement** after φημί, *I say* (A 119),
and νομίζω, *I think*, is put into the **Infinitive**.

(1) If the **Subject** of the Infinitive is **different** from the Subject
of the Verb of *saying* or *thinking*, then, as in Latin, we have
the **Accusative and Infin.** construction:

ἔφη τὸν ἀδελφὸν εἶναι σοφόν (ἀπελθεῖν).
He said that his brother was wise (*had departed*).

(2) If the **Subjects** are the **same**, then (*a*) if the Subject of the
Infin. (which would be a Pronoun) is not required for emphasis,

it is omitted; (*b*) if it **is** required for emphasis, it goes into the **Nominative**; in both (*a*) and (*b*) a Complement is in the **Nom.**:

(*a*) ἐνόμιζεν εἶναι σοφός, *he thought he was wise.*
    (No emphasis, Pronoun omitted.)

(*b*) ἔφη αὐτὸς ἰέναι, *he said that he himself would go.*
    (Pronoun emphatic, placed in Nom.)

The Neg. with the Infinitive is οὐ, but when φημί is used, the Neg. **precedes** φημί:

  οὐκ ἔφη ἰέναι, *he said he would not go.*

The above construction is **always** used after φημί and νομίζω, and is found after many other Verbs of *saying* and *thinking*, but should **never** be used after λέγω to express an Indirect Statement.

The Tense of the Infinitive is the Tense used by the original speaker.

EXERCISE 148.

1. ὁ ἄγγελος ἔφη τοὺς πολεμίους ὀλίγους εἶναι.
2. ἐνομίζομεν τοὺς Πέρσας εὐθὺς ἀποχωρήσειν.
3. ὁ Σωκράτης οὐκ ἐνόμιζεν σοφὸς εἶναι.
4. ἡ Ἄλκηστις ἔφη αὐτὴ ἀποθανεῖσθαι.
5. οἱ ναῦται ἔφασαν ἀπολιπεῖν τὸν Ἀρίονα εὖ πράσσοντα ἐν τῇ Ἰταλίᾳ.
6. ὁ τύραννος οὐκ ἔφη πέμψειν στρατιώτας εἰς τὴν Ἑλλάδα.
7. ἆρα νομίζετε τοῦτο εἶναι ἀληθές;
8. ὁ ἁλιεὺς ἔφη αὐτὸς λαβεῖν τὸν ἰχθύν.
9. ὁ Ξέρξης ἐνόμισε δουλώσειν τοὺς Ἕλληνας.
10. οὔ φαμεν σύμμαχοι εἶναι τῶν Περσῶν.

EXERCISE 149.

1. The soldiers said that the enemy were fleeing.
2. We do not think that the orator is wise.
3. Polycrates said that he had thrown away his ring.
4. The tyrant said that he wanted to lead the Greeks himself
5. Surely you do not think that you will capture the city?

6. The Athenians said that they would build more triremes.
7. The citizens said that they did not trust the general.
8. The messenger said that the fleet had sailed away.
9. Even the Persians thought that the Spartans were brave.
10. The citizen said that he himself would educate his children.

2. Verbs of 'knowing' and 'perceiving'

Verbs of *knowing* and *perceiving* (e.g. οἶδα, *I know* (A 120); αἰσθάνομαι, *I perceive*; ἀκούω, *I hear*; ὁρῶ, *I see*), when introducing an Indirect Statement (a *that* Clause), are followed by a Participle, instead of by an Infinitive.

The Subject of the Participle goes into the same Case as it would with φημί, and the Participle agrees with its Subject in Gender, Number, and Case; as with φημί, when the two Subjects in the sentence are the same, the word αὐτός is omitted unless emphasis is required; the Neg. is οὐ:

(a) οἶδα τὸν ἐμὸν ἀδελφὸν ὄντα σοφόν.
   I know that my brother is wise.

(b) οἶδα οὐ σοφός ὤν.
   I know I am not wise.

(c) οἶδεν αὐτὸς ποιήσας τοῦτο.
   He knows that he himself did this.

In (b) αὐτός is omitted as the Subject of ὤν because there is no emphasis on the Subject. Compare the examples given above with φημί and νομίζω.

EXERCISE 150.

1. ὁ τύραννος οἶδεν ὢν εὐτυχέστατος.
2. ὁ ἁλιεὺς εἶδε τὸν ἰχθὺν ὄντα μέγαν.
3. ὁ Πολυκράτης ᾔσθετο τὴν σφραγῖδα σωθεῖσαν.
4. εἴδομεν τοὺς πολεμίους προχωροῦντας πρὸς τὸν ποταμόν.
5. ὁ Σωκράτης οὐκ ᾔδει αὐτὸς ὢν σοφώτατος.
6. ὁ Κροῖσος ᾔσθετο τοὺς ἵππους φοβουμένους τὰς καμήλους.

7. ἡ Ἀρτεμισία ὁρᾷ αὐτὴ οὖσα ἐν κινδύνῳ.
8. ἠκούσαμεν τοὺς Πέρσας τὸν ποταμὸν διαβάντας.
9. ᾐσθόμεθα οὐχ οἷοί τε ὄντες ἀποφυγεῖν.
10. οἱ Πέρσαι ᾔδεσαν οὐ πολλοὺς ἐνόντας ἐν τῇ ἀκροπόλει.

EXERCISE 151.

1. We know that we are not safe.
2. The Athenians perceived that the enemy had departed.
3. We saw that the enemy were on the mountain.
4. Cyrus did not know that he himself was the son of a king.
5. The general saw that the island would be useful.
6. The Athenians heard that the Spartans would not come at once.
7. We perceived that we were being pursued by the enemy.
8. The sailors did not know that Arion had been saved.
9. Xenophon perceived that many of the soldiers were ill.
10. Who does not know that the Greeks were saved by their fleet?

3. ὅτι or ὡς Construction

As was stated above, λέγω (Aorist εἶπον) should never be followed by the Acc. and Infin. construction in Indirect Statement. It is followed by ὅτι or ὡς (*that*) and a **Finite Verb**. This construction is commonly used with several other Verbs, including ἀγγέλλω, *I announce*; ἀποκρίνομαι, *I answer*. It is **not** used with φημί or with Verbs of *thinking*.

With the ὅτι or ὡς construction it is always correct to keep the **Indicative Tense** which was **used in the original Direct Speech** (Neg. οὐ):

Direct Speech—ὁ Σωκράτης σοφός ἐστιν.
    Socrates is wise.

Indirect Speech—(*a*) λέγουσιν ὅτι ὁ Σωκράτης σοφός ἐστιν.
    They say that Socrates is wise.

    (*b*) εἶπον ὅτι ὁ Σωκράτης σοφός ἐστιν.
    They said that Socrates was wise.

When, however, as in example (*b*) above, the Verb of *saying* is in a **Historic** Tense, the Verb in the ὅτι Clause is **sometimes** put in the **Optative Mood,** though it is still kept in the **same Tense** as was used in the Direct Speech:

(*c*) εἶπον ὅτι ὁ Σ. σοφὸς εἴη.
They said that S. was wise.

So also ἀπεκρίνατο ὅτι οἱ πολέμιοι ἀπῆλθον.
(Tense and Mood of Direct Speech.)
He replied that the enemy had gone away.

or ἀπεκρίνατο ὅτι οἱ πολέμιοι ἀπέλθοιεν.
(Tense the same, Mood now Optative.)

The **Graphic** or **Vivid Construction** of keeping the original Indicative Tense of the speaker is more often used than not, but both Constructions are equally good Greek.

EXERCISE 152.

1. ὁ ἄγγελος λέγει ὅτι οἱ πολέμιοι πάρεισιν.
2. ὁ "Αμασις εἶπεν ὅτι ὁ Πολυκράτης ἐστὶν εὐτυχής.
3. ὁ Γέλων εἶπεν ὅτι οὐ βοηθήσει τοῖς "Ελλησιν.
4. ὁ 'Αρισταγόρας ἤγγειλεν ὡς οἱ βάρβαροι οὐκ ἀνδρεῖοι εἶεν.
5. οἱ 'Αθηναῖοι εἶπον ὅτι ἐν μεγάλῳ κινδύνῳ εἰσίν.
6. ὁ ἡγεμὼν ἀπεκρίνατο ὅτι τοὺς "Ελληνας ἀπάξει πρὸς τὴν θάλασσαν.
7. ὁ Θεμιστοκλῆς εἶπεν ὅτι δεῖ τοὺς 'Αθηναίους πιστεύειν τῷ ναυτικῷ.
8. ἠγγέλθη ὡς ὁ Λεωνίδας ἀπέθανεν.
9. ὁ ἄγγελος εἶπεν ὅτι οἱ 'Αθηναῖοι τειχίσαιεν τὴν Πύλον.
10. οἱ Λακεδαιμόνιοι ἀπεκρίναντο ὡς πέμψοιεν πρέσβεις.

EXERCISE 153. Use ὅτι or ὡς construction.

1. The prisoner announces that the Persians are fleeing.
2. The sailors said that the ship was ready.
3. Cyrus said that he had punished the boy justly.
4. Aristagoras said that it was easy to conquer the Persians.

5. Admetus' father replied that he would not save his son.
6. The messenger announced that ten ships had been captured.
7. His friends said that Socrates was not worthy of death.
8. The Athenians said that the enemy would easily capture the city.
9. I replied that I had not heard this.
10. Some say that this is true, others that it is false.

EXERCISE 154.

PYLOS AND SPHACTERIA: (2) STALEMATE

οἱ δὲ πρέσβεις ἀφικόμενοι εἰς τὰς Ἀθήνας ἔφασαν τοὺς Λακεδαιμονίους προκαλεῖσθαι μὲν τοὺς Ἀθηναίους εἰς εἰρήνην καὶ συμμαχίαν, ἀνταιτεῖν δὲ τοὺς ἐκ τῆς νήσου ἄνδρας. οἱ γὰρ Λακεδαιμόνιοι ἐνόμισαν τοὺς Ἀθηναίους, ἤδη πολλάκις νικηθέντας, εἰρήνην ἀσμένως δέξεσθαι. οἱ δέ, ἔχοντες τοὺς ἄνδρας τοὺς ἐν τῇ νήσῳ, ἔτι πλείονα ἕξειν ἤλπιζον. μάλιστα δὲ αὐτοὺς ἐνῆγε Κλέων, ἀνὴρ πιθανώτατος· οἱ δὲ πρέσβεις ἀνεχώρησαν ἐκ τῶν Ἀθηνῶν ἄπρακτοι.

Ἀφικομένων δὲ αὐτῶν εἰς τὴν Πύλον, αἱ σπονδαὶ εὐθὺς διελύοντο. οἱ δὲ Ἀθηναῖοι ἔτι ἐπολιόρκουν τοὺς ἐν τῇ νήσῳ Λακεδαιμονίους, καὶ ἡ τῶν Λακεδαιμονίων στρατιὰ ἔμενεν οὗ ἦν ἐν τῇ ἠπείρῳ. χαλεπὴ δ' ἦν τοῖς Ἀθηναίοις ἡ φυλακὴ δι' ἀπορίαν σίτου τε καὶ ὕδατος. πρὸς δὲ τούτῳ μάλιστα ἠθύμουν, ὡς ἐνόμιζον ἐκπολιορκήσειν τοὺς πολεμίους ἡμερῶν ὀλίγων. οἱ δὲ Λακεδαιμόνιοι ὑπέσχοντο πολὺ ἀργύριον τοῖς βουλομένοις εἰς τὴν νῆσον εἰσάγειν σῖτόν τε καὶ οἶνον· μάλιστα δὲ εἰσῆγον οἱ Εἵλωτες.[1]

Ἐν δὲ ταῖς Ἀθήναις πυνθανόμενοι ὅτι ἡ στρατιὰ οὐκ εὖ πράσσει, καὶ σῖτος τοῖς ἐν τῇ νήσῳ εἰσάγεται, οἱ πολῖται ἠπόρουν. Κλέων δὲ πρῶτον μὲν οὐκ ἔφη τοὺς ἀγγέλλοντας τὰ ἀληθῆ λέγειν, ὕστερον δὲ εἶπε τῷ Νικίᾳ, στρατηγῷ ὄντι, ὅτι

[1] The Helots were the original inhabitants of territory taken over by Sparta; they were reduced to the position of serfs and in war-time served as light-armed troops.

ῥᾴδιόν ἐστι λαβεῖν τοὺς ἐν τῇ νήσῳ καὶ αὐτὸς οἷός τε ἔσται τοῦτο ποιῆσαι. ὁ δὲ Νικίας ἐκέλευε τὸν Κλέωνα στρατιὰν λαβόντα ἐπιχειρεῖν ἀντὶ τῶν στρατηγῶν. ὁ δὲ ἀνεχώρει καὶ οὐκ ἔφη αὐτὸς ἀλλ᾽ ἐκεῖνον στρατηγὸν εἶναι. οἱ δὲ Ἀθηναῖοι ἐβόων ὅτι δεῖ τὸν Κλέωνα πλεῖν· τέλος δὲ ἔφη τοῦτο ποιήσειν καὶ ἡμερῶν εἴκοσιν ἢ ἄξειν τοὺς Λακεδαιμονίους ζῶντας ἢ ἐκεῖ ἀποκτενεῖν.

Adapted from Thucydides, IV, 16–28.

Chapter 29
Indirect Questions

Indirect Questions are expressed in exactly the same way as Indirect Statements of the ὅτι or ὡς type (see Ch. 28, 3), with the same preference for the Indicative Mood, i.e. the Graphic or Vivid Construction. They are introduced by an Interrogative word (either Direct or Indirect; see A 59; εἰ means *whether* or *if*; πότερον . . . ἤ, *whether . . . or*; a Neg. after ἤ can be either οὐ or μή :

ἐρωτᾷ τὸν ἄγγελον ὅπου οἱ πολέμιοί εἰσιν.
He asks the messenger where the enemy are.

ἤρετο ὅπου οἱ πολέμιοι εἰσιν (or εἶεν).
He asked where the enemy were.

ἠρόμεθα αὐτοὺς τί προσέβαλον (or προσβάλοιεν).
We asked them why they had attacked.

τί ποιήσουσιν (or ποιήσοιεν).
what they would do.

πότερον ἐνίκησαν ἢ οὔ (or μή).
whether they had won or not.

Note. The past tense of ἐρωτάω, *I ask (someone a question)*, is usually ἠρόμην (Strong Aorist), though ἠρώτησα is also found. It should be particularly noticed that the Verb which intro-

Indirect Questions 129

duces an Indirect Question in Greek, as in Latin, is very often not a Verb of *asking* at all. Verbs of *saying, warning, seeing, hearing, finding out, knowing,* etc., can all introduce Indirect Questions.

Distinguish οἶδα αὐτὸν πάροντα, *I know that he is here,* from οἶδα τί πάρεστιν, *I know why he is here.*

EXERCISE 155.

1. ἐρωτήσω τοὺς ἄνδρας τίνες εἰσίν.
2. οὐκ ἴσμεν ὅποι οἱ πολέμιοι ἔφυγον.
3. ὁ τύραννος ἤρετο τὸν ἁλιέα ὅπου τὸν ἰχθὺν εὗρεν.
4. ἐβουλόμεθα εὑρίσκειν ποῖ οἱ Πέρσαι πορεύοιντο.
5. εἰπὲ ἡμῖν πότερον βούλει βοηθεῖν τοῖς Ἕλλησιν ἢ οὔ.
6. ἠρόμεθα τὸν ἡγεμόνα ποτέρα ὁδός ἐστιν ἀσφαλεστέρα.
7. ἐπειρώμεθα εὑρίσκειν εἰ οἱ πολέμιοι προσβαλοῦσιν ἡμῖν ἐκείνῃ τῇ ἡμέρᾳ.
8. ὁ Ἀρισταγόρας ἤγγειλε τῷ βασιλεῖ ὁπόσα χρήματα εἴη τοῖς Πέρσαις.
9. οὐκ ᾖσμεν εἰ οἱ σύμμαχοι ἀφίξονται.
10. οἱ πολῖται ἤροντο τίνες ἐσμὲν καὶ πόθεν ἤλθομεν.
11. ἆρ' οἶσθα εἰ ὁ στρατηγὸς νενίκηκε τοὺς Πέρσας;
12. οἱ Ἀθηναῖοι ἠρώτων εἰ ἡ γέφυρα καταλυθήσεται.

EXERCISE 156.

1. We are asking who he is.
2. The enemy wanted to know where the road was.
3. We tried to discover where the allies had gone.
4. I asked the sailor whether the ship had arrived.
5. We asked the guide where we were.
6. The Greeks did not know whether the Persians had crossed the river or not.
7. We could not find out what the enemy would do.
8. The general asked the messenger how big the enemy's camp was.
9. Demosthenes asked the Athenians whether they wanted to save their country.
10. The scout told us where the enemy had encamped.

11. Have you heard where the ships are being sent?
12. The king asked the boy why he had done this.

Exercise 157.

PYLOS AND SPHACTERIA: (3) A BOAST FULFILLED

Ἐν δὲ τούτῳ, ἐπεὶ ἡ ἐν τῇ νήσῳ ὕλη ὑπὸ στρατιώτου τινὸς ὡς ἐπὶ τὸ πολὺ[1] κατεκαύθη, ῥᾷον ἦν τῷ Δημοσθένει εὑρίσκειν ὁπόσοι εἰσὶν οἱ Λακεδαιμόνιοι καὶ ὅπου ἔξεστιν ἀποβαίνειν. Κλέων δὲ, ὃς τὸν Δημοσθένη προσείλετο, ἔχων στρατιὰν ἀφικνεῖται εἰς Πύλον. οἱ δὲ στρατηγοί, πάντας τοὺς ὁπλίτας νυκτὸς ἐπιβιβάσαντες ἐπ’ ὀλίγας ναῦς, ἑκατέρωθεν τῆς νήσου ἀπέβαινον καὶ ἐχώρουν δρόμῳ ἐπὶ τὸ πρῶτον φυλακτήριον· τοὺς δὲ φύλακας εὐθὺς διαφθείρουσιν ἔτι ἀναλαμβάνοντας τὰ ὅπλα. ὕστερον δὲ πᾶς ὁ ἄλλος στρατὸς ἀπέβαινε πλὴν τῶν ἐν τῇ Πύλῳ φυλάκων. οἱ δὲ Λακεδαιμόνιοι, ὡς εἶδον τὸ φυλακτήριον διεφθαρμένον καὶ στρατὸν ἐπιόντα, τοῖς ὁπλίταις τῶν Ἀθηναίων ἐπήεσαν, βουλόμενοι εἰς χεῖρας ἐλθεῖν. οἱ δὲ Ἀθηναῖοι, αἰσθόμενοι αὐτοὶ πολλῷ πλείονες ὄντες τῶν πολεμίων, ἔβαλλον λίθοις τε καὶ τοξεύμασιν. τέλος δὲ οἱ Λακεδαιμόνιοι ἐχώρησαν εἰς τὸ ἔσχατον ἔρυμα τῆς νήσου.

Χρόνον μὲν οὖν πολὺν ἀμφότεροι ἐμάχοντο, πιεζόμενοι τῇ μάχῃ καὶ δίψῃ καὶ ἡλίῳ· προσελθὼν δὲ ὁ τῶν Μεσσηνίων[2] στρατηγὸς Κλέωνι καὶ Δημοσθένει ἔφη ἐκείνους μὲν μάτην πονεῖν, αὐτὸς δέ, εἰ βούλονται ἑαυτῷ παρέχειν τοξότας καὶ ψιλούς, περιιέναι κατὰ νώτου. λαβὼν δὲ τούτους λάθρα περιῆλθεν, ὥστε τοὺς πολεμίους μὴ ἰδεῖν, καὶ αὐτοὺς ἐξέπληξεν. καὶ οἱ Λακεδαιμόνιοι βαλλόμενοι ἑκατέρωθεν οὐκέτι ἀντεῖχον. ὁ δὲ Κλέων καὶ ὁ Δημοσθένης, βουλόμενοι λαβεῖν αὐτοὺς ζῶντας, ἔπαυσαν τὴν μάχην. καὶ οὕτως ὁ Κλέων εἴκοσιν ἡμερῶν ἤγαγε τοὺς ἄνδρας Ἀθήναζε, ὥσπερ ὑπέσχετο.

Adapted from Thucydides, IV, 29–39.

[1] ὡς ἐπὶ τὸ πολύ, *for the most part.*
[2] Helots in Messenia had revolted in 464 B.C.; when Sparta suppressed the rebellion, they were given a settlement by the Athenians at Naupactus on the Corinthian Gulf.

Chapter 30
Sentences for Revision

EXERCISE 158. (Chapters 3–5)

1. They hunt and pursue.
2. The Muse has honour.
3. We trust the goddess.
4. He is writing a letter.
5. The army flees to the sea.
6. They will loose the wagon.
7. They flee from the land.
8. We do not flee, but pursue.
9. I shall stop the contest.
10. You do not honour the Muse.
11. You will set free the land.
12. They will hinder the army.
13. He rules in the land.
14. We will set free the village.
15. They do not trust the goddess.
16. The sea hinders the army.
17. You will not stop the battle.
18. They are writing letters.
19. We flee from the sea.
20. They will march into the land.
21. The sailors were sacrificing to the north wind.
22. The soldier was setting free the citizens.
23. We were pursuing the soldiers from the land.
24. Citizens, we will trust the sailors.
25. We were keeping the soldiers from the door of the house.
26. The soldiers and sailors were hindering the citizens.
27. They trusted the slave's words.
28. Judges seek after justice.
29. They were sacrificing to the goddess in the market-place.
30. The river did not hinder the army.
31. We were pursuing the soldiers from the gates of Athens.
32. The judges set free the young man.
33. Poets pursue glory.
34. The steward of the house does not trust the soldiers.
35. We kept the Persians from the islands.
36. Xerxes' army was fleeing from Athens.

37. We will honour the goddess of the country.
38. The general of the Persians stopped the battle.
39. You did not sacrifice to the goddess of the island.
40. The Athenians were fleeing to the river.
41. The citizens honour poets and generals.
42. The wagons hindered the soldiers on the road.
43. We are pursuing the army of the Persians.
44. The doctor is writing the words in the book.
45. The young men were seeking after wisdom in Athens.
46. The doctors did not stop the plague.

EXERCISE 159. (Chapters 6–8)

1. The young man has loosed the horses' yokes.
2. The children are injuring the tree.
3. The Athenians are hostile to the generals.
4. Seek after wisdom, children.
5. The soldier has trained the horse.
6. Friendship is good.
7. The enemy have long weapons.
8. We are not rich, citizens.
9. The general ordered the herald to announce the victory.
10. The trees have hindered the enemy.
11. He had not educated his children in Athens.
12. Some are fleeing, others are pursuing.
13. Always seek after justice, citizens.
14. We have set free the slaves.
15. The steward ordered the children not to injure the fruit.
16. Money is useful in war.
17. It is easy to pursue the enemy, difficult to capture them.
18. We provide arms for the guards.
19. The enemy's general has trusted his soldiers.
20. The citizens have not kept the enemy from the gate.
21. It is not difficult to guard the camp.
22. We are cutting down the bad trees.
23. The guards have breast-plates.
24. There are dangerous animals in the island.
25. We set free the general himself.
26. Fine is the Athenians' victory.

27. Trust both the soldiers and the sailors.
28. He told some to flee, others to remain.
29. The animal's body is small.
30. The Persians had not set free the citizens.

EXERCISE 160. (Chapters 9–11)

1. The citizens will not be hostile to the exiles.
2. The wild beasts were crossing the river.
3. The enemy were waiting for the night.
4. We hear, but do not believe, the orator's words.
5. You were brave in the battle, sailors.
6. The father heard his daughter's voice.
7. It will not be easy to save Greece.
8. The guard at the gate hindered the soldiers.
9. We pursued the enemy into the harbour.
10. We were hunting a lion in the wood.
11. On account of the storm the general did not draw up the army.
12. The road through the island was not long.
13. The Athenians wish to save their country.
14. Some pursued the Persians, others were guarding the camp.
15. The soldiers in the harbour were ready.
16. We do not feel grateful to the allies.
17. The herald was announcing a fine victory.
18. The general has drawn up the Greeks for battle.
19. Neither the old men nor the children wish to stay.
20. The Spartans fared well in the contest.
21. The women in the house were training the slaves.
22. The arms were ready for the soldiers.
23. The people there are friendly to the Greeks.
24. There were beautiful statues in the market-place.
25. The allies will guard the arms of the Greeks.
26. The shepherd led the goats from the meadow.
27. The fathers were sending away their sons to the islands.
28. We were once free, O citizens.
29. The statues in the market-place are beautiful.
30. Xerxes drew up the fleet for battle.

EXERCISE 161. (Chapters 12–14)

1. For six days we were guarding the harbour.
2. The Athenians have saved their country.
3. The men in the city threw stones from the wall.
4. We shall be in Athens within ten days.
5. The words of Demosthenes did not persuade them.
6. The army was crossing the river by night.
7. The mountains are high and dangerous.
8. No one will send an army in the winter.
9. The storm compelled the sailors to flee to the harbour.
10. Some of the cities sent triremes, others soldiers.
11. Both earth and water were being sent by the cities.
12. No one was able to persuade him.
13. We will hide the pigs in the wood.
14. We will send a letter to the king himself.
15. The old man threw the little fish into the sea.
16. The plague will be stopped within a few days.
17. The enemy are being pursued by the cavalry.
18. They planted the trees in the fourth month.
19. The ships in the harbour are now ready.
20. We stayed in the camp for one day.
21. The Spartans sent ambassadors to Athens.
22. The women and children will be set free.
23. The citizens honour the king.
24. Sacrifice ten oxen to Zeus.
25. The men on the bridge are being compelled by the enemy to flee.
26. Ten of the ships were hindered by the storm.
27. The Persians damaged the cities of the Greeks.
28. We have persuaded the allies to send triremes.
29. The oxen were being loosed by the old woman.
30. The cavalry cannot pursue the enemy on the mountain.
31. The enemy left guards in the camp.
32. Ambassadors are being sent by the king to the Athenians.
33. The Spartans damaged the Athenians' trees.
34. The king's daughter was being sacrificed by the priest.
35. The enemy were waiting on the walls of the city.
36. I have written three letters and sent them to Athens.

EXERCISE 162. (Chapters 15–17)

1. The son is wiser than his father.
2. We have braver soldiers than the Persians.
3. Obey your fathers, children.
4. Order the soldiers to be ready.
5. We will ransom the general before night.
6. Socrates is very worthy of honour.
7. The walls of our city are high.
8. It is good to have stopped a war.
9. I am a soldier, you are a general.
10. The Athenian was winning the prize.
11. Nothing is more terrible than war.
12. Let the messenger stay in the camp.
13. The enemy's ships had not been hindered by the storm.
14. No one ransomed the prisoners.
15. Be brave, my son, and remain in the battle.
16. We admire the judge and his wisdom.
17. It was difficult to stop the battle.
18. Let the prisoner be set free at once.
19. My father is teaching your son.
20. The guide led us to the sea.
21. They hoped to be ransomed by their friends.
22. We were pursuing the Persians and their allies.
23. Send help to the allies at once.
24. We deliberated about the war for three days.
25. It was shameful to have been hindered by a few soldiers.
26. We think the Athenians more wise than the Spartans.
27. Let them cease from the battle on account of the storm.
28. We are about to encamp near the wood.
29. The general's horse has not been trained for war.
30. The Athenians ransomed us on the third day.

EXERCISE 163. (Chapters 18–20)

1. The Greeks are defeating the Persians by land.
2. Socrates was seeking justice.
3. The walls round the city were weak.
4. The general himself is never seen by the citizens.

5. The men on the island were being defeated by the Athenians.
6. The road to the harbour is short.
7. Those who sent help will be honoured (τιμάω) by many Greeks.
8. Wise men speak the truth.
9. The prisoner was being sought in a big wood.
10. The steward is freeing many slaves.
11. The boy on the mountain is shouting.
12. While pursuing the enemy, we were crossing a river.
13. The wall was made in ten days.
14. I was showing the way to the old man.
15. We do not admire those who trust riches.
16. The enemy were treating the prisoners well.
17. The rivers of the land are both wide and deep.
18. There was a big camp outside the city.
19. The Athenians used to honour (τιμάω) poets.
20. When they had defeated the enemy, they encamped.
21. The plan was being shown to the scouts.
22. He punished the children who had cut down the tree.
23. Even the old men are being enslaved.
24. The citizens trust those who will guard their country.
25. The water of the river seemed to be black.
26. The prisoners who had been set free were already in the camp.
27. Neither the women nor the children were enslaved.
28. We feel grateful to those who are fighting.
29. The island has at last been freed.
30. We will honour (τιμάω) the soldiers who saved the city.
31. While marching home, the Greeks were hindered by the snow.
32. The poet will be honoured (τιμάω) by many citizens.
33. Those who have been set free are rejoicing.
34. We do not think Admetus fortunate.
35. The enemy enslaved our city.
36. We honour (τιμάω) those who treated us well.
37. He sent into battle those who had been well trained.
38. We were marching towards a big river.

39. It is not prudent to attack the Persians today.
40. We were seeking the enemy's cavalry for a long (πολύς) time.
41. The enemy pursued us with swift ships.
42. It was not safe to stay near the river.
43. The king did not trust the man who had written the letter.
44. A large wall is being made round the city.
45. We see the enemy fleeing to the mountains.
46. After stopping the battle, the general sent away all the allies.
47. We were fleeing to the city, still being pursued by the enemy.
48. All the women went away with the children.

EXERCISE 164. (Chapters 21–23)

1. A large army has been drawn up near the river.
2. Many soldiers were sent by the allies.
3. The door will be guarded by two soldiers.
4. The queen has saved herself.
5. We will conquer that army in three days.
6. We wish to make the city bigger.
7. Athens was a very beautiful city.
8. The same messenger was bringing the letter.
9. That ship was sunk by the queen herself.
10. Our arms are very heavy.
11. The enemy's ships were very swift.
12. We admire the queen and her bravery.
13. The Greeks were marching faster than the enemy.
14. The allies have been left in the island.
15. These trees are more beautiful than those.
16. We have been saved from a great danger.
17. Demosthenes himself always says the same.
18. The citizens appeared to be more hostile than the soldiers.
19. These soldiers will guard the harbour bravely.
20. We were compelled to stay there a long (πολύς) time.
21. Many citizens have been persuaded to fight.

22. We could not save the general himself.
23. On that day the Greeks conquered the enemy both by land and by sea.
24. The citizens were not persuaded even by many words.
25. The guide went away to his own country.
26. Our ships are safer than the walls.
27. We shall be compelled to build a large house.
28. Most of the soldiers were fighting very bravely.
29. We think our city more beautiful than yours.
30. Many names had been written on the stone.
31. The worst of the ships were left in the harbour.
32. The generals managed the city's affairs more wisely than the tyrants.
33. The sailors were in very great danger.
34. The Athenians have more ships than the Spartans.

EXERCISE 165. (Chapters 24–29)

1. Let us save the women and children.
2. Let not the children stay in the city.
3. Do not hinder those who are crossing the river.
4. Surely you are willing to fight for us, aren't you?
5. Polycrates, who was a tyrant, was most fortunate.
6. When the Persians had entered Greece, we were in great danger.
7. The citizens are fighting in order that they may not be enslaved.
8. The messenger said ($\phi\eta\mu\iota$) that the enemy had gone away.
9. The Greeks said ($\lambda\acute{\epsilon}\gamma\omega$) that they wanted to be free.
10. Let us not cease from the battle before night.
11. When Cyrus had given the order, the Persians attacked the enemy.
12. The enemy were so few that we easily defeated them.
13. The prisoners saw that they could not escape.
14. Let nobody depart from the camp today.
15. We asked the boy who he was.
16. Do not send help to the Persians.
17. As the enemy are few, we shall easily defeat them.
18. The danger was so great that we did not fight on that day.

19. Never trust those who say such things.
20. We wanted to know why he had done that.
21. Do you wish to encamp at once?
22. Let nobody be persuaded by such an orator.
23. May our army conquer the Persians!
24. After the city had been captured, the citizens fought no
     longer.
25. Let us advance to attack the enemy.
26. The orator is so foolish that no one believes him.
27. May this danger not hinder us!
28. We know that the boy always speaks the truth.
29. We did not know where the enemy had encamped.
30. A certain Greek showed the Persians the way.
31. Xerxes said ($\phi\eta\mu\iota$) that he himself would lead the army.
32. When they had captured the city, the Persians enslaved
     all the citizens.
33. He was too brave to flee from the battle.
34. I knew that I had seen you before.
35. Who ordered the allies to go away?
36. Would that someone might save the ships!
37. Do not think that he knows everything.
38. We are present to honour the god.
39. Athens, which is the greatest city of Greece, is also the
     most beautiful.
40. We heard that the army was already advancing.
41. The general asked whether the ships would arrive or not.
42. We think that Socrates is very wise.
43. The tyrant said ($\lambda\acute{\epsilon}\gamma\omega$) that he would not help the Greeks.
44. The general perceived that he was himself in danger.
45. As the storm was dangerous, we did not go out of the
     harbour.
46. Is he so clever as to say that?
47. Surely we shall not be defeated?
48. Ambassadors were sent to receive earth and water.
49. Let us not fear this danger.
50. The general said ($\phi\eta\mu\iota$) that he would not send the allies
     away.
51. The prisoner answered that the enemy had not gone away.

52. Who are these men? Where are they marching to?
53. Do not treat badly those who treat you well.
54. The messenger told us what the Persians were doing.
55. The allies sent ships so that we might not be defeated.
56. The soldiers said (λέγω) that the wall was very weak.
57. The herald announced that Darius was dead.
58. I did not know whether Themistocles would be able to persuade the Greeks or not.

Commoner uses of Prepositions

The following list does not include all Prepositions nor all the uses of those that are given. Those marked with an asterisk are only found with one Case.

With Accusative Case:

*ἀνά, up	ἀνὰ τὸν ποταμόν	up the river
*εἰς, into, to	εἰς τὴν χώραν	into the country
*ὡς, to (a person)	ὡς τὸν βασιλέα	to the king
διά, on account of	διὰ τὸν πόλεμον	on account of the war
κατά, down-along	κατὰ τὸν ποταμόν	down the river
according to	κατὰ τὸν νόμον	according to the law
by way of	κατὰ γῆν	by land
ὑπέρ, beyond	ὑπὲρ δύναμιν	beyond one's power
ἐπί, against	ἐπὶ τοὺς πολεμίους	against the enemy
μετά, after	μετὰ τὴν μάχην	after the battle
παρά, to (the side of)	παρὰ τὸν βασιλέα	to the court of the king
contrary to	παρὰ τὸν νόμον	contrary to the law
περί, round	περὶ τὴν πόλιν	round the city
πρός, to, towards	πρὸς τὰς 'Αθήνας	to Athens
against	πρὸς τοὺς βαρβάρους	against the barbarians

With Genitive Case:

*ἀντί, in place of	ἀντὶ τῆς εἰρήνης	instead of peace
*ἀπό, from	ἀπὸ τῆς πόλεως	from the city
*ἐκ,[1] out of	ἐκ τῆς πόλεως	out of the city
after	ἐκ τούτων	after this

[1] ἐξ before a vowel.

*πρό, in front of 　before	πρὸ τῆς πύλης πρὸ τοῦ πολέμου	in front of the gate before the war
*ἕνεκα,[1] for the sake 　of	τῆς φιλίας ἕνεκα	for the sake of friendship
*πλήν, except	πλὴν ἐμοῦ	except me
διά, through	διὰ τῆς χώρας	through the coun- try
ὑπέρ, on behalf of	ὑπὲρ τῆς πατρίδος	on behalf of one's country
ἐπί, on	ἐπὶ τοῦ ὄρους	on the mountain
μετά, with	μεθ' ἡμῶν	with us
περί, concerning	περὶ τῆς εἰρήνης	concerning peace
ὑπό, by (Agent)	ὑπὸ τοῦ στρατηγοῦ	by the general

[1] ἕνεκα is placed *after* the Gen.

With Dative Case:

*ἐν, in	ἐν τῇ πόλει ἐν τούτῳ	in the city meanwhile
among	ἐν τοῖς πολίταις	among the citizens
ἐπί, on condition of	ἐπὶ τούτῳ	on this condition
πρός, in addition to	πρὸς τούτοις	in addition to this
ὑπό, under	ὑπὸ τῷ ὄρει	under the moun- tain

Greek–English Vocabulary

Tenses of Irregular Verbs are only given so far as they occur in this. book

ἀγαθός, -ή, -όν, good; n. pl., good things, goods.

Ἀγαμέμνων, -ονος, m., Agamemnon.

ἀγγεῖον, -ου, n., vessel, pail.

ἀγγέλλω, ἤγγειλα, ἠγγέλθην, I announce, report.

ἄγγελος, -ου, m., messenger.

ἄγκιστρον, -ου, n., hook.

ἀγορά, -ᾶς, f., market-place.

ἄγω, ἄξω, ἤγαγον, ἤχθην, I lead, bring.

ἀγών, -ῶνος, m., contest, game.

ἀδικία, -ας, f., wrongdoing.

Ἄδμητος, -ου, m., Admetus.

ἀδύνατος, -ον, impossible.

ἀεί, always.

ἀείδω, ᾖσα (ἀείσας, aor. partic.), I sing.

Ἀθήναζε, to Athens (Advb.).

Ἀθῆναι, -ῶν, f. pl., Athens.

Ἀθηναῖος, -ου, m., an Athenian.

Ἀθήνη, -ης, f., Athene, goddess of wisdom.

ἆθλον, -ου, n., prize.

ἀθροίζω, I collect.

ἀθυμέω, I am despondent.

ἀθυμία, -ας, f., despondency.

Αἴγινα, -ης, f., Aegina.

Αἰγινήτης, -ου, m., an Aeginetan.

Αἰγύπτιοι,-ων,m. pl.,Egyptians.

Αἴγυπτος, -ου, f., Egypt.

αἴθω, I burn.

αἴξ, αἰγός, c., goat.

αἱρέω, αἱρήσω, aor. pass. ᾑρέθην, I capture.

αἰσθάνομαι, ᾐσθόμην, I perceive.

αἴσχιστος, superl. of αἰσχρός.

αἰσχρός, -ά, -όν, shameful, disgraceful.

αἰτέω, I ask, beg, ask for.

αἰχμάλωτος, -ου, m., prisoner (of war).

αἰχμή, -ῆς, f., spear.

ἀκούω, ἤκουσα, I hear, listen to.

ἄκρον, -ου, n., top, summit.

ἀκρόπολις, -εως, f., citadel, esp. the Acropolis at Athens.

ἀκτή, -ῆς, f., shore.

ἄλγος, -ους, n., pain, grief.

ἀληθής, -ές, true.

ἁλιεύς, -έως, m., fisherman.

Ἁλικαρνασσεύς, -έως, m., a Halicarnassian.

Ἄλκηστις, -ιδος, f., Alcestis.

ἀλλά, but.

ἀλλήλους, -ας, -α, each other.

ἄλλος, -η, -ο, other, another; ὁ ἄλλος, the rest of.

ἄλλως, otherwise.

Ἅλυς, -υος, m., (river) Halys.

ἅμα, at the same time.

ἅμαξα, -ης, ƒ., wagon.

Ἄμασις, -ιος, m., Amasis.

ἀμείνων, -ον, *comp. of* ἀγαθός, better.

ἅμιλλα, -ης, ƒ., contest.

ἀμφίβληστρον, -ου, n., net.

ἀμφότερος, -α, -ον, both.

ἀναβαίνω, I mount, climb up.

ἀναγιγνώσκω, I read.

ἀναγκάζω, ἠνάγκασα, ἠναγκάσθην, I compel.

ἀναγκαῖος, -α, -ον, necessary.

ἀναγνωρίζω, I recognize.

ἀνάγομαι, I put out to sea.

ἀναλαμβάνω, I take up.

ἀναλίσκω, I spend.

ἀναξυρίδες, -ων, ƒ. pl., trousers.

ἀναχωρέω, I retire, withdraw.

ἀνδραποδίζω, ἠνδραπόδισμαι, ἠνδραποδίσθην, I enslave.

ἀνδράποδον, -ου, n., slave.

ἀνδρεία, -ας, ƒ., bravery.

ἀνδρεῖος, -α, -ον, brave.

ἀνδρείως, bravely.

ἀνδρίας, -αντος, m., statue.

ἄνεμος, -ου, m., wind.

ἄνευ (Gen.), without.

ἀνήρ, ἀνδρός, m., man, husband.

ἄνθρωπος, -ου, m., man.

ἀνταιτέω, I ask for in return.

ἀντέχω (*imperf.* ἀντεῖχον), I hold out, resist.

ἀντί (Gen.), instead of.

ἄνω (Gen.), above.

ἄξιος, -α, -ον, worthy, worth.

ἀξιόω, I think it right.

ἀπάγω, I lead away, lead back.

ἀπαλλάσσομαι, (Gen.) I get rid of.

ἄπειμι (*infin.* ἀπιέναι), I go away.

ἀπελαύνω, I drive away.

ἀπέρχομαι, ἀπῆλθον, I depart.

ἀπιστία, -ας, ƒ., disbelief.

ἀπό (Gen.), from.

ἀποβαίνω, I go away, disembark.

ἀποβάλλω, ἀποβαλῶ, ἀπέβαλον, I throw away, throw overboard.

ἀποθνήσκω, ἀποθανοῦμαι, ἀπέθανον, I die, am killed.

ἀποικία, -ας, ƒ., colony.

ἀποκρίνομαι, ἀποκρινοῦμαι, ἀπεκρινάμην, I answer.

ἀποκρύπτω, I hide, hide from view.

ἀποκτείνω, ἀποκτενῶ, I kill.

ἀπολαμβάνω, ἀπέλαβον, I cut off.

ἀπολείπω, ἀπολείψω, ἀπέλιπον, I leave, leave behind.

Ἀπόλλων, -ωνος, m., Apollo.

ἀποπέμπω, ἀπέπεμψα, ἀπεπέμφθην, I send away.

ἀποπλέω, ἀπέπλευσα, I sail away.

ἀπορέω, I am at a loss.

ἀπορία, -ας, ƒ., difficulty, lack.

ἀπορρέω, I flow away.

ἀποτέμνω, I cut off.

ἀποφαίνω, I display.

ἀποφεύγω, ἀπέφυγον, I flee away.

ἀποχωρέω, I go away, depart.

ἄπρακτος, -ον, unsuccessful.

ἆρα; ἆρ᾽ οὐ; (*interrog. particles*); *for use and examples see p. 107 under Direct Questions.*

Ἄργειοι, -ων, m. pl., Argives, people in N.E. of Peloponnese.

ἀργύριον, -ου, n., money.

ἄργυρος, -ου, m., silver.

ἀργυροῦς, -ᾶ, -οῦν, made of silver.

ἀρέσκω (Dat.), I please.

ἀρετή, -ῆς, f., courage.

ἀριθμός, -οῦ, m., number.

ἄριστα, superl. of εὖ, best.

Ἀρισταγόρας, -ου, m., Aristagoras.

ἀριστεύω, I am best, superior.

ἄριστος, superlat. of ἀγαθός, best.

Ἀρίων, -ονος, m., Arion.

Ἀρμενία, -ας, f., Armenia.

Ἀρμένιοι (m. pl.), Armenians.

ἀροτήρ, -ῆρος, m., ploughman.

ἁρπάζω, I snatch.

Ἀρτεμβάρης, -ους, m., Artembares.

Ἀρτεμισία, -ας, f., Artemisia.

ἀρχαῖος, -α, -ον, ancient.

ἀρχή, -ῆς, f., rule, empire, command.

ἄρχω, ἄρξω (Gen.), I rule, rule over, am in command of.

ἄρχων, -οντος, m., ruler, chief, magistrate.

ἀσθενής, -ές, weak.

Ἀσία, -ας, f., Asia.

ἀσμένως, gladly.

ἀσπίς, -ίδος, f., shield.

ἄστυ, -εως, n., town.

Ἀστυάγης, -ους, m., Astyages.

ἀσφαλής, -ές, safe.

ἀτιμάω, I slight.

Ἀττική, -ῆς, f., Attica, country in Greece of which Athens was the capital.

Ἀττικός, -ή, -όν, Attic.

αὖθις, again.

αὐλίζομαι, I encamp.

αὐξάνω, I increase; αὐξάνομαι, I increase (intrans.).

αὐτόμολος, -ου, m., deserter.

αὐτός, -ή, -ό, self (all cases); in all cases except Nom., him, her, it, them; ὁ αὐτός, the same.

ἄφθογγος, -ον, speechless.

ἀφικνέομαι, ἀφίξομαι, ἀφικόμην, ἀφῖγμαι, I arrive.

Βαβυλών, -ῶνος, f., Babylon.

Βαβυλώνιοι, -ων, m. pl., Babylonians.

βαδίζω, I walk.

βαθύς, -εῖα, -ύ, deep.

βάλλω, I throw; often, I pelt.

βάρβαροι, -ων, m. pl., barbarians.

βαρύς, -εῖα, -ύ, heavy.

βασίλεια, -ας, f., queen.

βασίλεια, -ων, n. pl., palace.

βασιλεύς, -έως, m., king; without article, the king of Persia.

βασιλεύω, I reign, am king; with Gen., I am king of.

βέβαιος, -α, -ον, sure, trusty.

βία, -ας, f., force; πρὸς βίαν, by force.

βίβλος, -ου, f., book.

βίος, -ου, m., life.

βλάπτω, ἔβλαψα, βέβλαφα, βέβλαμμαι, ἐβλάβην, I harm, injure, damage.
βλέπω, ἔβλεψα, I look.
βοάω, I shout.
βοή, -ῆς, f., shout.
βοήθεια, -ας, f., help.
βοηθέω (Dat.), I help.
Βορέας, -ου, m., North Wind.
βουκόλος, -ου, m., herdsman.
βουλεύω, I plan; βουλεύομαι, I deliberate.
βουλή, -ῆς, f., plan.
βούλομαι, I wish, am willing.
βοῦς, βοός, c., ox.
βραδύς, -εῖα, -ύ, slow.
βραδυτής, -ῆτος, f., slowness.
βραχύς, -εῖα, -ύ, short.

γάρ (2nd word), for.
γαστήρ, γαστρός, f., belly.
γείτων, -ονος, c., neighbour.
Γέλων, -ωνος, m., Gelon.
γέρων, -οντος, m., old man.
γέφυρα, -ας, f., bridge.
γῆ, γῆς, f., land, earth.
γίγας, -αντος, m., giant.
γίγνομαι, γενήσομαι, ἐγενόμην, I become; of events, happen; of time, arrive.
γλυκύς, -εῖα, -ύ, sweet.
γλῶσσα, -ης, f., tongue.
γνάθος, -ου, f., jaw.
γραῦς, γραός, f., old woman.
γράφω, ἔγραψα, γέγραφα, γέγραμμαι, I write.
γυμνός, -ή, -όν, lightly clad.
γυνή, -αικός, f., woman, wife.

δάκνω, I bite.
δακρύω, I weep.
δαρεικός, -οῦ, m., daric (Persian coin).
Δαρεῖος, -ου, m., Darius.
δέ, but, and.
δεῖ (with Acc. foll. by infin.), it is necessary.
δειλία, -ας, f., cowardice.
δειλός, -ή, -όν, cowardly.
δεινός, -ή, -όν, strange, terrible, clever.
δεῖπνον, -ου, n., dinner.
δέκα, ten.
δεκαετής, -ές, ten years old.
δέκατος, -η, -ον, tenth.
δελφίς, -ῖνος, m., dolphin.
Δελφοί, -ῶν, m., Delphi.
δένδρον, -ου, n., tree.
δεσμωτήριον, -ου, n., prison.
δεσπότης, -ου, m., master.
δεῦρο, hither.
δευτεραῖος, -α, -ον, on the second day.
δεύτερος, -α, -ον, second.
δέχομαι, δέξομαι, ἐδεξάμην, I receive.
δή, indeed.
δηλόω, I show, point out.
δῆμος, -ου, m., people.
Δημοσθένης, -ους, m., Demosthenes.
διά (Acc.), on account of; (Gen.), through.
διαβαίνω, διαβήσομαι, διέβην (partic. διαβάς), I cross.
διαβατός, -ή, -όν, fordable.

διαβιβάζω, διεβίβασα, I take across.

διάγω, I spend (*time*).

διακόσιοι, -αι, -α, two hundred.

διαλέγομαι (Dat.), I converse with.

διαλύω (*also* διαλύομαι), I destroy, break off.

διατρίβω, I spend (*time*).

διαφεύγω, I escape.

διαφθείρω, *perf. pass.* διέφθαρμαι, I destroy, kill.

διδάσκαλος, -ου, *m.*, master (*of school*).

διδάσκω, I teach.

Διηνέκης, *m.*, Dieneces.

δίκαιος, -α, -ον, just.

δικαιοσύνη, -ης, *f.*, justice.

δισμύριοι, -αι, -α, twenty thousand.

δισχίλιοι, -αι, -α, two thousand.

δίψα, -ης, *f.*, thirst.

διώκω, ἐδίωξα, ἐδιώχθην, I pursue.

διῶρυξ, -υχος, *f.*, trench.

δοκέω, ἔδοξα, I seem; δοκεῖ ἐμοί, it seems good to me, I am resolved.

δόκιμος, -ον, notable.

δόξα, -ης, *f.*, glory.

δορυφόροι, -ων, *m. pl.*, bodyguards.

δοῦλος, -ου, *m.*, slave.

δουλοσύνη, -ης, *f.*, slavery.

δουλόω, I enslave.

δράκων, -οντος, *m.*, dragon.

δρομεύς, -έως, *m.*, runner.

δρόμος, -ου, *m.*, running; δρόμῳ, at the double.

δρόσος, -ου, *f.*, dew.

δύναμις, -εως, *f.*, power.

δυνατός, -ή, -όν, powerful.

δύο, two.

δυσμαί, -ῶν, *f. pl.*, setting.

δῶρον, -ου, *n.*, present, gift.

ἑαυτόν, -ήν, -ό, himself, herself, itself, (*reflex.*); *pl.*, themselves.

ἐάω, I allow.

ἐγγύς (Advb.), near; (Prep. with Gen.), near.

ἐγώ, I.

ἐθέλω, I am willing, wish.

εἰ, if; whether (*in Ind. Q.*); εἰ γάρ, would that.

εἰδέναι, *see* οἶδα.

εἶδον, *see* ὁράω.

εἴθε, would that.

εἴκοσι, twenty.

Εἵλως, -ωτος, *m.*, Helot (a Spartan serf).

εἰμί, ἔσομαι, *imperf.* ἦν, I am.

εἶπον, *see* λέγω.

εἰργαζόμην, *see* ἐργάζομαι.

εἰρήνη, -ης, *f.*, peace.

εἰς (Acc.), into, to, for, up to.

εἷς, μία, ἕν, one.

εἰσάγω, εἰσήγαγον, I bring into.

εἰσβαίνω, I go on board.

εἰσβάλλω, I throw into, I invade.

εἰσβολή, -ῆς, *f.*, pass.

εἴσειμι, I enter, εἰσῆλθον.

εἴσοδος, -ου, *f.*, entrance.

εἰσρέω, I flow into.

εἶτα, then.

ἐκ (Gen.), out of, from.

ἐκάς, far.

ἕκαστος, -η, -ον, each.

ἑκάτερος, -α, -ον, each of two.

ἑκατέρωθεν, on both sides.

ἑκατόν, a hundred.

ἐκβάλλω, I throw out.

ἐκεῖ, there.

ἐκεῖνος, -η, -ο, that (*yonder*).

ἐκεῖσε, thither.

ἐκκλησία, -ας, *f*., assembly.

ἐκλέπω, I hatch.

ἐκκομίζω, ἐξεκόμισα, I bring out.

ἐκπηδάω, I leap out.

ἐκπλήσσω, ἐξέπληξα, I scare.

ἐκπολιορκέω, I capture by siege.

ἔκπωμα, -ατος, *n*., drinking-cup.

ἕκτος, -η, -ον, sixth.

ἐλάσσων, *comp. of* ὀλίγος, fewer.

ἐλαύνω, I drive.

ἐλάχιστος, *superl. of* ὀλίγος, smallest.

ἐλεύθερος, -α, -ον, free.

ἐλευθερόω, I free.

ἐλέγχω, I convict.

Ἐλεφαντίνη, -ης, *f*., Elephantine, city in Egypt.

ἐλθεῖν, *see* ἔρχομαι.

ἕλκω, I drag.

Ἑλλάς, -άδος, *f*., Greece.

Ἕλλην, -ηνος, *m*., a Greek.

Ἑλλήσποντος, -ου, *m*., the Hellespont.

ἕλος, -ους, *n*., marsh.

ἐλπίζω, I hope, expect.

ἐλπίς, -ίδος, *f*., hope.

ἔλυτρον, -ου, *n*., basin (reservoir).

ἐμβάλλω (Dat.), I ram.

ἔμπροσθε (Gen.), in front of.

ἐν (Dat.), in, among, at; ἐν τούτῳ, meanwhile.

ἐνάγω, I lead on, urge.

ἔνδον, inside.

ἔνειμι, I am within.

ἕνεκα (*after* Gen.), for the sake of.

ἐνθάδε, here.

ἐννέα, nine.

ἐνταῦθα, there.

ἐντεῦθεν, from there.

ἕξ, six.

ἐξάγω, I lead out.

ἐξάλλομαι, I leap out.

ἔξεστι, it is allowed, possible.

ἐξηγέομαι, I explain, recount.

ἐξήκοντα, sixty.

ἔξω (Gen.), outside.

ἔξω, *see* ἔχω.

ἑορτή, -ῆς, *f*., feast.

ἐπάγω, ἐπάξω, I lead against.

ἐπανέρχομαι, ἐπανῆλθον, I return.

ἐπεί, when, since.

ἐπείγομαι, I hasten.

ἔπειμι, *infin.* ἐπεῖναι (Gen.), I am upon.

ἔπειμι, *infin.* ἐπιέναι (Dat.), I attack.

ἔπειτα, then.

ἐπί (Acc.), against, on to; (Gen.), on, upon; (Dat.), on; ἐπὶ τούτῳ, on this condition.

ἐπιβάτης, -ου, *m*., marine.

ἐπιβιβάζω, ἐπεβίβασα, I put on board.

ἐπιβουλεύω, I plot.

ἐπικεῖμαι (Dat.), I lie opposite.

ἐπιπίπτω, I fall (upon).

ἐπιστάτης, -ου, m., overseer.

ἐπιστολή, -ῆς, f., letter.

ἐπιτήδειος, -α, -ον, fit.

ἐπιτρέπω, ἐπέτρεψα, I entrust.

ἐπιφαίνομαι, I appear.

ἐπιχειρέω, I make an attempt.

ἐποτρύνω, I urge on.

ἑπτακαίδεκα, seventeen.

ἐργάζομαι, *imperf.* εἰργαζόμην, I work.

ἔργον, -ου, n., work, deed.

ἔρχομαι, ἦλθον, I go.

ἔρυμα, -ατος, n., fort.

ἐρωτάω, *aor.* ἠρόμην or ἠρώτησα, I ask.

ἐσθίω, I eat.

ἑσπέρα, -ας, f., evening.

ἔσχατος, -η, -ον, last.

ἔσω, inside.

ἕτερος, -α, -ον, other.

ἔτι, still.

ἑτοῖμος, -η, -ον, ready.

ἔτος, -ους, n., year.

εὖ, well.

εὐγενής, -ές, of noble birth, noble.

εὐδαίμων, -ον, happy.

εὐεργέτης, -ου, m., benefactor.

εὐθύς, immediately.

εὔνοια, -ας, f., kindness.

εὐπορία, -ας, f., plenty.

εὑρίσκω, εὗρον, I find, find out.

Εὐριβιάδης, -ου, m. Eurybiades.

εὐρύς, -εῖα, -ύ, wide.

Εὐρώπη, -ης, f., Europe.

εὐτυχέω, I prosper.

εὐτυχής, -ές, fortunate.

εὐτυχία, -ας, f., good fortune, prosperity.

Εὐφράτης, m., (river) Euphrates.

ἔφη, see φημί.

ἐχθίων, -ιον, comp. of ἐχθρός.

ἐχθρός, -ά, -όν, hostile.

ἔχω, ἕξω, I have, hold, keep.

ἕως, while, until.

ζάω, I live.

Ζεύς, Διός, m., Zeus.

ζητέω, I seek.

ζυγόν, -οῦ, n., yoke.

ζῷον, -ου, n., animal.

ζωός, -ή, όν, alive.

ἤ, or; ἤ . . .ἤ, either . . . or; than.

ᾗ, where.

ἡγεμονεύω (Gen.), I command.

ἡγεμονία, -ας, f., leadership.

ἡγεμών, -όνος, m., guide.

ἡδέως, gladly.

ἤδη, already.

ᾔδη, see οἶδα.

ἥδομαι (Dat.), I am pleased with.

ἡδύς, -εῖα, -ύ, sweet, pleasant.

ἥκω, I am come.

ἦλθον, see ἔρχομαι.

ἥλιος, -ου, m., sun.

ἡμεῖς, we.

ἡμέρα, -ας, f., day.

ἡμέτερος, -α, -ον, our.

ἤπειρος, -ου, f., mainland, continent.

Ἡρακλῆς, m., Heracles.

ἠρόμην, see ἐρωτάω.

ᾐσθόμην, see αἰσθάνομαι.

ἡσυχάζω, ἡσυχάσω, I remain quiet.

θάλασσα, -ης, f., sea.
θάνατος, -ου, m., death.
θάπτω, I bury.
θάσσων, -ον, comp. of ταχύς, faster.
θαῦμα, -ατος, n., wonder.
θαυμάζω, I wonder at, admire, wonder.
θεά, -ᾶς, f., goddess.
Θεμιστοκλῆς, m., Themistocles.
θεός, -οῦ, m., god.
θεράπαινα, -ης, f., maidservant.
θεραπεύω, I honour, worship, heal, cure, look after.
θεράπων, -οντος, m., servant.
Θερμοπύλαι, -ῶν, f. pl., Thermopylae.
θερμός, -ή, -όν, warm.
θέρος, -ους, n., summer.
θέω, I run.
Θῆβαι, -ῶν, f. pl., Thebes, name of cities, (i) in Boeotia, (ii) in Egypt.
θῆλυς, -εια, -υ, female.
θήρ, θηρός, m., wild beast.
θηρευτής, -οῦ, m., hunter.
θηρεύω, I hunt.
θηρίον, -ου, n., beast.
θησαυρός, -ου, m., treasure-house.
Θήχης, Theches, mountain in Armenia.
θόρυβος, -ου, m., uproar.
θρόνος, -ου, m., throne.
θυγάτηρ, θυγατρός, f., daughter.

θύρα, -ας, f., door.
θύω, I sacrifice.
θώραξ, -ακος, m., breastplate.

Ἰάσων, -ονος, m., Jason, leader of the Argonauts.
ἰατρός, -οῦ, m., doctor.
ἰδέα, -ας, f., appearance.
ἰδών, see ὁράω.
ἱερεύς, -έως, m., priest.
ἱερόν, -οῦ, n., temple.
ἱερός, -ά, -όν, sacred.
ἱμάτιον, -ου, n., cloak.
ἵνα, in order that.
ἱππεύς, -έως, m., cavalryman; pl., cavalry.
Ἱππίας, -ου, m., Hippias.
ἵππος, -ου, m., horse; ἡ ἵππος, cavalry.
Ἰσθμός, -οῦ, m., the Isthmus of Corinth.
ἰσχυρός, -ά, -όν, strong.
Ἰταλία, -ας, f., Italy.
ἰχθύς, -ύος, m., fish.
Ἴωνες, -ων, m. pl., Ionians.

καθεύδω, I sleep.
καθίζω, I sit.
καί, and, also, even.
καιρός, -οῦ, m., right time, opportunity.
καίω, I burn, kindle.
κάκιστος, superl. of κακός.
κακός, -ή, -όν, bad, wicked.
κακῶς, badly.
κάλαμος, -ου, m., reed.
καλέω, I call, summon.

Καλλίμαχος, -ου, m., Callimachus.

κάλλιστος, *superl. of* καλός.

καλός, -ή, -όν, beautiful, fine.

καλύπτω, I cover.

κάμηλος, -ου, c., camel.

καρπός, -οῦ, m., fruit.

Καρχηδόνιοι, -ων, m. pl., Carthaginians.

κατά (Acc.), by way of, according to; κατὰ γῆν, by land; (Gen.), under.

καταβαίνω, I go down.

καταδύω, I sink (*trans.*); καταδύομαι, I sink (*intrans.*).

κατακαίω, κατεκαύθην, I burn down.

καταλαμβάνω, I capture.

καταλείπω, κατέλιπον, I leave behind.

καταλύω, I destroy.

καταμένω, I stay behind.

κατασκευάζω, I build.

καταστρέφομαι, I subdue.

κατάστρωμα, -ατος, n., deck.

καταφεύγω, I flee for refuge.

κατήγορος, -ου, m., accuser.

κάτω, underneath.

κελεύω, I order.

κενός, -ή, -όν, empty.

κέρας, κέρατος, n., wing (*of army*).

κεφαλή, -ῆς, f., head.

κῆρυξ, -υκος, m., herald.

κιθάρα, -ας, f., harp.

κιθαρῳδός, -οῦ, m., harp-player.

κινδυνεύω, I run risks.

κίνδυνος, -ου, m., danger.

κινέω, I move.

κλείω, I shut.

Κλεομένης, -ους, m., Cleomenes.

κλέπτω, ἔκλεψα, I steal.

Κλέων, -ωνος, m., Cleon.

κλῖμαξ, -ακος, f., ladder.

κλίνη, -ης, f., couch.

κοινόν, -οῦ, n., public treasury.

κοίτη, -ης, f., bed.

κολάζω, κολάσω, ἐκόλασα, ἐκολάσθην, I punish.

κολωνός, -οῦ, m., cairn.

κομίζω, ἐκόμισα, I convey; κομίζομαι, I recover.

κόπτω, κόψω, ἔκοψα, I cut, cut down, shatter.

Κορίνθιος, -α, -ον, Corinthian.

Κόρινθος, -ου, f., Corinth.

κόρυς, -υθος, f., helmet.

κοσμέω, I adorn.

κοῦφος, -η, -ον, light.

κρατέω (Gen.), I conquer, become master of.

κρατήρ, -ῆρος, m., bowl.

κραυγή, -ῆς, f., shout.

κριτής, -οῦ, m., judge.

Κροῖσος, -ου, m., Croesus.

κροκόδειλος, -ου, m., crocodile.

κρύπτω, ἔκρυψα, κέκρυφα, I hide.

κτῆμα, -ατος, n., possession.

κυβερνήτης, -ου, m., helmsman.

κυρβασία, -ας, f., turban.

κύριος, -α, -ον, appointed.

κωλύω, I hinder, prevent, keep *someone* from.

κώμη, -ης, f., village.

κώνωψ, -ωπος, m., gnat.

λάθρα, secretly.
Λακεδαιμόνιος, -ου, m., a Spartan.
λαμβάνω, ἔλαβον, ἐλήφθην, I take, capture, catch, arrest.
λανθάνω, I escape the notice of.
λέγω, aor. εἶπον, I say, speak.
λειμών, -ῶνος, m., meadow.
λείπω, λείψω, ἔλιπον, λέλειμμαι, ἐλείφθην, I leave.
Λέσβιοι, -ων, m. pl., Lesbians.
λέων, -οντος, m., lion.
Λεωνίδας, m., Leonidas.
λῃστής, -οῦ, m., robber.
λίθινος, -η, -ον, of stone.
λίθος, -ου, m., stone.
λιμήν, -ένος, m., harbour.
λίμνη, -ης, f., marsh, lake.
λόγος, -ου, m., word.
λοιπός, -ή, -όν, rest, remaining.
λοχαγός, -οῦ, m., captain.
Λυδοί, -ῶν, m. pl., Lydians.
λύω, I loose, set free; I break; λύομαι, I ransom.

μακρός, -ά, -όν, long.
μάλιστα, very much, exceedingly, especially.
μᾶλλον, more.
μανθάνω, ἔμαθον, I learn.
μαντεῖον, -ου, n., oracle.
Μαραθών, -ῶνος, m., Marathon.
μάστιξ, -ιγος, f., whip.
μάτην, in vain.
μάχη, -ης, f., battle.
μάχομαι, ἐμαχεσάμην, I fight.
μέγας, μεγάλη, μέγα, large, big, great.

μέγεθος, -ους, n., size.
μέγιστος, superl. of μέγας.
μείζων, -ον, comp. of μέγας.
μέλας, μέλαινα, μέλαν, black.
μέλλω (with fut. infin.), I am about to.
μέμνημαι (Gen.), perf. mid., I remember.
μέν, on the one hand; οἱ μέν ... οἱ δέ, some ..., others.
μέντοι (2nd word), however.
μένω, ἔμεινα, I remain; wait for.
μέρος, -ους, n., part.
μεσογεία, -ας, f., the interior.
μέσος, -η, -ον, middle.
Μεσσήνιοι, -ων, m. pl., Messenians, people in S.W. of Peloponnese.
μετά (Acc.), after; (Gen.), with.
μέταλλον, -ου, n., mine.
μεταξύ, between; ἐν τῷ μεταξύ, meanwhile.
μεταπέμπομαι, μετεπεμψάμην, I send for.
μή, not.
μηδέ, and not.
μηδείς, (Gen.) μηδενός, no one.
Μῆδοι, -ων, m. pl., Medes.
μήν, μηνός, m., month.
μήτε ... μήτε, neither ... nor.
μήτηρ, μητρός, f., mother.
μία, see εἷς.
μικρός, -ά, -όν, small.
Μιλήσιος, -α, -ον, Milesian, of Miletus.
Μίλητος, -ου, f., Miletus, city in Caria, in Asia Minor.

Μιλτιάδης, -ου, m., Miltiades.
μισέω, I hate.
μισθόομαι, I hire.
μοῖρα, -ας, f., part.
μόνον, only.
μόνος, -η, -ον, alone, only.
Μοῦσα, -ης, f., Muse.
μύζω, I suck.
μωρία, -ας, f., folly.
μῶρος, -α, -ον, foolish.

ναυμαχέω, I fight a sea-battle.
ναυμαχία, -ας, f., sea-battle.
ναῦς, νεώς, f., ship.
ναύτης, -ου, m., sailor.
ναυτικόν, -οῦ, n., fleet.
νεανίας, -ου, m., young man.
νῆσος, -ου, f., island.
νικάω, I conquer; win.
νίκη, -ης, f., victory.
Νικίας, -ου, m., Nicias.
Νίτωκρις, f., Nitocris, a queen of Babylon.
νομίζω, ἐνόμισα, I think.
νόμος, -ου, m., law.
νόσος, -ου, f., disease, illness.
νῦν, now.
νύξ, νυκτός, f., night.
νῶτον, -ου, n., back; κατὰ νώτου, in the rear.

ξενίζω, I entertain.
ξένος, -ου, m., friend, stranger.
Ξενοφῶν, -ῶντος, m., Xenophon.
Ξέρξης, -ου, m., Xerxes.
ξύλινος, -η, -ον, wooden.
ξύλον, -ου, n., wood, firewood.

ὁ, ἡ, τό, the; ὁ δέ, and he, he; οἱ μέν . . . , οἱ δέ, some . . . , others.
ὅδε, ἥδε, τόδε, this (near me).
ὀδμή, -ῆς, f., smell.
ὁδός, -οῦ, f., road, way, journey.
ὀδούς, ὀδόντος, m., tooth.
Ὀδυσσεύς, -έως, m., Odysseus.
ὅθεν, whence.
οἶδα, imperf. ᾔδη, infin. εἰδέναι, I know.
οἴκαδε, homewards.
οἰκεῖος, -α, -ον, related; so οἱ οἰκεῖοι, relations.
οἰκέτης, -ου, m., member of household, slave; pl., family.
οἰκέω, I inhabit; live, dwell.
οἰκία, -ας, f., house.
οἰκίζω, ᾤκισα, I found.
οἰκοδομέω, I build.
οἰκτείρω, ᾤκτειρα, I pity.
οἶνος, -ου, m., wine.
οἷός τέ εἰμι, I am able, can.
ὀκτώ, eight.
ὀλίγος, -η, -ον, little, few.
ὅλος, -η, -ον, whole.
ὁμαίμων, -ον, related by blood.
ὄνομα, -ατος, n., name.
ὄνος, -ου, m., ass.
ὀξύς, -εῖα, -ύ, sharp.
ὄπισθε (Gen.), behind.
ὅπλα, -ων, n. pl., arms.
ὁπλίζω, I arm.
ὁπλίτης, -ου, m., hoplite (heavy-armed soldier).
ὅποι, whither.
ὁπόσος, -η, -ον, how much, how many.

ὅπου, where.

ὅπως, in order that.

ὁράω, εἶδον (ἰδών, *aor. partic.*), I see.

ὀργίζομαι, I grow angry.

ὁρμάομαι, I start.

ὄρνις, -ιθος, *c.*, bird.

ὄρος, -ους, *n.*, mountain.

ὀρυκτός, -ή, -όν, dug out.

ὀρύσσω, ὤρυξα, ὠρύχθην, I dig.

ὅς, ἥ, ὅ, who, which.

ὅτε, when.

ὅτι, because; that (*after Verbs of 'saying', etc.*).

οὐ, οὐκ (*before smooth breathing*), οὐχ (*before rough breathing*), not.

οὗ, where.

οὐδέ, and not, nor (*after preceding neg. clause*).

οὐδείς, οὐδεμία, οὐδέν, no one, nothing; *Gen.* οὐδενός, *etc.*; (*Adj.*), no.

οὐκέτι, no longer.

οὖν (*2nd word*), therefore.

οὔποτε, never.

οὔπω, not yet.

οὖς, ὠτός, *n.*, ear.

οὔτε ... οὔτε, neither ... nor.

οὗτος, αὕτη, τοῦτο, this.

οὕτω, οὕτως (*with Adj. or Advb.*), so.

οὕτως, thus, in this way.

ὀφθαλμος, -ου, *m.*, eye.

ὄψις, -εως, *f.*, sight, presence.

παιδεύω, I train, educate.

παίζω, I play.

παῖς, παιδός, *c.*, child, boy, son, daughter.

πάλαι, of old, long ago.

πάλιν (*Advb.*), back.

πανσέληνος, -ου, *f.*, full moon.

πανταχοῦ, everywhere.

παρά (*Acc.*), to the presence of, to; (*Gen.*), from; (*Dat.*), at the side of, at the court of.

παρακαλέω, I summon.

παρασκευάζω, I prepare; παρασκευαζομαι, I get ready.

πάρειμι, I am present, have arrived.

παρέχω, I cause, produce, provide.

πᾶς, πᾶσα, πᾶν, all, every, whole.

πάσχω, ἔπαθον, I suffer.

πατήρ, πατρός, *m.*, father.

πατρίς, -ίδος, *f.*, fatherland, country.

παύω, I stop (*trans.*); παύομαι (*Gen.*), I cease (from).

πέδη, -ης, *f.*, fetter.

πεζοί, -ῶν, *m. pl.*, infantry.

πείθω, πείσω, ἔπεισα, πέπεισμαι, ἐπείσθην, I persuade; πείθομαι, πείσομαι, ἐπιθόμην (*Dat.*), I obey.

πειράομαι, I try.

πέλαγος, -ους, *n.*, sea.

πέλεκυς, -εως, *m.*, axe.

Πελοποννήσιοι, -ων, *m. pl.*, Peloponnesians.

πελταστής, -οῦ, *m.*, targeteer (*soldier with light shield*).

πέμπτος, -η, -ον, fifth.

πέμπω, πέμψω, ἔπεμψα, πέπομφα, ἐπέμφθην, I send.

πέντε, five.

πεντήκοντα, fifty.

πεντηκόντερος, -ου, f., ship with fifty oars.

περί (Acc.), round; (Gen.), concerning.

Περίανδρος, -ου, m., Periander.

περιβάλλω, I embrace.

περίειμι, I survive.

περιέρχομαι, infin. περιιέναι, περιῆλθον, I go round.

περίοδος, -ου, f., map.

περιπλέω, I sail round.

Πέρσης, -ου, m., a Persian.

Περσικός, -ή, -όν, Persian.

πηλός, -οῦ, m., mud, clay.

πῆχυς, -εως, m., cubit (*about* 18 *inches*).

πιέζω, I weigh down, press hard, distress.

πιθανός, -ή, -όν, persuasive.

πιθέσθαι, *see* πείθομαι.

πίναξ, -ακος, m., tablet.

πίνω, I drink.

πίπτω, I fall.

πιστεύω (Dat.), I trust, believe.

πιστός, -ή, -όν, faithful.

πλεῖστος, -η, -ον, *superl. of* πολύς, very much, very many, most.

πλείων, -ον, *comp. of* πολύς, more.

πλέω, ἔπλευσα, I sail.

πληγή, -ῆς, f., blow.

πλήν (Gen.), except.

πληρόω, I man.

πλοῖον, -ου, n., boat.

πλούσιος, -α, -ον, rich.

πλοῦτος, -ου, m., wealth.

πόθεν; from where?

ποῖ; whither?

ποιέω, I make, do; treat.

ποιητής, -οῦ, m., poet.

ποιμήν, -ένος, m., shepherd.

πολεμέω, I make war upon.

πολέμιοι, -ων, m. pl., enemy.

πολέμιος, -α, -ον, hostile.

πόλεμος, -ου, m., war.

πολιορκέω, I besiege.

πόλις, -εως, f., city.

πολίτης, -ου, m., citizen.

πολλάκις, often.

πολλῷ, by much, far.

Πολυκράτης, -ους, m., Polycrates.

πολύς, πολλή, πολύ, much, many.

πονέω, I toil.

πορεύομαι, I march.

πόσος, -η, -ον; how much? *in plur.*, how many?

ποταμός, -οῦ, m., river.

ποτέ, once (*upon a time*).

πότερον . . . ἤ, whether . . . or.

πότερος, -α, -ον, which of two.

ποῦ; where?

πούς, ποδός, m., foot.

πρᾶγμα, -ατος, n., matter, affair.

Πραξιτέλης, -ους, m., Praxiteles, a famous Greek sculptor.

πράσσω, πράξω, ἔπραξα, πέπραχα (*I have done*), πέπραγα (*I have fared*), πέπραγμαι, ἐπράχθην, I do, transact; I fare.

πρέσβυς, -εως, *m.*, old man;
πρέσβεις, ambassadors.

πρίν (Advb.), before.

πρό (Gen.), before, in front of.

προαιρέομαι, I prefer.

προκαλέομαι, I invite.

πρός (Acc.), to, towards, against
(*of fighting*); πρὸς βίαν, by
force; (Dat.), in addition to.

προσάγω, I move *something* towards.

προσαιρέομαι, προσειλόμην, I
choose as colleague.

προσβάλλω, προσβαλῶ, προσέβαλον (Dat.), I attack.

προσειλόμην, *see* προσαιρέομαι.

προσέρχομαι, προσῆλθον (Dat.),
I approach.

προσπίπτω, προσέπεσον (Dat.),
I attack.

προστάσσω, προσέταξα, I order.

πρόσωπον, -ου, *n.*, face.

πρότερον, formerly, before.

προχωρέω, I advance.

πρύμνα, -ης, *f.*, stern.

πρωτεύω, I hold the first place.

πρῶτον (Advb.), first, at first.

πρῶτος, -η, -ον, first.

πύλη, -ης, *f.*, gate.

Πύλος, -ου, *f.*, Pylos.

πυνθάνομαι, I learn, ascertain.

πῦρ, πυρός, *n.*, fire.

πύργος, -ου, *m.*, tower.

ῥάδιος, -α, -ον, easy.

ῥᾷστα, *superl. of* ῥᾳδίως, very
easily.

ῥᾴων, -ον, *comp. of* ῥᾴδιος, easier.

ῥήτωρ, -ορος, *m.*, orator.

ῥίπτω, ἔρριψα, I throw.

Σαλαμίς, -ῖνος, *f.*, Salamis,
island opposite Athens.

σάλπιγξ, -γγος, *f.*, trumpet.

Σάμιοι, *m. pl.*, Samians.

Σάμος, -ου, *f.*, Samos.

σαφής, -ές, clear.

σεαυτόν, -ήν, -ό, yourself (*sing.
reflexive*).

σημαίνω, I signify, mean, signal.

σήμερον, today.

Σικελία, -ας, *f.*, Sicily.

Σίκιννος, -ου, *m.*, Sicinnus.

σῖτος, -ου, *m.*, food.

σκευή, -ῆς, *f.*, dress, attire.

σκηνή, -ῆς, *f.*, tent.

σκιά, -ᾶς, *f.*, shade.

σός, σή, σόν, your (*s.*).

Σοῦσα, -ων, *n. pl.*, Susa, royal
city in Persia.

σοφία, -ας, *f.*, wisdom.

σοφός, -ή, -όν, wise.

Σπάρτη, -ης, *f.*, Sparta.

σπείρω, I sow.

σπεύδω, I hasten.

σπονδαί, -ῶν, *f.*, truce.

στέγη, -ης, *f.*, roof.

στέφανος, -ου, *m.*, crown.

στόμα, -ατος, *n.*, mouth, entrance.

στράτευμα, -ατος, *n.*, army.

στρατεύω, I march, go upon an
expedition.

στρατηγός, -οῦ, *m.*, general.

στρατιά, -ᾶς, *f.*, army.

στρατιώτης, -ου, *m.*, soldier.

στρατοπεδεύομαι, I encamp.

στρατόπεδον, -ου, *n.*, camp.

στρατός, -οῦ, *m.*, army.

Στρυμών, -όνος, *m.*, the Strymon, a river in Thrace.

σύ, you (*s.*).

συγγιγνώσκω (Dat.), I pardon.

συλάω, I ravage.

συλλαμβάνω, I arrest.

συμβουλεύω (Dat.), I advise.

συμμαχία, -ας, *f.*, alliance.

σύμμαχος, -ου, *m.*, ally.

συμφορά, -ᾶς, *f.*, misfortune, disaster.

συνάγω, συνήγαγον, I lead together, assemble, draw together.

Συρακόσιοι, -ων, *m. pl.*, Syracusans.

Συράκουσαι -ῶν, *f. pl.*, Syracuse.

συχνός, -ή, -όν, *in plur.*, many.

Σφακτηρία, -ας, *f.*, Sphacteria.

σφραγίς, -ῖδος, *f.*, ring.

σχίζω, I split.

σῴζω, σώσω, ἔσωσα, σέσωκα, σέσωσμαι, ἐσώθην, I save; σῴζομαι, I get safely back.

Σωκράτης, -ους, *m.*, Socrates.

σῶμα, -ατος, *n.*, body.

σωτηρία, -ας, *f.*, safety.

σώφρων, -ον, prudent.

ταμίας, -ου, *m.*, steward.

Τάρας, -αντος, *m.*, Tarentum, a city in south Italy.

ταράσσω, ἐτάραξα, I throw into confusion.

τάσσω, τάξω, ἔταξα, τέταχα, τέταγμαι, ἐτάχθην, I draw up.

τάφος, -ου, *m.*, tomb.

τάφρος, -ου, *f.*, ditch.

ταχέως, quickly.

τάχιστα, *superl. of* ταχέως.

ταχύς, -εῖα, -ύ, swift.

τε, both (*before* καί).

τειχίζω, ἐτείχισα, I fortify.

τείχισμα, -ατος, *n.*, fortification.

τεῖχος, -ους, *n.*, wall.

τέκνον, -ου, *n.*, child.

τέλος, at last.

τέμνω, I cut.

τέσσαρες, -α, four.

τέταρτος, -η, -ον, fourth.

τέχνη, -ης, *f.*, skill.

τίκτω, I breed, lay (*eggs*).

τιμάω, I honour.

τίμη, -ης, *f.*, honour.

τίς, τί; who? what?

τις, τι, a certain; someone, anyone.

τοίνυν (2nd word), therefore.

τοιοῦτος, τοιαύτη, τοιοῦτο, such.

τολμάω, I dare.

τόξευμα, -ατος, *n.*, arrow.

τοξεύω, I shoot (*with an arrow*).

τόξον, -ου, *n.*, bow.

τοξότης, -ου, *m.*, archer.

τόπος, -ου, *m.*, place.

τοσοῦτος, τοσαύτη, τοσοῦτο, so great; *pl.*, so many; ἐς τοσοῦτο(ν), so much (*used as* Advb.).

τότε, then, at that time.

τράπεζα, -ης, *f.*, table.

τρεῖς, τρία, three.

τρέπω, ἔτρεψα, I turn, rout.

τρέφω, I feed.

τρέχω, I run.

τριακόσιοι, -αι, -α, three hundred.

τριήραρχος, -ου, m., captain of trireme.

τριήρης, -ους, f., trireme.

Τροιζήν, -ῆνος, f., Troezen, a city in Argolis.

τρόπος, -ου, m., way.

τύπτω, ἔτυψα, τέτυμμαι, I beat, hit.

τύραννος, -ου, m., tyrant.

τύχῃ, by chance.

ὑβρίζω, ὕβρισα, ὕβρισμαι, I insult.

ὕδωρ, ὕδατος, n., water.

υἱός, -οῦ, m., son.

ὕλη, -ης, f., a wood.

ὑμεῖς, you (pl.).

ὑμέτερος, -α, -ον, your (pl.).

ὑπείκω, ὑπείξω, I yield, give in.

ὑπέρ (Acc.), beyond; (Gen.), on behalf of.

ὑπερβαίνω, I climb over.

ὑπερβάλλω, I cross.

ὑπισχνέομαι, ὑπεσχόμην, I promise.

ὑπό (Gen.), by (Agent); (Dat.), under.

ὑποζύγιον, -ου, n., beast of burden.

ὑπολαμβάνω, ὑπέλαβον, I take on my back.

ὑπολείπω, ὑπολέλειμμαι I leave behind.

ὑπομένω, I stand firm.

ὗς, ὑός, c., pig.

ὕστερον, later.

ὑψηλός, -ή, -όν, high.

φαίνομαι, I seem.

φανερός, -ά, -όν, visible.

φανερῶς, obviously.

Φεραί, -ῶν, f. pl., Pherae.

φέρω, I carry, bear, endure; φέρομαι, I win.

φεύγω, ἔφυγον, I flee.

φημί, imperf. ἔφην, I say.

φθείρω, I lay waste.

φθονέω, I am jealous.

φιάλη, -ης, f., drinking-bowl.

φιλέω, I love.

φιλία, -ας, f., friendship.

φίλιος, -α, -ον, friendly.

Φιλιππίδης, m., Philippides.

φοβέομαι, I fear.

φόβος, -ου, m., fear.

Φοῖνιξ, -ικος, m., a Phoenician.

Φοίνισσα (f. Adj.), Phoenician.

φορέω, I wear.

φυγάς, -άδος, c., exile.

φυλακή, -ῆς, f., custody, watch.

φυλακτήριον, -ου, n., guard-post.

φύλαξ, -ακος, m., guard.

φυλάσσω, φυλάξω, ἐφύλαξα, πεφύλαχα, ἐφυλάχθην, I guard.

φωνή, -ῆς, f., voice.

χαίρω, I rejoice; κελεύω χαίρειν, I bid farewell to.

χαλεπαίνω, I grow annoyed.

χαλεπός, -ή, -όν, difficult, dangerous.

χαλκοῦς, -ῆ, -οῦν, of bronze.

χαρίζομαι (Dat.), I curry favour with.

χάρις, χάριτος, f., thanks; χάριν ἔχω, I feel grateful.

χειμών, -ῶνος, m., storm, winter.

χείρ, χειρός, f., hand; εἰς χεῖρας ἐλθεῖν, to come to grips.

χήν, χηνός, f., goose.

χίλιοι, -αι, -α, a thousand.

χιλός, -οῦ, m., grass.

χιτών, -ῶνος, m., tunic.

χιών, -όνος, f., snow.

χορεύω, I dance.

χράομαι (Dat.), I use.

χρήματα, -άτων, n. pl., money.

χρήσιμος, -η, -ον, useful.

χρόνος, -ου, m., time.

χρυσός, -οῦ, m., gold.

χρυσοῦς, -ῆ, -οῦν, golden.

χώρα, -ας, f., country.

χωρέω, I advance, withdraw.

χωρίον, -ου, n., place.

ψευδής, -ές, false.

ψηφίζομαι, I vote, vote for.

ψιλοί, -ῶν, m. pl., light troops.

ψυχή, -ῆς, f., life.

ὦ (with Voc.), O.

ὧδε, thus.

ὦμος, -ου, m., shoulder.

ᾠόν, -οῦ, n., egg.

ὥρα, -ας, f., right time, season.

ὡς, when; since, because; as; in order that; that (after Verbs of 'saying', etc.).

ὡς (Acc.), to (a person).

ὡς τάχιστα, as quickly as possible.

ὥσπερ, just as.

ὥστε, that, so that (consecutive).

ὦτα, see οὖς.

English–Greek Vocabulary

Tenses of Irregular Verbs are only given so far as they are needed in the exercises

Able, I am, οἷός τέ εἰμι.

about to, I am, μέλλω with fut. infin.

about (*concerning*), περί (Gen.).

absent, I am, ἄπειμι.

accomplish, I, πράσσω, perf. pass. πέπραγμαι.

account of, on, διά (Acc.).

Acropolis, Ἀκρόπολις, -εως, f.

act, I, πράσσω.

Admetus, Ἄδμητος, -ου, m.

admire, I, θαυμάζω.

advance, I, προχωρέω.

advise, I, συμβουλεύω (Dat.).

affairs of, the, τὰ with Gen.

afraid, I am, φοβέομαι.

after, μετά (Acc.).

against, ἐπί (Acc.).

Alcestis, Ἄλκηστις, -ιδος, f.

all, πᾶς, πᾶσα, πᾶν.

allies, σύμμαχοι, -ων, m. pl.

already, ἤδη.

also, καί.

always, ἀεί.

am, I, εἰμί, ἔσομαι, ἦν; infin. εἶναι, partic. ὤν, οὖσα, ὄν.

ambassador, πρέσβυς, -εως, m.

among, ἐν (Dat.).

ancient, ἀρχαῖος, -α, -ον.

and, καί.

angry, I grow, ὀργίζομαι.

animal, ζῷον, -ου, n.

announce, I, ἀγγέλλω, ἤγγειλα.

answer, I, ἀποκρίνομαι, ἀπεκρινάμην.

Apollo, Ἀπόλλων, -ωνος, m.

appear, I, φαίνομαι.

Arion, Ἀρίων, -ονος, m.

Aristagoras, Ἀρισταγόρας, -ου, m.

Armenia, Ἀρμενία, -ας, f.

Armenians, Ἀρμένιοι, -ων, m. pl.

arms (*weapons*), ὅπλα, -ων, n. pl.

army, στρατιά, -ᾶς, f.; στράτευμα, -ατος, n.

arrive, I, ἀφικνέομαι, ἀφίξομαι, ἀφικόμην.

as (*since*), ἐπεί.

ask for, I, αἰτέω (Acc.).

ask (*question*), I, ἐρωτάω, ἠρόμην or ἠρώτησα.

assembly, ἐκκλησία, -ας, f.

at, ἐν (Dat.).

Athenian, an, Ἀθηναῖος, -ου, m.

Athens, Ἀθῆναι, -ῶν, (f. pl.); to Athens, Ἀθήναζε (Advb.).

attack, I, προσβάλλω, προσέβαλον (Dat.).

Attica, Ἀττική, -ῆς, f.

axe, πέλεκυς, -εως, m.

160

Babylon, Βαβυλών, -ῶνος, f.

bad, κακός, -ή, -όν.

badly, κακῶς.

barbarians, βάρβαροι, -ων, m. pl.

battle, μάχη, -ης, f.

bear, I, φέρω.

beautiful, καλός, -ή, -όν; comp. καλλίων,-ον; superl. κάλλιστος.

because, ὅτι.

because of, διά (Acc.).

become, I, γίγνομαι.

before (Prep.), πρό (Gen.).

before (Advb.), πρότερον.

beg, I, αἰτέω, ᾔτησα.

behind, ὄπισθε (Gen.).

believe, I, πιστεύω (Dat.).

best, ἄριστος, -η, -ον.

better, ἀμείνων, -ον.

big, μέγας, μεγάλη, μέγα; comp. μείζων, -ον; superl. μέγιστος.

bird, ὄρνις, -ιθος, c.

bitter, ὀξύς, -εῖα, -ύ.

black, μέλας, μέλαινα, μέλαν.

body, σῶμα, -ατος, n.

book, βίβλος, -ου, f.

both ... and, -τε καί.

bowl, κρατήρ, -ῆρος, m.

boy, παῖς, παιδός, m.

brave, ἀνδρεῖος, -α, -ον.

bravery, ἀνδρεία, -ας, f.

breastplate, θώραξ, -ακος, m.

bridge, γέφυρα, -ας, f.

bring, I, φέρω; (back), ἀπάγω.

broad, εὐρύς, -εῖα, -ύ.

build, I, οἰκοδομέω.

burn, I, καίω.

bury, I, θάπτω.

but ἀλλά in a corresponding or contrasting clause, δέ, after a previous μέν.

by (Agent), ὑπό (Gen.).

by (way of), κατά (Acc.), e.g. by sea, κατὰ θάλασσαν; by land, κατὰ γῆν.

Call (by name), I, ὀνομάζω.

camel, κάμηλος, -ου, c.

camp, στρατόπεδον, -ου, n.

can, I, οἷός τέ εἰμι.

captain, λοχαγός, -οῦ, m.

capture, I, λαμβάνω, λήψομαι, ἔλαβον, ἐλήφθην; αἱρέω, εἷλον, ᾑρέθην.

carry, I, φέρω, ἤνεγκα; κομίζω, ἐκόμισα.

catch, I, see capture.

cavalry, use pl. of ἱππεύς, -έως, m., horseman.

cease from, I, παύομαι with Gen.

certain, a, τις, τι (after a Noun).

child, τέκνον, -ου, n.; παῖς, παιδός, c.

citizen, πολίτης, -ου, m.

city, πόλις, -εως, f.

clear, σαφής, -ές.

Cleon, Κλέων, -ωνος, m.

clever, δεινός, -ή, -όν.

colony, ἀποικία, -ας, f.

come, I, ἔρχομαι, fut. εἶμι.

command, I am in, ἄρχω.

compel, I, ἀναγκάζω, ἀναγκάσω, ἠνάγκασα, ἠναγκάσθην.

conquer, I, νικάω.

contest, ἅμιλλα, -ης, f.; ἀγών, -ῶνος

country, χώρα, -ας, f.; (*native land*), πατρίς, -ίδος, f.

courage, ἀνδρεία, -ας, f.; ἀρετή, -ῆς, f.

cowardly, δειλός, -ή, -όν.

Croesus, Κροῖσος, -ου, m.

cross (*river*), I, διαβαίνω, διέβην; (*mountain*), ὑπερβαίνω.

cure, I, θεραπεύω.

cut, cut down, I, κόπτω.

Cyrus, Κῦρος, -ου, m.

Damage, I, *see* harm.

danger, κίνδυνος, -ου, m.

dangerous, χαλεπός, -ή, -όν.

Darius, Δαρεῖος, -ου, m.

daughter, θυγατήρ, θυγατρός, f.

day, ἡμέρα, -ας, f.

death, θάνατος, -ου, m.

deed, ἔργον, -ου, n.

deep, βαθύς, -εῖα, -ύ.

defeat, I, νικάω.

deliberate, I, βουλεύομαι.

Demosthenes, Δημοσθένης, -ους, m.

depart, I, ἀπέρχομαι, ἀπῆλθον.

destroy, I, καταλύω.

die, I, ἀποθνήσκω, ἀπέθανον.

difficult, χαλεπός, -ή, -όν.

discover, I, εὑρίσκω, εὗρον.

do, I, ποιέω.

doctor, ἰατρός, -οῦ, m.

door, θύρα, -ας, f.

drag, I, ἕλκω.

draw up, I, τάσσω, τάξω, ἔταξα, τέταχα, τέταγμαι, ἐτάχθην.

drive, I, ἐλαύνω.

Earth, γῆ, γῆς, f.

easily, ῥαδίως; comp. ῥᾷον.

easy, ῥάδιος, -α, -ον; superl. ῥᾷστος.

eat, I, ἐσθίω.

educate, I, παιδεύω.

Egyptians, Αἰγύπτιοι, -ων, m. pl.

empty, κενός, -ή, -όν.

encamp, I, στρατοπεδεύομαι.

enemy, πολέμιοι, -ων, m. pl.; (*a private enemy*), ἐχθρός, -οῦ, m.

enslave, I, δουλόω.

enter, I, εἰσέρχομαι, εἰσῆλθον.

escape, I, ἀποφεύγω, ἀπέφυγον.

even, καί.

evening, ἑσπέρα, -ας, f.

every, *see* all.

exile, φυγάς, -άδος, c.

Faithful, πιστός, -ή, -όν.

fall, I, πίπτω.

false, ψευδής, -ές.

fare, I, πράσσω, πράξω, ἔπραξα, πέπραγα.

faster (Advb.), θᾶσσον.

father, πατήρ, πατρός, m.

fear, I, φοβέομαι.

feel grateful, I, χάριν ἔχω.

few, ὀλίγοι, -αι, -α.

fewer, ἐλάσσονες, -α.

fight, I, μάχομαι, ἐμαχεσάμην.

find, find out, I, εὑρίσκω.

fine, καλός, -ή, -όν.

fish, ἰχθύς, -ύος, m.

fisherman, ἁλιεύς, -έως, m.

five, πέντε.

flee, I, φεύγω, ἔφυγον.

fleet, ναυτικόν, -οῦ, n.

food, σῖτος, -ου, m.

foolish, μῶρος, -α, -ον.

for (*on account of*), διά (Acc.).

for (*on behalf of*), ὑπέρ (Gen.).

for (*a purpose*), εἰς (Acc.).

fortunate, εὐτυχής, -ές.

found, I, οἰκίζω.

fourth, τέταρτος, -η, -ον.

free, I, ἐλευθερόω.

free, ἐλεύθερος, -α, -ον.

freedom, ἐλευθερία, -ας, f.

friend, φίλος, -ου, m.

friendly, φίλιος, -α, -ον.

friendship, φιλία, -ας, f.

from, ἀπό (Gen.).

fruit, καρπός, -οῦ, m.

Gate, πύλη, -ης, f.

general, στρατηγός, -οῦ, m.

giant, γίγας, -αντος, m.

gift, δῶρον, -ου, n.

girl, παῖς, παιδός, f.

glory, δόξα, -ης, f.

gnat, κώνωψ, -ωπος, m.

go, I, ἔρχομαι, εἶμι, ἦλθον;
(away), ἀποχωρέω; ἀπέρχομαι; (out), ἐξέρχομαι.

goat, αἴξ, αἰγός, c.

god, θεός, -οῦ, m.

goddess, θεά, -ᾶς, f.

good, ἀγαθός, -ή, -όν.

grateful, I feel, χάριν ἔχω.

great, μέγας, μεγάλη, μέγα;
comp. μείζων, -ον; *superl.*
μέγιστος.

Greece, Ἑλλάς, -άδος, f.

Greek, a, Ἕλλην, -ηνος, m.

guard, I, φυλάσσω, φυλάξω, ἐφύλαξα, πεφύλαχα, ἐφυλάχθην.

guard, φύλαξ, -ακος, m.

guide, ἡγεμών, -όνος, m.

Harbour, λιμήν, -ένος, m.

harm, I, βλάπτω, βλάψω, ἔβλαψα, βέβλαφα, βέβλαμμαι.

harsh, χαλεπός, -ή, -όν.

hate, I, μισέω.

have, I, ἔχω; *or express by* ἐστὶν ἐμοί.

heal, I, θεραπεύω.

hear, I, ἀκούω, ἤκουσα.

heavy, βαρύς, -εῖα, -ύ; *superl.*
βαρύτατος.

helmet, κόρυς, -υθος, f.

help, I, ὠφελέω (Acc.); βοηθέω (Dat.).

help, βοήθεια, -ας, f.

her (*possess. pron.*), αὐτῆς; her own (*reflex.*), ἑαυτῆς.

Heracles, Ἡρακλῆς, -έους, m.

herald, κῆρυξ, -υκος, m.

here, ἐνθάδε.

here, I am, πάρειμι.

herself (*ipsa*), αὐτή.

herself (*reflex.*) ἑαυτήν.

hide, I, κρύπτω, κρύψω, ἔκρυψα, κέκρυφα, κέκρυμμαι.

high, ὑψηλός, -ή, -όν.

hill, ὄρος, -ους, n.

him, *oblique Cases of* αὐτός.

himself, herself, itself (*ipse, etc.*),
αὐτός, -ή, -ό.

hinder, I, κωλύω.

his, αὐτοῦ.

his own (*reflex.*), ἑαυτοῦ.

home (*homewards*), οἴκαδε.
honour, I, θεραπεύω, τιμάω.
honour, τίμη, -ης, *f.*
hope, I, ἐλπίζω, ἤλπισα.
hope, ἐλπίς, -ίδος, *f.*
horse, ἵππος, -ου, *m.*
hostile, ἐχθρός, -ά, -όν; *comp.*
  ἐχθίων, -ον; *superl.* ἔχθιστος.
house, οἰκία, -ας, *f.*
how? πῶς;
how big (*indir.*), ὁπόσος, -η, -ον
  (*or use* πόσος).
hunt, I, θηρεύω.
hurry, I, σπεύδω.
husband, ἀνήρ, ἀνδρός, *m.*

I, ἐγώ.
ill, I am, νοσέω.
illness, νόσος, -ου, *f.*
in, ἐν (Dat.).
infantry, οἱ πεζοί, -ῶν.
injure, I, βλάπτω.
intend, I, μέλλω *with fut. infin.*
into, εἰς (Acc.).
island, νῆσος, -ου, *f.*
it, *oblique Cases of* αὐτός, -ή, -ό.

Journey, ὁδός, -οῦ, *f.*
judge, κριτής, -οῦ, *m.*
justice, δικαιοσύνη, -ης, *f.*
justly, δικαίως.

Keep from, I, κωλύω ἀπό (Gen.).
kill, I, ἀποκτείνω.
king, βασιλεύς, -έως, *m.*
know, I, οἶδα, *imperf.* ᾔδη.

Lake, λίμνη, -ης, *f.*

land, γῆ, γῆς, *f.*
large, μέγας, μεγάλη, μέγα.
last, at, τέλος.
law, νόμος, -ου, *m.*
lead, I, ἄγω, ἄξω, ἤγαγον, ἦχα,
  ἤχθην.
leave (behind), I, λείπω, λείψω,
  ἔλιπον, λέλοιπα, λέλειμμαι,
  ἐλείφθην; καταλείπω.
Leonidas, Λεωνίδας, *m.*
letter, ἐπιστολή, -ῆς, *f.*
life, βίος, -ου, *m.*
lion, λέων, -οντος, *m.*
listen to, I, ἀκούω (Acc. *of thing*;
  Gen. *of person*).
little, μικρός, -ά, -όν.
long, μακρός, -ά, -όν.
loose, I, λύω.
love, I, φιλέω.

Make, I, ποιέω.
man (*opposed to* woman), ἀνήρ,
  ἀνδρός, *m.*; (*human being*),
  ἄνθρωπος, -ου, *m.*
manage, I, πράσσω, πράξω,
  ἔπραξα, πέπραχα, ἐπράχθην.
many, πολύς, πολλή, πολύ;
  superl. πλεῖστος.
march, I, στρατεύω; πορεύομαι.
market, market-place, ἀγορά,
  -ᾶς, *f.*
master (*of household*), δεσπότης,
  -ου, *m.*
meadow, λειμών, -ῶνος, *m.*
messenger, ἄγγελος, -ου, *m.*
Miltiades, Μιλτιάδης, -ου, *m.*
money, χρήματα, -ων, *n. pl.*
month, μήν, μηνός, *m.*

moon, σελήνη, -ης, f.
more (Adj.), πλείων, -ον.
more (Advb. *of degree*), μᾶλλον.
most, πλεῖστοι.
mother, μήτηρ, μητρός, f.
mountain, ὄρος, -ους, n.
much, πολύς, πολλή, πολύ.
Muse, Μοῦσα, -ης, f.
my, ἐμός, -ή, -όν (*preced. by article*).
myself (*reflex.*), ἐμαυτόν, -ήν.

Name, ὄνομα, -ατος, n.
narrow, στενός, -ή, -όν.
native land, πατρίς, -ίδος, f.
navy, ναυτικόν, -οῦ, n.
near, ἐγγύς (Gen.).
neighbour, γείτων, -ονος, c.
neither . . . nor, οὔτε . . . οὔτε; μήτε . . . μήτε.
net, ἀμφίβληστρον, -ου, n.
never, οὔποτε, μήποτε.
night, νύξ, νυκτός, f.
nobody, οὐδείς; μηδείς.
no longer, οὐκέτι.
no one, *see* nobody.
North Wind, Βορέας, -ου, m.
not, οὐ, οὐκ (*before smooth breathing*), οὐχ (*before rough breathing*); (*in indir. command, with imperative, subjunctive, wish clauses, final clauses, infin. in consecutive clauses*) μή.
not yet, οὔπω.
nothing, οὐδέν.
now, νῦν.

O, ὦ (*with* Voc.).

obey, I, πείθομαι (Dat.).
Odysseus, Ὀδυσσεύς, -έως, m.
old man, γέρων, -οντος, m.
old woman, γραῦς, γραός, f.
on, ἐν, (Dat.); ἐπί (Gen.).
on to, εἰς (Acc.).
once (*upon a time*), ποτέ.
once, at, εὐθύς.
one, εἷς, μία, ἕν.
only, μόνον.
orator, ῥήτωρ, -ορος, m.
order, I, κελεύω.
order that, in, ἵνα, ὡς, ὅπως.
other, ἄλλος, -η, -ο.
our, ἡμέτερος, -α, -ον (*preced. by article*).
ourselves (*reflex.*), ἡμᾶς αὐτούς.
out of, ἐκ (Gen.).
outside, ἔξω (Gen.).
overcome, I, νικάω.
owing to, διά (Acc.).
ox, βοῦς, βοός, c.

Palace, βασίλεια, -ων, n. pl.
pass, εἰσβολή, -ῆς, f.
peace, εἰρήνη, -ης, f.
people, δῆμος, -ου, m.
perceive, I, αἰσθάνομαι, ᾐσθόμην.
Pericles, Περικλῆς, -έους, m.
Persian, a, Πέρσης, -ου, m.
persuade, I, πείθω, πείσω, ἔπεισα, πέπεικα, πέπεισμαι, ἐπείσθην.
pig, ὗς, ὑός, c.
pity, I, οἰκτείρω.
place, τόπος, -ου, m.
plague, νόσος, -ου, f.
plan, βουλή, -ῆς, f.

plant, I, φυτεύω.
pleasant, ἡδύς, -εῖα, -ύ.
poem, ποίημα, -ατος, n.
poet, ποιητής, -οῦ, m.
Polycrates, Πολυκράτης, -ους, m.
power, δύναμις, -εως, f.
present, I am, πάρειμι.
prevent, I, κωλύω.
priest, ἱερεύς, -έως, m.
prison, δεσμωτήριον, -ου, n.
prisoner (of war), αἰχμάλωτος, -ου, m.
prize, ἆθλον, -ου, n.
protect, I, σῴζω, ἔσωσα.
provide, I, παρέχω.
prudent, σώφρων, -ον.
punish, I, κολάζω, κολάσω, ἐκόλασα.
pursue, I, διώκω, διώξω, ἐδίωξα, δεδίωχα, ἐδιώχθην.

Queen, βασίλεια, -ας, f.
quick, ταχύς, -εῖα, -ύ.
quickly, ταχέως; superl. τάχιστα.

Ransom, I, λύομαι.
reach, I, ἀφικνέομαι, ἀφικόμην, εἰς (Acc.).
ready, ἑτοῖμος, -η, -ον.
receive, I, δέχομαι, ἐδεξάμην.
rejoice, I, χαίρω.
remain, I, μένω.
reply, I, ἀποκρίνομαι, ἀπεκρινάμην.
rest, I, ἡσυχάζω.
rest, the, οἱ ἄλλοι.
retreat, I, ἀναχωρέω.

return, I, ἐπανέρχομαι, fut. ἐπάνειμι.
rich, πλούσιος, -α, -ον.
riches, πλοῦτος, -ου, m.
ring, σφραγίς, -ῖδος, f.
river, ποταμός, -οῦ, m.
road, ὁδός, -οῦ, f.
round, περί (Acc.).
rower, ἐρέτης, -ου, m.
rule, I, ἄρχω, ἄρξω, ἦρξα, ἦρχα (Gen.).
rule, ἄρχη, -ης, f.
run, I, τρέχω; (away), ἀποτρέχω.
run risks, I, κινδυνεύω.
runner, δρομεύς, -έως, m.

Sacrifice, I, θύω.
safe, ἀσφαλής, -ές.
sail, I, πλέω; (away), ἀποπλέω, ἀπέπλευσα.
sailor, ναύτης, -ου, m.
same, the, ὁ αὐτός, ἡ αὐτή, τὸ αὐτό.
save (from), I, σῴζω, σώσω, ἔσωσα, σέσωκα, σέσωσμαι, ἐσώθην (ἐκ).
say, I, φημί, imperf. ἔφην; λέγω, εἶπον.
scout, κατάσκοπος, -ου, m.
sea, θάλασσα, -ης, f.
sea-battle, ναυμαχία, -ας, f.
second, δεύτερος, -α, -ον.
see, I, ὁράω, εἶδον.
seek, seek for, I, ζητέω.
seek after, I, διώκω.
seem, I, φαίνομαι.
send, I, πέμπω, πέμψω, ἔπεμψα,

πέπομφα, πέπεμμαι, ἐπέμφθην; (away), ἀποπέμπω.

send for, I, μεταπέμπομαι, μετεπεμψάμην.

set free, I, λύω.

seven, ἑπτά.

shameful, αἰσχρός, -ά, -όν; comp. αἰσχίων, -ον.

sharp, ὀξύς, -εῖα, -ύ; comp. ὀξύτερος.

she, ἐκείνη.

shepherd, ποιμήν, -ένος, m.

shield, ἀσπίς, -ίδος, f.

ship, ναῦς, νεώς, f.

shoot, I, τοξεύω.

short, βραχύς, -εῖα, -ύ.

shout, I, βοάω.

show, I, δηλόω.

Sicinnus, Σίκιννος, -ου, m.

since (because), ὅτι, ἐπεί.

sink, I (trans.), καταδύω.

six, ἕξ.

slave, δοῦλος, -ου, m.

slow, βραδύς, -εῖα, -ύ.

slowly, more, βραδύτερον.

small, μικρός, -ά, -όν; superl. μικρότατος.

snake, δράκων, -οντος, m.

snow, χιών, -όνος, f.

so (with Adj. or Advb.), οὕτω, οὕτως (before vowel).

so, so much, ἐς τοσοῦτο(ν).

so big, so great, τοσοῦτος, τοσαύτη, τοσοῦτο.

so many, τοσοῦτοι.

so that (final), ἵνα, ὡς, ὅπως.

Socrates, Σωκράτης, -ους, m.

soldier, στρατιώτης, -ου, m.

some . . . , others, οἱ μέν . . . , οἱ δέ (acc. to gender).

some (indef. Pron. or Adj.), τις, τι.

someone, τις.

sometimes, ἐνίοτε.

son, υἱός, -οῦ, m.; παῖς, παιδός, m.

Sparta, Σπάρτη, -ης, f.

Spartans, Λακεδαιμόνιοι, -ων, m. pl.

speak, I, λέγω.

spring, κρήνη, -ης, f.

statue, ἀνδρίας, -αντος, m.

stay, μένω, ἔμεινα.

steward, ταμίας, -ου, m.

still, ἔτι.

stone, λίθος, -ου, m.

stop, I (trans.), παύω.

storm, χειμών, -ῶνος, m.

strange, δεινός, -ή, -όν.

strike, I, τύπτω, τύψω, ἔτυψα.

strong, ἰσχυρός, -ά, -όν.

such, τοιοῦτος, τοιαύτη, τοιοῦτο.

summer, θέρος, -ους, n.

surely? ἆρ' οὐ (with answer 'yes' or 'no') ; for use and examples see p. 107 under Direct Questions.

sweet, γλυκύς, -εῖα, -ύ; superl. γλυκύτατος; ἡδύς, -εῖα, -ύ; superl. ἥδιστος.

swift, ταχύς, -εῖα, -ύ; superl. τάχιστος.

sword, ξίφος, -ους, n.

Take, I, λαμβάνω, ἔλαβον.

taught, I get (someone), διδάσκομαι.

teach, I, διδάσκω.

tell (*order*), I, κελεύω.

tell (*inform*), I, ἀγγέλλω, ἤγγειλα (*with* Dat.).

tell (*say*), I, λέγω.

temple, ἱερόν, -οῦ, n.

ten, δέκα.

tenth, δέκατος, -η, -ον.

terrible, δεινός, -ή, -όν.

terribly, δεινῶς.

than, ἤ.

that, ἐκεῖνος, -η, -ο.

that (*in order that*), ἵνα, ὡς, ὅπως.

that, so that (*consecutive*), ὥστε.

them, *oblique cases of pl. of* αὐτός.

Themistocles,   Θεμιστοκλῆς, -έους, m.

themselves (*reflex.*), ἑαυτούς, -άς, -ά.

there, ἐκεῖ.

think, I, νομίζω, ἐνόμισα.

thirst, δίψα, -ης, f.

this, ὅδε, ἥδε, τόδε; οὗτος, αὕτη, τοῦτο.

three, τρεῖς, τρία.

through, διά (Gen.).

throw, I, ῥίπτω, ῥίψω, ἔρριψα, ἔρριφα; βάλλω; (away), ἀποβάλλω, ἀπέβαλον.

throw into disorder, I, ταράσσω, ταράξω, ἐτάραξα.

time, χρόνος, -ου, m.

to (*motion towards*), εἰς (Acc.); (*with persons*), ὡς (Acc.).

to, in order to, ἵνα, ὡς, ὅπως.

today, σήμερον.

tomb, τάφος, -ου, m.

tongue, γλῶσσα, -ης, f.

tooth, ὀδούς, -όντος, m.

torch, λαμπάς, -άδος, f.

towards, πρός (Acc.).

town, ἄστυ, -εως, n.

train, I, παιδεύω.

traitor, προδότης, -ου, m.

treat well, badly, I, εὖ, κακῶς, ποιέω.

tree, δένδρον, -ου, n.

trireme, τριήρης, -ους, f.

true, ἀληθής, -ές.

trumpet, σάλπιγξ, -ιγγος, f.

trust, I, πιστεύω (Dat.).

truth, the, τὸ ἀληθές.

try, I, πειράομαι, ἐπειρασάμην.

two, δύο.

tyrant, τύραννος, -ου, m.

Use, I, χράομαι (Dat.).

useful, χρήσιμος, -η, -ον.

Vain, in, μάτην.

victory, νίκη, -ης, f.

village, κώμη, -ης, f.

voice, φωνή, -ῆς, f.

Wagon, ἅμαξα, -ης, f.

wait, I, μένω, ἔμεινα.

wait for, I, μένω (Acc.).

wall, τεῖχος, -ους, n.

want, I, ἐθέλω, ἠθέλησα.

war, πόλεμος, -ου, m.

water, ὕδωρ, -ατος, n.

way (*road*), ὁδός, -οῦ, f.

we, ἡμεῖς.

weak, ἀσθενής, -ές.

weapons, ὅπλα, -ων, n. pl.

weep, I, κλαίω.

weigh down, I, πιέζω.

well, εὖ.

well-born, εὐγενής, -ές.

what? τί; (*indir.*), ὅτι.

where? ποῦ; (*indir.*) ὅπου; (whither?), ποῖ; (*indir.*), ὅποι.

where, from? πόθεν;

whether (*interrog.*), εἰ; whether . . . or (not), πότερον . . . ἢ (μή or οὐ).

which (*rel.*), ὅς, ἥ, ὅ.

who? τίς; (*indir.*), ὅστις.

why? τί; διὰ τί;

wide, εὐρύς, -εῖα, -ύ.

wife, γυνή, -αικός, f.

wild beast, θήρ, θηρός, m

willing, I am, ἐθέλω.

win (*prize*), I, φέρομαι.

win (*victory*), I, νικάω.

wine, οἶνος, -ου, m.

winter, χειμών, -ῶνος, m.

wisdom, σοφία, -ας, f.

wise, σοφός, -ή, -όν.

wisely, σοφῶς; *comp.* σοφώτερον.

wish, I, ἐθέλω, βούλομαι.

with, μετά (Gen.).

woman, γυνή, -αικός, f.

wood (*forest*), ὕλη, -ης, f.

wooden, ξύλινος, -η, -ον.

word, λόγος, -ου, m.

work, ἔργον, -ου, n.

worship, I, θεραπεύω.

worst, κάκιστος, -η, -ον; χείριστος.

worthily, ἀξίως.

worthy, ἄξιος, -α, -ον.

would that! εἰ γάρ, εἴθε.

write, I, γράφω, γράψω, ἔγραψα, γέγραφα, γέγραμμαι.

Xenophon, Ξενοφῶν, -ῶντος, m.

Xerxes, Ξέρξης, -ου, m.

Year, ἔτος, -ους, n.

yoke, ζυγόν, -οῦ, n.

you, σύ; *pl.* ὑμεῖς.

young man, νεανίας, -ου, m.

your (*s.*), σός, σή, σόν; (*pl.*) ὑμέτερος, -α, -ον (*both; :ced. by article*).

yourselves (*reflex.*), ὑμᾶς αὐτούς.

Zeus, Ζεύς, Διός, m.